BUGABOO
DREAMS

Topher Donahue

BUGABOO DREAMS

A STORY OF SKIERS, HELICOPTERS & MOUNTAINS

Rocky
Mountain Books
VANCOUVER · VICTORIA · CALGARY

Rocky Mountain Books   Rocky Mountain Books
#108 – 17665 66A Avenue   PO Box 468
Surrey, BC V3S 2A7   Custer, WA
www.rmbooks.com   98240-0468

Library and Archives Canada Cataloguing in Publication

Donahue, Topher
    Bugaboo dreams : a story of skiers, helicopters and mountains / Topher
Donahue.

Includes bibliographical references.
ISBN 978-1-897522-11-0

    1. Gmoser, Hans. 2. Grillmair, Leo. 3. Skis and skiing—Canada,
Western. 4. Ski mountaineering—Canada, Western. 5. Skiers—Canada,
Western—Biography. I. Title.
GV854.8.C3D65 2008   796.93   C2008-902781-7

Library of Congress Control Number: 2008930511

Printed and bound in Canada

Rocky Mountain Books gratefully acknowledges the financial support of the Government of Canada through the Book Publishing Industry Development Program (BPIDP); the Canada Council for the Arts; and the province of British Columbia through the British Columbia Arts Council and the Book Publishing Tax Credit for our publishing activities.

BRITISH COLUMBIA ARTS COUNCIL   Canada Council   Conseil des Arts
                                      for the Arts   du Canada

This book has been produced on 100% post-consumer recycled paper, processed chlorine free and printed with vegetable-based dyes.

To the mountain guide who introduced me
to life and the mountains: my father,
Mike Donahue (1946–2005)

CONTENTS

PREFACE

A story like this has a thousand characters, and each character has a story that is worthy of a book. Like a legend passed on around campfires for generations, this is just one version of the tale. I heard the story for the first time at a celebration of friends and skiing in the Bugaboos during the spring of 2005. It was an event called the Nostalgia Weeks, a celebration of the people who were a big part of the outrageous adventure of learning to ski with a helicopter for a lift. By then, the story had been evolving for 40 years, and during the Nostalgia Weeks, skiing was secondary to telling stories and debating how it really happened.

I first encountered the Columbia Mountains as a young rock climber drawn to the vertical walls of the Bugaboo Spires in the Purcell Range. I spent a week climbing every day during a spell of good weather that allowed my climbing partner and me to stand on top of most of the main spires. The view from the summit of Snowpatch Spire presented my aspiring alpinist's eyes with the kind of vista I had always dreamed of seeing: a 360-degree panorama of black mountains and blinding white glaciers fading over the horizon. By looking closely into the valley below I could see a few tiny dots of human establishment. The first was the collection of climbers' tents perched on the rock slabs of Applebee Dome. The second was the Kain Hut, where climbers with a little more money slept. The third was a single, plane roofline and wall of windows reflecting sunlight from far in the valley bottom past the toe of Bugaboo Glacier. The reason for the building's existence was a mystery to me at the time. I asked around camp and some climbers told me it was a base area for heli-skiing. For the rest of my climbing trip I found myself thinking about skiing in the area. While resting on a ledge, coiling a rope, or sitting at camp waiting for water to boil, and eventually hiking away from the spires under knee-shuddering backpacks loaded with ropes and climbing hardware, I looked out over the nearby peaks and imagined what it would be like to ski between the massive granite walls in deep powder snow.

My dad was a climbing guide in Colorado, so I was introduced to the mountains as a kid with the idea that the three main elements of mountaineering – skiing, rock climbing and alpinism – were all one sport. Eventually I learned them all, and by the time I was in college I was spending summers and holidays guiding technical climbs in Colorado and Alaska. Mountain sport eventually took me all over the globe, but as I looked out over the Bugaboos and envisioned skiing huge mountain faces with a helicopter to take me effortlessly to the top again, I realized there was an element of mountain sport I had never really considered.

Fifteen years later, an unusual series of events put me in the Bugaboo lodge, listening to a great story by night and skiing between the spires by day. It began when my wife-to-be, Vera Schulte-Pelkum, tore one of her anterior cruciate ligaments while skiing deep powder in Alta, Utah. During her recovery, I went climbing with an old friend from Colorado named Kyle Lefkoff. When he heard of her injury, he said, "You should go to the Adamants with us this summer. We'll go do first ascents with a helicopter to take us to the base so she won't have to walk."

By then I was making a living as a photojournalist, writing stories and taking pictures of mountain adventures. While I couldn't pay for heli-sport, I could work for it, so I landed an assignment from *Climbing* magazine to document the trip and, after a conversation with Jane Carswell in the marketing department of Canadian Mountain Holidays, I had the job of climbing, writing and shooting photos of a week of vertical exploration out of the most luxurious base camp I had ever encountered, the Adamants lodge. We did several first ascents, including the south face of Mt. Colossal, the hardest rock climb in the area, but I was far more stunned by the remote wildness of the area and that the most successful mountain guide service in the world had somehow been built around taking people skiing and hiking in the middle of nowhere.

The next summer, Carswell hired me to photograph a hiking trip in the Cariboos. Coincidentally, a couple named Hans and Margaret Gmoser were there at the same time, hiking with their grandkids. We hiked together for three days, and I watched Hans stand in a stream to help hikers across, the mountain guide in him pouring out even in his retirement. I learned from everyone else that they were the founders of the business, the first of its kind anywhere in the world. From Hans and Margaret I learned only how much they loved both the mountains and the people they spent time with while skiing and hiking. We talked about our common history of being part of a guiding family, and I was bursting with curiosity about how they had built a humble guide service like my father's into such a vast network of skiing and hiking areas. At some point Margaret told me about the Nostalgia Weeks planned for the following year, when many of the people involved in the project would meet in the Bugaboos to celebrate their friendships. I remember saying, "I'd love to be a fly on the wall for that."

To which Hans replied, "You should join us."

Nine months later, in April, I was looking out the window of a Bell 212 helicopter as it powered past the very cracks in the Bugaboo granite I had jammed my hands into years before. The spires looked bigger under their cloak of snow, and the way my stomach felt as I thought of skiing among them reminded me of the nights before Christmas when I still had faith in Santa Claus. I had an assignment from *Powder* magazine to report on the party celebrating 40 years of heli-skiing in North America, but it didn't take long to realize the story was of far greater magnitude than could fit in a magazine article. It was some time between ski legend Ethan Compton's 88th birthday party – when all the women in the lodge paraded topless with paper bags on their heads past the birthday boy – and when I straight-lined down a section of untracked powder, inspiring guide Rudi Gertsch to say, "Taking you heli-skiing is like feeding caviar to a pig" – that I realized I was at the edge of the most intriguing, diverse mountain story I had ever encountered in my life.

After a few nights of taking notes about one unbelievable story after another, and watching the shared passion for skiing and mountain friendships form a nearly visible haze in the room, I turned to Marc Piché, a guide and climber I'd met in the Bugaboos years earlier, and said, "I'd be happy to contribute what I'm getting here to whoever is writing the book."

Marc said, "People have talked about it, but nobody has done it yet."

For the rest of the 2005 Nostalgia Weeks, I savoured the experience of skiing with a group of people who cherished the mountains and each other with childish enthusiasm. During the day it was like being on a high-school ski trip again, with everyone laughing, joking and having the time of their lives; at dinner every night I looked around the room full of white-haired seniors and found it hard to believe these were the same youthful people I skied with all day. As the Nostalgia Weeks drew to a close, the urgency of putting these people's story into a book grew on me. Regardless of who wrote it, it had to be done.

Later, I spoke with Hans about the idea and asked him if he wanted to write it. He just chuckled and shook his head. When I told him I was considering writing a book telling the story of the many adventures and the many people involved, he agreed to help. Hans told me in no uncertain terms that he did not want a book written exclusively about him, but that he was interested in helping to tell other people's stories. Connie MacDonald, the communications director at Canadian Mountain Holidays, was enthusiastic and arranged financial support for the project.

The next two years passed in a mix of unpredictable tragedy and beauty such as only life can concoct. First, my father passed away, leaving me with renewed motivation to do justice to this story that is, at the heart of it, a glimpse into his profession of mountain guiding. Second, Hans Gmoser passed away, leaving me without his guidance for writing this book but inspiring everyone I spoke with to dig deeper for memories. Third, my wife, Vera, gave birth to twin brother and sister, filling our life to overflowing. I began to wonder if I would finish this book before the infants became toddlers and ripped this very keyboard from under my hands. There were times I wrote with my son or daughter, and sometimes both, sitting on my lap. I would put a second keyboard in front of them, and let them pound on it while I composed on the first keyboard just out of their reach.

Over the course of two winters I visited most of the areas covered in this book and listened to stories from hundreds of people. Many guides I spoke with had the common characteristic of young eyes peering out from old skin wrinkled from laughter and concern chiselled into their expressions by the sun and wind. The younger guides' eyes sparkled with excitement of their new profession. Many of the skiers and hikers had the common characteristic of being business visionaries who found the mountains offered something even money can't buy, and everyone respected Hans greatly for his perseverance and boldness in business. When I started writing, I tried to honour Hans's desire to be a minor part of the story, but it was impossible; everyone I spoke with primarily credited Hans with the forward progress of the endeavour and painted him as the force that made it all happen.

However, there were many people besides Hans who committed vast swaths of their lives to his wilderness vision. This book is only the tip of the iceberg of the decades of human effort involved in the project. As the writer, I realized from the beginning that including everyone would have distilled the project down to no more than a yearbook, a collection of faces and names for the thousands of people involved. Conversely, telling only one person's story would miss much of the multi-faceted element that is the spice of this story. I chose to write a version somewhere in between. I conducted interviews more as conversations and recorded mostly with a pen and notebook to create the most comfortable atmosphere possible, and as a result many discussions extended over several days. I attempted to go deeper with fewer people rather than conducting short, journalistic interviews with many.

After listening to the old-timers, and some not so old, debate "how it really happened," I decided that if someone told me something happened, I would just write it as it was told to me, rather than cross-examine someone else to prove the story as absolute truth. The result is not the history of heli-skiing, hiking or mountain guiding, but a glimpse into the passions that inspire people to make mountain adventure a part of their lives, and the mishaps and tragedies as well as fun and friendships found along the way. It is the kind of story best told on a long ski tour or road trip, over a casual dinner with a few friends, or on the way to the bottom of a bottle of wine while sitting around a roaring fire in a mountain hut.

—Topher Donahue, February 25, 2008

ACKNOWLEDGEMENTS

Some writers take everyday events and make a great story out of them. Others are merely at the right place at the right time to capture a great story before it is too late. As the author of this book, I fell into the latter category. Throughout the writing I was frequently struck with the feeling that my role was that of a porter assigned the task of carrying this story to the world. The story already existed, a legend across Western Canada, full of wild tales passed by word of mouth on ski lifts from Gstaad to Bariloche. As with any legend, the tale changed with each telling, and I was fortunate to be able to talk to many people who were part of the story from the beginning. I stumbled into this story at the twilight of its living history and am grateful to have had the opportunity to delve into such a project while most of the protagonists are still telling stories.

First, I would like to thank Hans and Margaret Gmoser and Leo and Lynne Grillmair. Were it not for the Gmosers' enthusiasm for my idea of gathering the stories of many people involved, I would have merely thought about it and let it pass like many other ideas. Were it not for the Grillmairs' hospitality and several evenings of good food and conversation in their home, I would have never understood the depth of the story I was endeavouring to write.

My deepest appreciation goes out to the guides with whom I had the opportunity to ski, hike, climb or at least share stories over a bottle of wine: Alison Andrews, Steve Chambers, Roger Laurilla, Thia Klebaur, Robert "Roko" Koell, Paul Vidalin, Erich Unterberger, Bernhard Ehmann, Rudi Gertsch, Peter Schlunegger, Rob Whalen, Stefan Blochum, Ken France, Thierry Cardon, Rudi Kranabitter, Lloyd "Kiwi" Gallagher, Kitt Redhead, Merrie-Beth Board, John Mellis, Ernst Buehler, Daniel Zimmerman, Peter Harvey, Martin Vogt, Brett Lawrence, Derek Marcinyshyn Pete Harvey, Bernie Wiatzka, Pete Arbic, Mike Welch, Duncan Brown, Roger Atkins, Diny Harrison, Claude Duchesne, Bob Geber, Gery Unterasinger, Carl Trescher, Marc Hammer, Tom Raudaschl, Bruce Howatt, Marc Piché, Tim Poochay, Kobi Wyss, Kirk Mauthner, Pierre Lemire, Buck Corrigan, Lilla Molnar, Kevin Christakos, Dean Walton, Dave Cochrane, Paul Langevin, Luke Griffith, JF Lacombe, Dave Gauley, Robson Gmoser, Brian Keefer, Otto Klimmer, Bob Sawyer, Anjan Truffer, Danny Stoffel, James Vickers, Karl Wieser, Jorg Wilz, Mike Wiegele, Jim Markin, Willy Trinker, Brad White, Sepp Renner, Hermann Frank, Martin Heuberger, HP Stettler and anyone else I may have inadvertently overlooked. You all have my utmost respect for how well you manage people in the harsh workplace of the mountains.

Thanks also to the helicopter pilots I watched fly, including Rob Askin, Rocky Cooper, Steve Stier, Alex Holliday, Doug Pascuzzo, Derek Robinson, Brian MacPherson, Matt Conant, Lyle Ledoux, Brian Wyatt, Dave Schwan, Don Wederfort, Simon Miederna, Gordon Grice, Steve Cote, Jeff Gotta and Roger Hoogendoorn for their almost unfathomable ability to fly helicopters in some of the snowiest mountains on earth and for explaining many of the intricacies of their craft; and to Jim Davies for showing it could be done.

For arranging the complicated logistics of the research and travel for this project, and helping sort through the vast archives in the basement of the CMH building in Banff, I thank Maggie Sterchi, Tyler Toohey, Laura Newsome, Nicole Koester and Nancy DaDalt. Thanks to Marion Kingsbury, Rob Rohn, Walter Bruns, Colani Bezzola, Lynda Murdock, Pat Aldous and Marty Von Neudegg for their advice and honesty in discussing the business of heli-sport. Special thanks to Connie MacDonald for her guidance throughout this project – and for having the confidence to let me run with the story and write it as I saw fit.

Everywhere I went to research this book, the hospitality was overwhelming. For that I thank Lianne Marquis, Chantal Gainer, Bruce Rainer, Brady and Fred Beruschi, Mike and Bonnie Wiegele, Carlee Hughes, Cheryl Cunningham, Marnie Frackleton, Vicki Hemmingson, Erin Teunissen, René Clark, Heidi Israelson, Cheryl White, Kelly Nadeau, Marie Hamm, Angelika Weder, Sheri McEwen and Adrienne Daniel.

Thanks to all the skiers, hikers and climbers who shared the powder, rock, tundra and stories, including Joe and Anne Jones, Betty MacRae, Enga Thompson, Don and Barbara Guild, Peter Lustenberger, Michel Dufresne, Kyle and Cindy Lefkoff, Maya Geber, Art Patterson, Roy and Barb Ostberg, Ethan Compton, Fran Gallagher, Brooks Dodge, Ken and Patti Ferrin, Junko Takashima, Dieter Von Hennig, Viet Erben, Freddy Weiss, Miguel Arias, Steve Komito, Cliff Milleman, Hank Brandtjen, Diane Soucheray, Olav Rudd, Alan Green, Hannelore Achenbach and Ary Dedet.

Of everyone I talked to during the writing of this book, nobody deserves more credit than the families of the guides and staff. I was fortunate to speak with a number of the children who grew up in the shadow of Canadian Mountain Holidays. For their insights, and for honesty and intelligence in discussing the business that took so much of their parents' time and energy, I thank Conrad and Robson Gmoser, Luke Griffith, Aita Bezzola, Tess Keefer and Troy, Abigail and Lydia Kingsbury.

I would also like to pass on a word of thanks from Hans and Margaret Gmoser to some of the other people who helped make it all happen: Alfred B. Saroni, Andy Epstein, Art Dion, Lloyd Nixon, Arthur Tauck, Mark Aubrey, Bernadette McDonald, Marty Flug, Bob Sutherland, Carolyn Damon, Cory Pollack, Charles Barlow, Chris Stetham, Dave Whyte, Dave Zemke, David and Tessa Brooksbank, Debbie Cooper, Dick Schrader, Don and Jean Stuart, Eric and Judy Disbrow, Evelyn Mathews, Franz Dopf, Fred Noble, Mary Walsh, Monique Luscher, Morton (Morty) Gurrentz, Pat Lever, Pauline Carr Gaines, Pepi Erben, Peter Fischer, Ralph Bogan, Rene Duss, Richard (Dick) Wright, Richard Verenneau, Roger Vernon, Tom Schrecker, Grant Statham, Herman and Myrna Frank, Jack White, Jeff Boyd, Jim Dalton, King Juan Carlos, Tony Noichl, Vic Van Isle and Willy Bogner.

For expertise in helicopters, guiding, photography and avalanches – and proofreading these technical aspects – I thank Marc Piché, Roger Atkins, Martin Heuberger, Pascal Hägeli, Lloyd "Kiwi" Gallagher, Rob Rohn, Chic Scott, Paul Lazarski and Dave Gubbels.

Thanks to Urs and Gerda Kallen, Don Gorman and the staff at Rocky Mountain Books and The Whyte Museum of the Canadian Rockies.

And finally, I would like to profusely thank my wife, Vera, for not only accommodating and enduring the writing of this book but also encouraging, advising and editing throughout our first chaotic year as parents of twins; my stepmother, Sorako Schulte-Pelkum, and her endless energy and good food; my mother, Peggy Donahue and her enduring youth; and my son and daughter, Keahi and Aya, for the motivation they inspire that only parents can understand.

1

IT'S ALL LEO'S FAULT

Like great sailing ships with towering masts and enormous keels, mountains are alive at their tallest peaks, humming in the elements, alive at hearts of stone floating on the fiery matrix which gave them birth. Perched on mountains, I am a human speck of an observer to this wild extravagance of creative force. It extends beyond my world, and time, to know that I cannot truly measure space, energy and beauty. In the face of mountains, measurement seems contrived, impertinent, dwarfed. But mountains do not dwarf the spirit; they present reaches that convene with the universal. I feel them renew and deepen my first transaction with nature. I have a covenant with mountains.

— Andrea Mead Lawrence, *A Practice of Mountains*

The mountain guide tensed his vocal cords in a way only men of the alpine can, and the chortle of a loud yodel left his lungs, spreading across the pristine white glacier to rebound against the sheer walls of black and white stone where the ice abruptly ended. Before the echo of the yodel had time to return to his ears, his world was transformed by a catastrophic change under his feet as the edge of a nearby crevasse collapsed into the bowels of the glacier.

The crevasse was one of many formed by the long battle between ice and stone. He was standing in a place where the rock forces the slowly moving ice between two monolithic spires, causing upheaval in the glacier as it squeezes through. Like a river flowing into a narrow canyon, the surface becomes chaotic and broken, changing daily in a rare display of geologic change moving in human time. The ice carves huge shards from the surrounding rock, mixing boulders into the ice. Within the crevasse wall, a massive boulder the size of an automobile was entombed, and when the weight of the yodeling climber, or maybe even the vibration of the yodel itself, was added to the pressure within the delicate sculpture, hundreds of tonnes of ice, the boulder and the guide dropped into the depths.

A second later, stillness returned. The guide – a young Austrian named Hans Gmoser – along with the ice he had been standing on and the boulder were rearranged at the bottom of the crevasse in a diabolical order. The ice was shattered into blocks and thrown about the chasm. The rock was leaning against the impenetrable ice of the inner glacier, and the guide was on the bottom, pinned between rock and ice.

To understand where this guide was trapped, imagine a mountain range built from ancient islands compressed and folded into a continent by the movement of the earth's crust before being shaped by an ice age that deposits two kilometres of ice over the region. After eons of carving, give the ice a few millennia to melt and expose the chaotic layers of rock, leaving jagged peaks and deep valleys at the edge of the biggest body of water on the planet.

Position winter cyclones with colossal violence and moisture content right off the coast to spin wave after wave of precipitation into the steep-sided mountains. The first blast of moisture falls on the coastal mountains, creating some of the heaviest rain and snow falls in the world. Then align a series of warmer, drier valleys running perpendicular to the prevailing winds to warm the storm cells, allowing them to pick up even more moisture from evaporation off numerous rivers and lakes. Finally, bring cold air down from the Arctic to freeze and dry the moisture as it runs headlong into ever taller mountain ranges, where the precipitation is dropped in the form of cold, light, dry snow before passing over the Continental Divide.

During the summer, waist-deep snows are replaced by waist-deep wildflowers. Stark granite spires jut from high ridges above valleys perched at the edge of deeper valleys. The vertical relief is overwhelmed by the sheer vastness of the mountains. From any summit, mountains stretch as far as the eye can see, many of them still unnamed, unclimbed, unskied and uninhabited. Dark castles of mountains built of every combination of rock imaginable, from blinding white quartz to jet-black shale. Some are cut as if chiselled from a single block of stone, while others contain uncountable fragments, not one rock bigger than you could move, all held together by the sheer grace of gravity.

Precipitation and geography combine to give the mountains of western Canada an almost mythical stature in the world of adventure destinations. Few who know the area would disagree that the heart of the region, both physically and philosophically, is the Columbia Mountains. Most people living outside of British Columbia think the range is part of the Rocky Mountains, while many have never even heard of the Columbias. It's hard to blame them; the geography of the region is so complicated, rugged and mountainous that even locals and geographers have differing definitions of the borders of the ranges. Other than a few broad river basins, mountains stretch for 700 kilometres from the Pacific Ocean to the edge of the Great Plains that make up the centre of the continent.

Rainforests cling to nearly vertical mountainsides. Turquoise-coloured lakes prone to easy reflections nestle at the bottom of steep valleys draped with veils of mist that cling to the forest canopy. Wildflowers and berries inject bursts of colour into the deep greens and browns of photosynthesis and decay.

These rainforests are the only ones on Earth that receive most of their precipitation between October and March in the form of snow. Short winter days hold the snow in a refrigerated state for much of the time, so it piles up to unbelievable depths. It's no mystery why these mountains have become one of the seven wonders of the world of skiing, but it took a series of events and concurrent technological breakthroughs before the ultimate recreational potential of those mountains and their powerful storm machine could be realized.

Returning to our guide, one essential factor in his fate was the trajectory of the boulder as it fell into the hole in the glacier. With enough force to smash a bomb shelter, the boulder landed on Hans Gmoser. A slight curve in the crevasse wall left enough space for most of his body to remain intact, and his backpack cushioned his torso from the iron hardness of the ice. His leg was twisted at a rakish angle where it disappeared under the boulder – but he was alive. With a slightly different trajectory of the boulder, Hans would have been dead before the echo from his yodel faded.

A second guide rappelled into the crevasse and spent several hours hacking at the ice around the broken leg. Eventually the leg dropped free. The rest of Hans's body was a mass of bruises, but his injuries were relatively minor considering the forces pounding the crevasse walls around him at the time of his fall. A rescue flight took him to the hospital where he was stabilized, bandaged and plastered.

Hans had no time to heal. He was scheduled to interview a potential cook, Lynne Seidler, for his new project of using a helicopter to ferry skiers to the summits of the mountains surrounding the very crevasse that had almost killed him. He conducted the interview from his hospital bed, hiring the cook on the spot. "I remember being horrified by how beat up he was," remembers Lynne, "and he didn't talk much, so I asked him a lot of questions and he seemed impressed that I was so interested in everything. He did ask me if I could cook for 44, and I figured if I could cook for one I could cook for 50. I got the job."

Neither Hans nor Lynne knew it at the time, but they were on the verge of changing mountain recreation forever. Through the next decade neither gave any thought to the magnitude of what they were involved with. The day-to-day adventure of running an unprecedented business in the mountains gave them little chance to step aside and consider the magnitude of the story engulfing them.

It all started with a chance meeting on another continent on the other side of a faraway ocean. It was a cold February day in 1951 when Hans bumped into his lifelong friend Leo Grillmair on the streets of Linz, Austria, on their way home from work. Neither one could have known that the simple choice of which street they took to return home that day would have such a profound effect on their lives. They exchanged pleasantries in the typical manner where no real groundbreaking news is expected.

In post-war Austria, good news was rare. Hours earlier, Leo had been warned by the friendly foreman at his plumbing job that a firing was imminent. Such news was commonplace and scarcely cause for discussion, but there was more to it this time. The foreman knew about an immigration offer for qualified tradesmen whereby the Canadian government would provide an interest-free loan for 90 per cent of the cost of immigration. Before even heading home, Leo had signed up.

Leo Grillmair was a gregarious 23-year-old with a wiry build and a singsong voice. For an extrovert like him, emigrating halfway around the world sounded a lot better with a friend at his side. So without much discussion, he blurted out, "I'm going to Canada! Why don't you come with me?"

Hans's head must have spun. With meagre career prospects and a penchant for adventure, seeking a life in Canada was the stuff of dreams. And with his training as an electrician, he would find the immigration offer ripe for the taking.

The die was cast. While Hans was filling out his paperwork at the immigration office, the official asked him where he wanted to live. Choosing a particular place in a country roughly the size of all of Europe was a tall order, so the only answer Hans could honestly give was, "In the mountains!"

Mountains were in the lifeblood of the two young men. Both had been born and raised within sight of the lofty peaks of the Alps. Both belonged to climbing clubs and spent their every free moment exploring the mountains with ropes and skis. But rising at the crack of dawn to work all day in the trades for a minimal wage didn't leave much time for play. They knew hard work would be the key to success in Canada, but they wanted to be surrounded by their beloved mountains whatever hardships were in store.

Leo was able to secure a berth on an earlier ship than Hans, so they agreed to meet in Canada. Before sailing, Leo and a group of fellow passengers decided to spend the last of their money partying like Romans. "It seemed like a good idea at the time," remembers Leo, "but it was a really bad idea because we arrived at the end of a horrendous rough voyage, seasick the whole time, with nothing."

After a more comfortable voyage on the later ship, Hans arrived in much better shape and with a few dollars in his pocket. There is no way the two mountaineers could have known, as they first considered the vastness of western Canada, that a

LEO GRILLMAIR CLIMBING IN
THE BUGABOOS, 1969.

technological maelstrom was about to engulf the world, affecting the most traditional professions and creating opportunity for new professions that even the wildest dreamers couldn't have predicted. It was the 1950s and the post-war era that had made their lives so miserable in Austria also caused massive innovation worldwide. It was the decade of the first satellite, the first silicon microchip and the first photovoltaic solar cell.

But it was far from instant gratification for the Austrian mountaineers. The first setback happened as soon as they got off the train in Edmonton: there were no mountains in sight. Years later, Hans told a reporter for the *Edmonton Journal* that when he got off the train and looked around at the endless prairie, he sat down and cried.

"It was as if somebody had sawed the world off!" Hans said. If you consider the perspective from someone who had grown up within sight of the Alps, his reaction was one of genuine shock and sudden homesickness. Flat broke, Leo and Hans took the first jobs that came their way: cutting trees with a logging crew northwest of Edmonton. The two skinny young men, malnourished for most of their teenage years in war-ravaged Austria, must have looked mighty weak among a group of burly, corn-fed loggers. Since they were paid 14 cents per tree, it was no skin off the company's back if the boys couldn't fell as many trees as the rest of the crew. While the locals were felling as many as 200 trees each week, Hans and Leo worked hard to bring home 70.

They took a big double-handled saw and went to work, Leo pushing and pulling on one side of the tree and Hans doing the opposite on the other. If there was one thing Hans and Leo could do, it was work. Hard work. After a week of logging from dawn to dusk, their hands were blistered, their backs were sore, and they were still not cutting enough trees to pay for their room and board at the logging camp. To increase their yield, they rapidly sawed through one tree and watched it fall into the branches of a second where it stopped. With no concern for the potential disaster unfolding, they cut the second tree and both trees fell into a third tree. They cut the third and it stuck in a fourth! Now even the neophyte loggers realized things were getting interesting. As they cut into the fourth tree, suddenly something gave way. Hans and Leo ran in different directions as the whole mess crashed to the ground. It was the first of many narrow escapes for the two, but their double-handled saw didn't fare so well and when the foreman saw the damage, they were kicked off the crew without a dime to take home.

Winter was just beginning and the two friends were in dire straits. Standing penniless nearly 8000 kilometres from home on the streets of Edmonton with minimal English just as the Canadian winter was setting in was not quite what they had envisioned when they signed up at the immigration office back in Linz. They had one hope for salvation. Hans knew his climbing partner from back home, Franz Dopf, had an uncle who drove a taxi in Edmonton, but that's all they knew. Desperately, they waved down taxi after taxi until they found someone who knew how to find Franz's uncle. They banged on his door in the middle of the night, and the uncle invited the boys to stay through the holidays and even loaned them some money to buy skis so they could learn to enjoy Canada.

Things were looking better for the two immigrants, and they excitedly climbed the nearest hill, above Whitemud Creek, to have a bit of fun with their new skis in their new country. Two hours later Leo wrapped himself around a tree and shattered his leg.

"We were always happy to break a leg instead of a ski," remembers Leo. "Legs heal on their own. Skis cost money!"

They spent their first winter together in Canada like an old married couple, with Hans working for both of them and Leo gimping around with his healing leg. It was the beginning of a friendship the likes of which the world sees only rarely, the kind that begins as children, endures hardships and a great war, travels to a new land together, builds an industry together, grows old together, and stays strong through it all.

"We never questioned our friendship," says Leo, eyes glinting with just a hint of moisture. In the spring of 1952 Hans got a job in Calgary at an electrical shop, rewiring electric motors, which, according to Hans, "wasn't much better than Edmonton but at least we could see mountains."

They finally found their mountains in the spectacular Bow Valley, where the striking peaks of the Canadian Rockies rise within walking distance from the mountain hamlet of Banff, one of the most scenic towns on Earth. With their classical European tradesman training, Hans was able to get work as an electrician and Leo as a plumber.

Hans knew no one the first time he visited Banff, and found himself walking the streets looking for a place to pitch his tent and sleep for the night. He located a bit of flat ground, set up his tent and crawled in to sleep with his feet jutting outside. In the morning he was awakened by someone roughly kicking his feet. After extracting himself from his sleeping bag, he found himself facing an irritated homeowner by the name of Elizabeth "Lizzie" von Rummel.

Lizzie was born the daughter of Baron von Rummel of the German aristocracy at the turn of the century. The ravages of the First World War had robbed the family of their estate except for one property Lizzie's mother had bought near Kananaskis, on the eastern slopes of the Rockies. Lizzie found herself in Canada and eventually became a Western Canadian legend for using her natural good humour to give people unmatched hospitality in mountain huts. After kicking Hans out of his sleeping bag, Lizzie realized he was a native German speaker struggling to make it as an immigrant, and before he packed his bags and walked off her lawn, she had offered him a job assisting her with the daily operation of the hut at Mt. Assiniboine, where she and Erling Strom ran a remote alpine hut reminiscent of the charismatic huts of Hans's and Leo's homeland in the European Alps.

From a meeting as random as a lightning strike – with a baroness committed to mountain hospitality – Hans Gmoser found himself taking the first steps down a path he would follow for the next 40 years. Through Lizzie Rummel, he was introduced to guiding at the base of one of the most beautiful peaks in the world, leading guests the 30 kilometres from the Sunshine ski resort near Banff to and from Mt. Assiniboine. Hans was part guide and part courier, skiing from the lodge to the Sunshine ski area as if the 27-kilometre trip were no more than a normal commute.

Under the wing of one of the most hospitable hut keepers the mountains had ever known, Hans found passion and a way of life as he watched Lizzie and Erling lead people to experience the greatest days of their lives. Lizzie's style was a hybrid of the food and cleanliness of traditional European alpine living, in a humble lodge Hans called "the most wonderful mountain hut you could imagine," combined with the family camaraderie born of isolation in the vast western North American wilderness. Visitors didn't just stay for a week – they lived there. The lodge was their home and the hut keepers were their family. After a hard day in the mountains, mealtimes were family affairs, with big, mouth-watering plates of hot food brought to the tables to be dished out in front of famished climbers and skiers. After eating, everyone helped clear the tables before gathering around the wood stove to tell tales and build strong friendships as only crackling fires can inspire.

At the base of a peak called the "Matterhorn of the Rockies," in a hut where everyone was close and every day was a chance to live nirvana, Hans found his calling. He would devote his life to giving as many people as possible a life-changing experience in the mountains. If a crystal ball could have told him just how many people that would amount to over the course of his life, he would have laughed, sworn, or most likely both. Lizzie herself opened Hans's eyes to a philosophy of caring for people and became his hero, mentor, teacher and parent away from home.

She encouraged him to learn to write well and to read from her vast library, where he applied his natural focus and work ethic to eventually learn English to a standard well beyond many native speakers. He was inspired by reading about the visionary adventurers who were the first climbers on the remote and difficult peaks of the Rockies and the seemingly endless and mysterious mountain ranges to the west. Many of them were guides imported from Europe by the Canadian Pacific Railway to take well-heeled tourists to a summit. One, however, inspired Hans more than all the rest combined: Conrad Kain, the black sheep of Canadian mountain guiding in the early 1900s, whose writing showed Hans what was possible.

Kain's rugged style and against-all-odds achievements inspired Hans to dream of wild adventures while leading climbers and skiers to the edges of human endurance and imagination. It's not hard to visualize the young climber reading Kain's autobiography, *Where the Clouds Can Go,* candlelight illuminating the focused expression on his chiselled, handsome face, the striking green eyes the colour of a glacial tarn, the pages of the book, and a few logs of the hut, while outside the moonlight painted stark contrasts on the pyramidal lines of Mt. Assiniboine. Kain was not only a great mountaineer; he also came from a similar background as Hans and shared a similar philosophy of minimalism, environmentalism and individualism. Kain was a poor Austrian whose first guiding work was showing footsore travellers a shortcut to Salzburg over the pass near his home. He always shared with them whatever food he had and asked for nothing in return. Although Kain started as something of a rogue guide – he once was run out of Chamonix, narrowly escaping bodily harm at the fists of enraged local guides protecting their turf – he eventually gained international acclaim as a superb climber and guide, raising professional standards on three continents with guided and solo first ascents in New Zealand, the Alps and North America at a time when long ocean voyages made it much harder to explore the world's alpine regions.

Hans's respect for Kain was so great that he not only modelled his approach to mountain adventure after Kain, he also named his sons, Conrad and Robson, after Kain and his greatest first ascent – the tallest peak in the Canadian Rockies, 3954-metre Mt. Robson, which Kain guided in 1913. The day before the ascent, he guided the second ascent of Mt. Resplendent and was nearly snow blind when he began the ascent of Mt. Robson. When he stepped onto the summit and turned to Billy Forrester and Albert McCarthy and stoically uttered the now immortal words, "Gentlemen, that's as far as I can take you," he left his mark forever on the face of world mountaineering and unknowingly inspired another Austrian to redefine mountain adventure in the mountains of western Canada 50 years later.

These stories of epic achievement must have fanned the flames of an already motivated Hans Gmoser, who came from a world where climbing was not a fringe frontier pursuit, but a normal mainstream sport. Hans explained his perspective in an interview in *Maclean's* magazine: "I grew up where rock climbing is as much a teenage pastime as ice-skating is in eastern Canada. Apart from that, I suppose we all enjoy doing things we do reasonably well. But that's only part of the story. I can't tell you why really. It's beyond words. I don't know why people climb, but I've never heard of a bad reason for doing it."

Kain's humble yet world-class approach to mountain sport, and the everyday normalcy of the game of mountaineering in Europe, contributed to Hans's motivation to push the limits in Canada's mountains and to share their wonders through guiding, photography and public speaking.

Inevitably, one mountain could only hold the attention of someone like Hans for so long, so he started guiding in other areas besides Assiniboine, taking people mountaineering all over the Rockies in the summer and during the winter leading ski tours in Little Yoho National Park northwest of Banff, and in Glacier National Park around Rogers Pass in the Columbia Mountains. In his quest to show people a great time in the outdoors, he unwittingly stumbled on some of the best skiing on earth.

There were no ski lifts, so ski touring was the only option. To go ski touring, according to Hans, "You need the perseverance of a bulldozer – and you almost have to work as hard as one." Before skiing, Hans and Leo would install climbing skins on everyone's skis. The climbing skin opened the mountains to skiing in ways even a helicopter cannot rival. The simple device, originally made of mohair clipped to the bottoms of skis, and later from a synthetic attached with an adhesive, allows the skis to slide easily uphill but hold fast under downward pressure. With skins, the steep terrain of the Columbias became a ski area for those willing to work for it. People who only ski downhill find it hard to believe, but skiing uphill holds an ephemeral pleasure and makes the eventual downhill rush exponentially more enjoyable than simply riding a lift or helicopter to the top.

Hans quickly earned a reputation as an extraordinary mountain guide and climber, and in 1955 he was invited to be an honorary member of the Victoria Outdoor Club. Their newsletter at the time read: "His humble and interested manner, coupled with an iron strength, has carried him into the hearts of our members and to the tops of many of the Canadian Rockies."

Hans wrote a letter of thanks to the club expressing his gratitude and sharing a philosophy of adventure that would stay with him throughout his life:

> I don't know what to say. Your making me an honorary member makes me very proud. I only hope you didn't pick the wrong man and I can live up to your expectations. I am really proud to wear your pin and I didn't miss to stick it right away on my climbing sweater. I guess this is the place where it belongs. Unfortunately I don't know too many of you folks but the ones I do know I really think a lot of and I like to call them my good friends.
>
> There are many different ways in which people climb and ski in our mountains. First of all of them is the one where they hope to gain fame. This I don't consider quite right. There is so much more to be found in our mountains than fame. Isn't it where we can forget about all the small things that seem so important in our lives and leave ourselves open to

all the great things the mountain world concerns us with? Isn't it here where in a hard and fair trial we can prove to ourselves the real and good qualities in our spirit and body? Doesn't it give you more satisfaction to be impressed yourself with your experiences on the mountain, than to impress others with your hair-raising tales?

We have to stand for a lot when we climb or ski. But the harder we have to work for a goal, the more we will appreciate it. It is easy to follow the good trails but yet we find it dull to walk on them. Where the route leads through forbidding cliffs, there we want to go, even though we are afraid. We don't mind the hardships and the danger, because we have confidence in ourselves and because of this confidence we don't fear what's ahead of us, and this confidence will help us all through our difficulties, may they be on a mountain or in everyday life.

With BERG HEIL
Yours,
Hans Gmoser

Notice that Hans's final sentence there mentions the word "confidence" not once, but three times. "Confidence" is Hans Gmoser in a single word. It characterizes precisely the nature of the man and the way he pursued both adventure and business. By the early sixties he was simultaneously managing an expedition schedule to some of the most difficult and remote peaks in North America, running a summer mountaineering school and a winter ski touring program, and through it all shooting and producing films about his mountain adventures. And still, somehow, every year he also made time to take his films on tour to packed auditoriums throughout Canada, the United States and Europe, where he regaled audiences with witty and awe-inspiring narration, dressed for the stage in stylish tweed and speaking with the vivacity of mountain spirit.

His confidence was not only in himself but also in his team, a trait that would set him apart from many other business and adventure leaders. In his late 20s Hans already had the leadership qualities of an older man but also had the fearlessness and enthusiasm of a teenager. Even before he ever set foot in a helicopter, he was an unstoppable force already known worldwide for his audacious ascents of both rock walls and remote alpine peaks.

Hans and Leo, and Hans's climbing partner from Austria, Franz Dopf, ignored the ethic of the day that frowned on the use of pitons. In doing their own thing, they pioneered one of the sheerest faces yet climbed in Canada, the southeast face of Yamnuska. Canadian purists scorned the technically advanced ascent, to which Dopf responded, "The places that we put a piton in, they wouldn't even get to."

Later, Hans and Heinz Kahl made their own statement of pure climbing style by doing the Lewis-Garner route on Brussels Peak without using the protection bolts previously thought necessary. These arguments over climbing style have been going on ever since, with modern climbers now skipping bolts on some of today's hardest routes – most of them having no idea that Hans and Heinz were making the same statement fully half a century earlier.

Momentum was building in Hans's career. In 1957 he incorporated Rocky Mountain Guides Ltd. Ski touring was the biggest aspect of the business, but guiding difficult technical climbs kept Hans busy through the summer months. In 1958 he was part of the first ascent of Alaska's heavily glaciated Mt. Blackburn. He followed that success in 1959 by leading the first Canadian ascent of Mt. Logan, Canada's tallest peak, in a style that even today would garner expedition sponsorship and news coverage. Most modern ascents of Mt. Logan begin with a ski plane flight onto the glacier at the base of the mountain. While the summit rises to just 41 metres short of the 6000-metre mark, it makes up for any lack of height with sheer mass. The summit plateau of Mt. Logan is 20 kilometres long with a dozen sub-summits, and at its base it has a girth of 120 kilometres. In this dimension, Mt. Logan is the largest mountain on earth.

The 1959 Canadian Mount Logan Expedition was led by Hans and included Ron Smylie, Willy Pfisterer, Karl Ricker, Don Lyon and Philippe Delesalle. It began 100 miles from the peak, at Kluane Lake, whence they hiked and skied up the Kaskawulsh Valley to the base of Mt. Logan. The team climbed the peak's east ridge, pushing the limits of their bodies' ability

HANS GMOSER WITH HIS CAMERA.
THIS PHOTO WAS USED TO PROMOTE
HANS'S FILM PROJECTS.

to acclimatize to the altitude while climbing 4000 metres of narrow, corniced ridge in just six days. When compared to the first ascent of the same route two years earlier, which took a group of five Americans 24 days in the equipment- and time-intensive style of the day, the Canadian ascent was decades ahead of its time. Then, as if the ascent was not enough, Hans led the team down an entirely different route via the Donjek Valley.

Delesalle, the eventual architect for most of the CMH lodges, remembers Hans's leadership style in the face of the unknown with awe. "I don't remember him telling any of us about his plan (to return a different way) until we were there! Hans just said, 'We're going back this way!'"

When they reached the Donjek River, where Hans had used an airplane to stash two inflatable rafts, their 30 days of supplies were long ago rationed and recently finished. "None of us knew a thing about rafting," remembers Delesalle, "but Hans was unquestionably the captain. He was there in the front of the boat telling us what to do. He didn't know a thing about boating either!"

The neophyte watermen made a nearly fatal mistake by lashing their skis to the rafts to create more surface area for the equipment, and the metal edges of the skis eventually cut through the rubber with the motion of the swift river. With one raft and no food remaining, the expedition split into two, with one group continuing down the river with the equipment and the other walking for the road. Eventually they all reached the Alaska Highway safely with little more than their threadbare clothing and their lives. Near the road, the last raft capsized and disappeared, taking with it hundreds of priceless photographs and thousands of dollars in equipment, but the climbers escaped unscathed. Hans wrote of the epic adventure: "Now we head home. We lost most of our gear and many pictures. Financially speaking, we are poor – broke. But this does not mean anything now. I think we are rich."

The few surviving photos and the film from Hans's movie camera were in his pack, which he had carried from the river when the group split. The footage from the trip is among the greatest expedition filming ever done, with sequences ranging from the gruelling approach, the meagre food and equipment, difficult climbing, easy midnight glacier descents riding their backpacks strapped to their skis, and finally the ill-fated raft trip and soggy struggles in the quickly rising Donjek River.

The next winter, Hans put together another team of six for an audacious traverse connecting the series of icefields and glaciers along the Continental Divide between Lake Louise and Jasper, an undertaking Hans felt would rival the famous Haute Route from Chamonix, France, to Zermatt, Switzerland – with a few minor differences. In Europe, a skier could glisse from hut to hut, gleaning information from the hut keepers, guides and other skiers along the way; and with the extensive hut amenities, all a skier needed was a daypack and a wad of cash. The Canadian version of such a traverse was entirely uninhabited, so the endeavour required airdrops of supplies, a bloodhound's sense of smell to find them again and legs strong enough to break trail for 150 miles in untouched snow.

The 1960 Canadian Icefields Expedition was a watershed project for Hans. With his natural entrepreneurial sense of purpose, he convinced the Duke of Edinburgh and the

Calgary Herald to support the undertaking financially, with hopes of eventually placing huts along the route to make it accessible to less masochistic skiers. The plan to cross five icefields and ten glaciers during one ski tour was ambitious enough, but Hans wanted to blaze a trail that not only would work for his team but also would bring skiers from all over the world. For the project he recruited his old friend and Mt. Logan partner Philippe Delesalle as well as Neil Brown, Pat Boswell, Pierre Garneau and Kurt Lukas.

Hans explained his intent to Stephen Franklin, a writer for *Weekend* magazine, by saying: "Once there are sufficient shelters along the route as there are along the [Haute Route], it would be quite easy for any good skier to make the trip. The Americans develop even the most limited ski areas to the utmost. Here, we have skiing country to throw away. It's a shame to have all this wonderful country for ski touring and ski mountaineering and not enjoy it or make use of it."

This underlying motivation to share the mountain experience, one Hans found so rewarding and life changing, had become a driving force in his life beyond his own adventure ambitions. More than one long-time friend has had the same comment about Hans: "He never did it for himself."

He found deeper motivation to break new ground for others to follow than the purely hedonistic reasons that drive many outdoor visionaries. Hans was willing to go to the limits of human tenacity to show the world not only what was possible in North America's most rugged ranges, but demonstrate it in a way that would make an industry out of appreciating and experiencing the wilderness on its own terms.

The expedition skied the most difficult part of the planned route, barely surviving most of the possible pitfalls of an unknown ski traverse. Blizzards trapped the team for days on end amid seas of ice, with dwindling food supplies threatening to starve them to death before the clouds lifted enough for visibility to grant them access to their next food cache. At one point, an avalanche thundered off a nearby peak with billowing snow and churning ice blocks heading straight for the skiers, only to lose momentum on the broken ice and séracs without reaching the terrified team. Hans took an 80-foot fall into a crevasse, and when the team pulled him out, the rope jammed, leaving the rescuers unsure of how to save their leader. While they were pondering the dilemma of the stuck rope, they looked to the side to see a ski punch up through the snow, then a second, followed by Hans who managed to climb out under his own power while the rest of the team worked to extricate his immense pack.

In the end, they didn't reach their goal of Jasper, due to the numerous delays of storms, deep snow and food reserves composed of mostly freeze-dried meals without enough calories to fuel the skiers and their massive energy output. Their effort opened eyes of adventure skiers to the potential of big ski traverses in the Rockies and the snowier ranges to the west. While the traverse today is still far less popular than its glamorous European sister, it was one of the first forays into western Canada's unmatched and untapped potential for rugged, expedition-scale ski traverses.

After Logan and the first ascent of Mt. Blackburn, Hans was confident enough to try big mountains much more quickly than other expeditions of the same era. A mountain wall on

North America's tallest peak, 6193-metre Mt. McKinley, known affectionately by modern climbers as Denali in honour of its original First Nations name, was a natural target for Hans's ambitious and ski-oriented style. The Wickersham Wall is one of the biggest mountain faces on the planet, with 14,000 feet of relief between the Peters Glacier and the summit. In comparison, the Kangshung face of Mt. Everest is 12,000 feet from the base to the summit and the North Face of the Eiger rises 5,000 feet above the high pastures of Switzerland. On Denali, with its higher altitude than Logan or Blackburn, the team's speedy approach nearly proved their undoing. In vintage Gmoser style, they balanced for weeks on the razor edge between unprecedented success and catastrophic failure, and in the end walked away with the success. To minimize exposure to avalanches, they climbed and skied from 10,000 feet to over 18,000 feet in three days, an altitude gain most Denali climbers take eight days to ascend. Half the team became nearly incapacitated by altitude sickness.

Dieter Raubach was paralyzed on one side of his body and was unable to talk or walk properly. Pat Boswell's intestines revolted, preventing him from keeping up with hydration and nutrition, and Hank Kaufman, typically an easy-going Alaskan, became so cantankerous that at times the rest of the team avoided his company entirely. A storm hit right after Gmoser, Gunti Prinz and Hans Schwarz summitted the peak, locking the team into a life or death battle that raged for days, pushing the hypoxic team to the point of vomiting if anyone mentioned food. With most of climbers unable to even drink a cup of tea, they knew if they didn't move they would die.

The descent that followed was more an act of primal survival than mountaineering prowess. Hans and Schwarz, the only healthy ones on the team, attempted to evacuate the others. Schwarz took Tom Spencer and Hans led Hank Kaufman, staggering with exhaustion and hypoxia into the tempest. In an interview with *Weekend* magazine, Hans recalled:

> The fact that I had a sick, staggering man on the end of the rope scared me to no end. I felt this was the next best thing to suicide, yet it had to be done. Halfway down Hank fell and I found myself hurtling through the air above his head. I was roped in 30 feet behind him. We rolled over and over on top of each other, both of us trying desperately to grab at something. It was a helpless feeling. We must have fallen 60 or 70 feet before plowing into a pile of soft snow.
>
> Hank wanted to curl up in the snow and sleep. I think he would have been quite happy to die at that stage. I had to kick him to make him move and this made me mad. I cursed the guy for using so much of my valuable energy.

Through the storm, Leo waited at high camp, and by the time the storm abated, Leo was blind in both eyes from cerebral edema, a deadly variation of altitude sickness, putting pressure on his brain. The one good thing about altitude edema is there is an easy cure so long as the victim can move – descend. Hans returned to high camp to help his old friend off the mountain, and after losing altitude Leo and the others improved quickly.

On the way down, they managed to ski all but one section of the West Buttress, the easiest way off the mountain and the most common route to the summit.

By this time, Hans and Leo were a committed team chasing a life of adventure. Each of these adventures, and many others on the cliffs and glaciers of the Rockies and the Columbias, built partnerships and forged a team of unwavering commitment. It was almost inevitable that the friendships formed in the hypoxia of Denali's high camp and the commitment of casting off down the Donjek River on rafts held together with skis, and the trust formed in shabby tents during fierce blizzards on the Lyell Icefield would somehow shape the future of mountain adventure. The early sixties were the last years Hans and Leo spent pushing the standards of ski mountaineering and climbing. They were unknowingly at the threshold of an enterprise that would devour their lives for the next three decades.

Franz Dopf remembers his perspective of Hans at the time: "I thought he was crazy. After ten years he had a Volkswagen and a movie camera. I told him he should get a job as an electrician."

The Denali expedition was at the end of the spring of 1963, a watershed season for Hans and Leo. While Leo led ski tours in Little Yoho, Hans was pushing the envelope of wilderness access in order to shoot a promotional film for his guide service by using a plane flown by one of the few mountain pilots at the time, Jim Davies, onto the glaciers in the inaccessible Cariboo Mountains. Most maps include the Cariboos in the Columbia Mountains, but technically the Columbias are the mountains draining into the Columbia river to the west of the Rockies, while the Cariboos drain farther west into the Fraser River. There are just too many mountains in the region to fuss over details, so even the cartographers have simplified the distinctions between the ranges.

As early as the late fifties, skiers in Europe and Alaska had experimented with using helicopters to access untracked snow in the high Alps and the Chugach. It didn't take a genius to see the obvious connection between downhill skiing and helicopter lift service, but it took the right combination of events in the right mountains for the idea to take hold. Unbeknownst to Hans, a geologist named Art Patterson from Calgary had been using helicopters to map geological formations. Patterson received a promotion, from field work to a desk job in Calgary, and explains his brainstorm to try what would become known as heli-skiing as more of a reaction to boredom than a vision of the ultimate snow sport: "After my 'promotion,' all of a sudden life became kind of dull. It sounded fun."

His idea was to try helicopter-supported skiing as a business and to base it out of established downhill ski areas. In 1962 Patterson applied to Banff National Park for a permit to fly helicopters out of Sunshine and Lake Louise but was turned down. Park officials were not about to let anyone loose with a helicopter in the most popular mountain area in Canada.

Patterson was disappointed but not ready to give up on the idea. Realizing he needed a professional guide as a partner to get the enterprise off the ground, he went to Calgary's local equipment store, Premier Cycle & Sport, to see if the owner, Ethan Compton, could recommend a mountain guide who would be up for the task. Hans

HANK KAUFMAN FACING STORM AND
ALTITUDE SICKNESS ON DENALI,
MAY TO JUNE 1963

recalls the story in typical humble prose: "Ethan had other incentives to recommend me to Art – I owed him for equipment he had given me on credit at his store."

Patterson remembers it differently, and based on Hans's reputation for humility and making good on his debts, as well as Compton's liberal loans to many young mountaineers, Patterson's version is the more believable. As he put it, "When I asked Ethan if he could recommend a good mountain guide, Ethan replied, "There is only one guy you want – Hans Gmoser.""

The deal was that Hans would take care of the mountain element and Patterson would take care of the business side. Art found 15 people ready to try using a helicopter ski lift, and charged them each $20 for the day. It sounds cheap, even considering that $20 in 1963 was the equivalent of $128 in today's dollars, but due to the rest of the package, it was not exactly an overnight sensation. The skiers met in Canmore, attached the skis to the helicopter the best way they could think of, with a car's ski rack mounted on the skids, and flew to the Old Goat Glacier just south of town. It took two hours to get everyone to the top of the run and then the snow was terrible. "Only Hans could ski it," remembers Patterson. Breakable crust from top to bottom made for horrendous skiing, and a bushwhack from the base of the run to the road completed a day of heli-skiing that today's discerning heli-skiers wouldn't consider doing even if it were free.

They tried again at Easter out of Golden in British Columbia, but Hans was unable to make the trip due to ski touring commitments in Little Yoho. He suggested veteran guide Peter Fuhrmann to lead the group, and the second attempt fared little better than the first. They flew up the Blaeberry River into the Mummery Mountains in windy conditions, and the engine in the small Bell 47 used every one of its 178 horses in a vain attempt to stay on course. Not only were they unable to reach their planned ski run, the helicopter was blown across the Freshfield Icefield into Alberta before it could land on the first safe-looking run with a suitable landing. Art learned that "you ski where the heli goes," an important lesson about heli-skiing that still holds true today even with helicopters with ten times the power.

After two days, Art decided to quit the business of heli-skiing because it was "too expensive and too chancy." But the seed had been planted. That same year, while Hans was touring the United States with a promotional film of skiing and mountaineering, and after a showing at the prestigious Massachusetts Institute of Technology, he was approached by a young Olympic skier named Brooks Dodge, who had been to several of Hans's screenings. Dodge had been leading ski trips to Europe and knew he could get enough people together to pay for a helicopter. He remembers the chain of events that led to the idea of using a helicopter lift: "On a flight back from Europe I was thinking how, by the sixties, (the Europeans) were powder pigs just like we were, so the good powder would get cut up in one day, and that we needed to go out into someplace like western Canada – maybe use a ski plane or a helicopter. The next year, Hans was touring, and in his film he showed a group ski touring (at Boulder Camp in the Bugaboos) and there was one picture of a helicopter unloading food and equipment. After the show I waited until everyone had gone. I asked Hans if it would be possible to use a helicopter for a couple of lifts on an especially nice day."

Hans wasn't exactly an easy sell. The first attempts at heli-skiing had turned out to be a bit of a disappointment, so it took something more to convince him to try it again. Brooks promised Hans he could keep the money for the trip even if the skiing didn't work out, and with a no-lose proposition in front of his nose, Hans agreed. In 1964, he tried to get permission to use a helicopter at Rogers Pass in Glacier National Park, the obvious spot for easy access to big-mountain powder stashes, but the park was no more accepting of Hans than they had been of Art Patterson two years earlier. It was becoming clear that an extremely remote area would be the place to go heli-skiing. That spring, Hans explored a relatively unknown area with a quirky name in the Purcell Mountains that had a reputation for spectacular rock climbing but no winter users whatsoever. A sawmill camp had been built in the area but it was only operational in the summer. Hans found excellent ski touring and with a team made up of top-notch skiers, including a hot young Austrian skier named Mike Wiegele, they skied most of the peaks and glaciers with reasonable ski access in the area.

THE GRANDFATHERS OF HELI-SKIING: HANS GMOSER, ETHAN COMPTON, BROOKS DODGE AND ART PATTERSON, AT THE BUGABOO LODGE.

Brooks still wanted to try the helicopter ski lift, and Hans had found the spot to try it out. He admitted at first that "when Art and Brookie approached us about using a helicopter to go skiing, we thought they were insane." But insanity and genius are not far apart. It was easy to get permission to use the sawmill camp, and with 46 kilometres of snow-drifted logging road between the helicopter and the nearest sensitive ear, no one would care if they flew all day long in and around the stunning spires with the name that would forever after be synonymous with the ultimate skiing experience: the Bugaboos.

It *was* the ultimate ski experience, and the Bugaboos were just the tip of the iceberg. The rest of the Columbia Mountains hid skier fantasies that took decades to realize and many are yet to be experienced. From the skier's ultimate, heli-hiking was gradually developed, allowing entire families of all ages and people of vastly different abilities and health to live a mountain fantasy built around helicopter access from intimate wilderness lodges with the hospitality learned from the baroness herself. Even with all this as Hans's most lasting contribution to the mountain world, most people who knew him are certain he did not think of himself as the creator of it at all.

"I'll always think of Hans as the climber, the mountaineer, not the heli-ski guru as he is known," says Lloyd "Kiwi" Gallagher, one of CMH's first employees and investors, who put his entire life savings of $5,000 and his heart and soul into the construction of the Cariboo lodge. Franz Dopf also credits climbing for the success of the project. "We did both (climbing and skiing) but climbing is what made us good friends. For making close friends, climbing is better (than skiing)." Indeed, there is no more literal bond between two people than a climbing rope used high on a vertical wall of rock.

Climbing is where it had begun for Hans and Leo, but skiing is where the path led. In 1960 Hans wrote an article for *SKI* magazine chronicling the Canadian Icefields Expedition. In it he gives the reader a clear insight – as he could not have known in 1960 that five years later he would be leading skiers out the door of a helicopter – into the blazing motivation he felt for skiing and why he was the natural leader to introduce the world to the thing we now call heli-skiing. He wrote:

> Every time I look from many mountaintops that I reach during the summer, I can see hundreds of fantastic ski runs, and the desire to skim over those distant snowfields grows so strong within me it hurts.
>
> Since the mountains are my profession, I suppose I should be more matter of fact about them. But the Canadian Rockies have a magnetic fascination, and as I look down from the peaks I get the feeling that a man should have wings to carry him where his dreams go. Since we are not angels, a pair of skis is a good substitute.
>
> Of course, there is plenty of skiing at our modern ski resorts, but this is not what I have in mind. I want to travel fast and free over the untouched, snow-covered country, to follow the lure of the tempting peaks which pierce the horizon and to be alone for a few days or even a few hours in the clear, mysterious surroundings.

2

BUGABOO MAGIC

We wanted to inhale and breathe life again . . . We were rebelling against an existence full of distorted values, against an existence where a man is judged by the size of his living room, by the amount of chromium in his car. But here we were ourselves again; simple and pure. We were ready to trust each other, help each other and give to each other our everything.

This mountain to us is not a sports arena. To us it is a symbol of truth and a symbol of life as it should be. This mountain teaches us that we should endure hardships and not drift along the easy way, which always leads down.

— Hans Gmoser

bug•a•boo (BUHG uh boo) n. 1. An object of obsessive, usually exaggerated, fear or anxiety.

— Oxford dictionary

THE BUGABOOS FROM THE AIR LOOKING SW. BUGABOO LODGE IS JUST OUT OF THE FRAME NEAR THE TOE OF BUGABOO GLACIER IN THE DEEP VALLEY AT THE BOTTOM LEFT OF THE PHOTO.

Time has a way of transforming what was once feared and worthless into something loved and valued. There is a little dead-end valley at the eastern edge of the Columbia Mountains where mining once proved to be an enterprise of such complete failure that one miner described the place as a "veritable bugaboo." The name was the only thing that stuck; the present day Bugaboos are one of the most revered mountain features on the planet for hikers, climbers, photographers and, of course, skiers.

The Bugaboo Spires are an anomaly of alpine beauty. They are made of granite, the stone that comprises most of the famous rock spires of the world, from the Himalaya to Patagonia, Yosemite to the Alps. It resists the carving power of glaciers better than most rock, so it tends to form smoother faces, as if the ice were a giant knife in the hand of a master sculptor cleaving great slices from the mountains to leave great cathedrals of stone. In the surrounding mountains, the glaciers shaped the softer sedimentary rocks as well, but left more rugged faces as if the carving force of the glacier were in the hands of a drunk with a bulldozer.

In all directions, thick forest and a morass of sedimentary rubble hide the spires from view. Hunters, loggers and miners all had their day attempting to pull something worthwhile from the area around the spires, and the difficult access prevented the place from becoming a tourist destination. Loggers had somewhat better luck harvesting the thick timber in the area, but the next enterprise in the valley transformed mountain recreation and uncovered the real treasure hiding in the snow-covered forest and across the extensive glaciers below the spires.

To allow loggers to process timber before transporting it down the long road to the Columbia River, a rudimentary sawmill camp had been built below Bugaboo Glacier. The plywood shacks with rough interiors were deserted during the winter, and situated as they were, within a day's ski of the Bugaboo Spires, they were ideal to serve as base camp for ski adventures. The sawmill camp was the first of a series of serendipitous coincidences that ultimately allowed remote heli-skiing to develop.

The potential for mountain adventure in the area was first realized when the spires drew the attention of mountaineers, including the climbing visionary Conrad Kain. After leading first ascents up more and more difficult peaks, he found himself in the Bugaboos facing climbing challenges at the cutting edge of the world standard of the day. In summarizing his experiences in the area, he wrote: "This summer came to an end with a trip to the Howser and Bugaboo spires, and it was in this group that we made an ascent as interesting and as difficult as any I have encountered in the Alps."

Today this concentration of inspiring and difficult summits is known worldwide as one of the finest climbing destinations on the planet, and each year the standards of alpine rock climbing are pushed higher on the steep faces, smooth rock and cleanly cleaved cracks of Bugaboo, Howser, Snowpatch and Pigeon spires. A logging road in the bottom of the valley makes it the most accessible alpine rock-climbing area in North America and the place for aspiring Canadian and American climbers to prepare for the world's most remote and difficult climbs.

Places like the legendary Mont Blanc massif in the Alps have similar climbing opportunities, but as a ski destination the Bugaboos became known worldwide as a place to have an experience unlike anything else on earth. The tectonic intrusion that pushed the granite into the sky also lifted the surrounding area into a high plateau, creating deep valleys on all sides and ski runs that begin within snowball-throwing distance of the surreal rock walls and go for miles down rolling steep glaciers into uninhabited valleys.

A second and perhaps more important coincidence was that the mid-sixties were blessed with big winters producing deep and stable snowpacks. Avalanche transceivers for finding buried avalanche victims were yet to be invented. Snow science was an oxymoron. Guides were more competitive with each other than the professional guide teams today, and they skied anything a helicopter could put them on top of. A different snowpack would almost certainly have meant a tragedy that would have crushed the fledgling industry. The unusually stable snowpack allowed every week, from the first one in 1965 until the booming popularity of heli-skiing in the early seventies, to be a festival of deep-powder skiing without serious avalanche incidents, ensuring nothing but rave reviews from all who experienced it.

Considering everything, it's hard to explain the development of Bugaboos skiing without considering a little magic. It began with Brooks and Ann Dodge, who convinced their ski club to join them on a rowdy adventure to the wilderness of British Columbia, and handed Hans Gmoser his first heli-ski week on a silver platter: a prepaid group with no refund no matter what happened. The adventure began in Banff, where Hans directed the group to don ski clothes before piling into the two Volkswagen station wagons for the drive to the Columbia Valley. Fortune smiled on the innovators and the first week of heli-skiing in the Columbias was seven days of perfect powder under bluebird skies. Enga Thompson, one of the skiers that first week, remembers the snow being "that effortless kind of powder where the skis just go wherever you look."

Those first flights into the spires, the small, slow Bell 47 helicopter pivoting back and forth beneath its rotor with the glass fuselage giving unobstructed views of the snow-cloaked spires, must have been an otherworldly experience and a glimpse into the future of skiing. Even the long wait on top while the two-passenger machine ferried the rest of the group up was a dream. It was worth the price of admission even without the skiing: to be transported effortlessly into the heart of the mountains – while the trails are buried in metres of snow, roads are impassable drifts, and trees are cloaked in ghoulish snow blankets – and left to stand as the only humans in a place where civilization did not exist. The group only skied a run or two each day, but it was more helicopter-accessed skiing than had ever been done before, on dizzyingly long runs that had never been skied – and no one was counting yet anyway.

Brooks Dodge found exactly what he had been looking for and word spread like wildfire as the interest in skiing the Bugaboos increased exponentially. The experience was more fascinating than any ski holiday ever sold, in part because each person who signed up for a week of skiing in the Bugaboos had a treat unlike anyone else's experience, and in part because it offered a mountain adventure to people who would never have had one without the helicopter to take them there. Just as every snowflake is different, every week of heli-skiing is different; the depth and texture of the snow, the runs chosen by the guides, the individual lines chosen by the skiers, and the congeniality and family relationships with the staff at the lodges gave every skier an experience unique to their time in the Bugaboos. To be able to offer a product whereby the buyer gets something no one else can have was an easy sell and cast a powerful spell over nearly everyone who tried it.

It was this elixir, seven days of skier's heaven, that Bugaboos skiing offered. People would arrive after travelling halfway around the world expecting the ultimate ski experience, only to have even those lofty expectations thoroughly surpassed with a quality of skiing and mountain living they had never dreamed could exist. And it happened in such remoteness that all the distractions of life ceased to matter. Isolation and exceeded expectations combined to make this an experience far more powerful than just using a helicopter for a ski lift.

It has been called "a nirvana that can be bought," but it was more than that – the price of admission also included the ability to ski, adding a ski team's athletic bond between participants that could never be found at the most expensive resort where anyone with enough cash can participate. It's the kind of experience often described as "beyond words," though some have come close. Kathryn Livingston wrote in *Town & Country*:

> Indeed, the adventure is dream realization of the highest order. The sensations eclipse superlatives. Weaving through the white wilderness resembles moon flights in that you have a sense of being out of this world, on some other plateau of existence, and in touch with eternities. It's the combination of the helicopter, the intensity of the action, and the knowledge that you are carving your tracks into virgin snow where sometimes no human has ever been before sends you into flights of ecstasy. As the sinisterly nice little James-Bondish helicopter swoops you up the valley and serves as a chair lift to take you from peak to peak, excitement begins. Your heart skips a beat and your

abdomen seems to leap as the chopper courses its way between sky-piercing granite spires, disappears into snow clouds, and suddenly tilts for touchdown on a patch of snow no larger than a living room to discharge you and your skis. Here starts the fantastic downhill voyage: skiing a run that might take three-quarters of an hour and take you from drops so steep you can't see the tips of your skis to stretches atop millennia-old glaciers and end in smooth, mild sunny vales punctuated by loops around pine trees. Bugaboo skiing is an experience that stands out like a bright gem to enrich a person's life.

It was the kind of skiing that backcountry skiers had been experiencing for years, but the helicopter made it accessible to an entirely new group of skiers. While the helicopter removed the difficulty and the rewards of working against gravity to get to the top on a muscle-powered ski tour, the beginning of heli-skiing was as tough a week as has ever been sold as a recreation excursion. The clientele came for the hardship and trials of the backcountry and the cost was $275, all-inclusive, round-trip from Calgary. The helicopter was a novel addition to the adventure, not a way around it. Hans remembers, "They were a pretty tough lot back then."

And they had to be. After a long journey from home, the final leg of the trip was a snowmachine-powered midnight ski from Spillimacheen for 43 twisting, drifted kilometres to reach the sawmill camp. Hans had hired Lloyd "Kiwi" Gallagher for the job of getting people from Spillimacheen to the Bugaboo lodge. The bluff New Zealander was just the kind of worker and partner Hans needed. He explains his role with a smirk: "I was a mechanic by trade and Hans saw I had a strong back, a weak mind and a warped sense of humour – he knew I'd make a good guide." In the beginning, Kiwi's sole job was to get skiers to the camp, no matter what it took. "We would drive as far as we could, get stuck, and from there walk, ski and skidoo in to the lodge."

The snowmobile had trouble pulling a group of skiers in deep snow, so Kiwi bought a little tank-like Nodwell snow machine from the Norquay ski area. Riding along, usually standing, packed in the short bed of the Nodwell on the road to the lodge, was the first taste of the unusual experience of Bugaboo skiing. If there wasn't enough room in the back of the Nodwell, there was a tow rope attached to the machine. Before jet lag would have a chance to set in, you're on your skis, holding on to the tow rope, being pulled through the darkness, trying to maintain your balance without getting too distracted by the ghostly winter forest on either side of the road. Jean Stuart, who lived in Brisco and for years helped with CMH logistics, remembers being towed to the lodge: "At first it seemed there was no way you could hang on that long. Then your body starts to relax and it's okay."

You arrived at ski nirvana as you should: on your skis, to find the lights of the cookhouse twinkling, the smell of the wood stove heavy in the air. Peeling your numb hands from the towrope, you walked into the rustic shelter at 3 a.m. to be greeted by a warm meal. You'd sit down to eat on a bench made from branches nailed across tree stumps at a table built with rough-cut trees. A few hours later you'd board the helicopter for your first flight into the spires.

The concept was simple: fly from the lodge to a safe landing zone, or drop-off, above a good ski run, land the helicopter, and everyone climbs out while the guide unloads the skis. Then, once everyone is ready, follow the guide down an immense mountain face through untracked snow to a second safe landing zone, or pickup, at the bottom of the valley, where the helicopter waits for everyone to board and the skis to be loaded. Repeat as many times as possible.

Today, the helicopter can handle 11 skiers at a time, and in the main CMH areas four such groups are on the mountain, supported by one helicopter flying almost non-stop to keep up with 44 skiers pounding as many fresh turns as their legs can handle. But in 1965 only two skiers could fit in the Bell 47 at the same time, so it took half a dozen trips to get everyone to the top. Women and children were flown last so they wouldn't have to wait as long in the wind and cold of the drop-off point. On a good day, the group would ski two big runs, one in the morning and one after lunch, for a weekly tally of 15,000 metres – a total frequently reached by today's heli-skiers in a single day.

It was untamed mountain terrain and snow conditions and there were no expectations, so the groups skied everything from the finest powder to the most hideous breakable crust Mother Nature could concoct. It was April, so often the conditions from summit to valley were variable. And it was all skied on long, skinny boards in 210–220 cm lengths later known as "misery sticks."

"I don't know why we never thought about wider skis," muses Sepp Renner, one of the early Bugaboos guides. "We wanted extra flotation, so we used longer skis. Sometimes you ignore the obvious (wider skis), eh?"

It helped that most of the glaciers went a lot farther then and had fewer broken sections of icefalls, séracs and crevasses. The glacial recession we are seeing today is not a subtle change. Joe Jones, one of the first heli-skiers, remembers the "Bugaboo Glacier probably went twice as far." As the glaciers have receded, their surfaces have deteriorated to a point where many sections that used to be safe to ski with abandon are now tricky, dangerous or impossible to navigate even with a rope and technical climbing equipment. A number of classic runs will never be skied again.

In the beginning, though, the snow was deep and stable, no one had ever done anything like heli-skiing before and there were no limits – so the guides and guests went out and found some. Every run started as high as they could land and went all the way to the valley bottom. Sepp Renner remembers, "We never even considered a high pickup." Jones recalls once skiing Baystreet, a run now infamous for the deadliest avalanche in CMH history, from a summit landing so tiny that Hans crawled under the nose of the helicopter to get to the ski basket on the other side of the machine.

Thierry Cardon, a philosopher of mountain sport and one of CMH's most experienced guides, known for his sharp intellect and for skiing alone with a cigarette dangling casually from his mouth, explains the contrast between then and now: "The runs we skied in the early days were sometimes totally different than today. There has been a mental shift in the way we use terrain. When I first lead guided, I tried to give people an Haute Route with a helicopter."

BUGABOO GLACIER AND
HOUNDSTOOTH IN THE SIXTIES.

It was about summits, big features, new terrain, long runs and adventure. There was an attitude of "let's see if we can get down this." The powder was not an end in itself as it is today, but rather a euphoric addition to a mountain odyssey.

To minimize helicopter time for the first few years, the guides chose the last run of the day to deposit the skiers on one of the logging roads near the lodge and to ski or be pulled by the Nodwell back to the camp. The last run was often the worst, with the fewest options. The sun had had plenty of time to melt the surface and the ensuing shadows froze it into a skier's nightmare – breakable crust. To handle the worst breakable crust, an awkward manoeuvre called the kick turn is used. Compared to the smooth, rhythmic motion of turning skis with momentum, the kick turn is like bowling while wearing a straitjacket: one ski at a time is lifted and awkwardly pointed in the opposite direction, all the while tangling in ski poles, the snow, tree branches and anything and anyone else within the radius of the skis' length. Jones remembers a day when he counted 150 kick turns on the last run of the day in bad conditions.

For guests, it was an adventure from the moment you stepped off the plane until you dragged your weary legs back on a week later. Success was not assured. Hard work and exploring the unknown were guaranteed. Terrain was encountered every week that had never been skied before.

Everyone involved – guests, guides and staff alike – worked hard to make the exotic adventure happen. Hans wrote of the project: "It seems to be all work and there is nothing wrong with work. I believe the more you like to work, the more enjoyment you will get out of everything you do."

Bob Geber was a rock climber from Bavaria who, like many European guides, came to Canada to work for Hans for "just one year." He remembers the typical day in the Bugaboos:

> We'd get up at 6 a.m. and the cabins would be freezing. There'd be frost on our sleeping bags. We'd build a fire and walk to the stream to get water in the dark. We cut steps in the snow to get to the stream but the steps would get icy. I remember busting my ass on those steps. Then we'd start fires in the wash shack and the cabins so people could get out of bed. We'd make breakfast, carry more firewood, set the tables and have breakfast ready at eight o'clock. Then we'd wash the dishes and have the first group ready to fly at nine. To begin with we had one cook, four guides and Jim Davies the pilot. That was it. After a storm we'd shovel the roof and the pathways. And it stormed a lot. At that time, guiding was the fun part – work was what happened after the skiing.

For no one did the experience just end when the ski boots came off. In the evening, singing and dancing were the name of the game. People brought their own instruments, and since CMH didn't have a liquor licence, people also packed booze. They would take their bottles of choice into the kitchen while cleaning up and then party until Hans sent everyone to bed at ten o'clock.

The crew of guides, cook, pilot and mechanic slept on the floor in the kitchen building, leaving the cabins for the skiers. The sawmill cabins were the very definition of rustic. A pot-bellied stove and bunk beds were the extent of the furnishings and the two outhouses were popular buildings. Skiers had to supply their own sleeping bags – very warm ones. The other popular building was the sauna, built like the rest of the camp with simple stick-frame plywood construction. Open rafters gave the skiers a place to perch in the hottest part of the sauna. Kiwi remembers one occasion when the men had been sitting in the rafters when the women came in giggling and naked, unaware of the boys just above. The lads in the rafters turned red from sweat and mirth until one of them burst out laughing and sent everyone into hysterics.

The lifestyle of the sawmill camp didn't last long. For three seasons it was a base camp for a group of people who knew they were involved in something unique in sport and time. Besides, they would have slept in holes in the ground if it meant they could ski the Bugaboos.

When Hans saw how people responded to this new experience of helicopter ski touring, and the way the numbers of skiers were growing exponentially each winter, he realized different lodging needed to be built but he was uncomfortable with any environmental impact of development in his beloved mountains. To help with his decisions, he fell back on a resource that proved to be the key to the success of his business: the perspective of his guests. He brought a group ski touring into the Bugaboos before the lodge was built, and while passing a knoll in the bottom of the valley, he pulled one of the skiers aside. It was Enga Thompson, an American in love with everything Hans held dear about the mountains and a veteran of half a dozen ski touring weeks with CMH.

Thompson remembers the day with pride at being chosen by Hans to provide counsel on this huge decision in his life. "Hans lagged behind the rest of the group for a while and then said, 'Come over here for a minute, there is something I have to show you.'"

Hans broke trail into an opening with a spectacular view of Houndstooth and Bugaboo Spires piercing both the sky above and the steep Bugaboo glacier below. Old-growth forest framed the peaks and completed an alpine vista of rarely matched artistic balance and natural splendour. He turned to Thompson and said solemnly, "I could buy this piece of Crown land and build a lodge for helicopter ski touring. What do you think?"

Thompson understood why Hans chose her to answer this crucial question. She explains: "He knew how much I loved the mountains. We had so much in common in the fascination of the wild. He just wanted my opinion."

Hans was a committed environmentalist before, as he put it, "there ever was such a word." His old friend and eventual competitor Mike Wiegele remembers Hans on early ski tours demanding minimalism and low-impact mountaineering. "There had to be hardship or it just wasn't worth it for Hans," Wiegele remembers. "He was a purist environmentalist even in (the early sixties)."

Years later, with a helicopter at his disposal and the tight schedule of a successful businessman, Hans would sometimes ski the 50 kilometres in to the Bugaboo lodge rather than be the only reason for a flight.

As usual, Hans chose his counsel carefully. Even when Thompson participated in the first week of heli-skiing with Brooks Dodge in April of 1965, a free trip as a gesture of thanks from the ever-thoughtful Hans Gmoser, she found it didn't quite suit her approach to the mountains. She forever preferred ski touring, although she felt heli-skiing was "remarkably glamorous" and remembers it as being akin to "landing on, and then skiing off, the top of an ice cream cone."

It is likely Hans felt Thompson would consider the prospect without being distracted by the novelty of the helicopter, and sought her advice because of her selfless perspective of utter respect for the mountain environment. She recalls the discussion through the haze of 43 years and a plane crash that left her with a wooden leg and a tenacious but patchy memory: "I don't remember talking about the noise of the helicopter. I do remember talking about the small impact of the lodge compared to a ski resort with lifts, roads and all that. I was overjoyed!"

Thompson's perspective may well have been a deciding factor for Hans. He told a group in Aspen, Colorado, in 1973: "I must admit that I wasn't concerned about intruding into the wilderness. In fact, I felt this was an ideal way to show a lot more people these mountains and let them ski there. There was a minimum of permanent fixtures: only a lodge and storage facilities in the valley; all we would leave behind on the mountain were ski tracks."

With Thompson's blessing the idea passed Hans's litmus test of minimizing impact on the natural world, and so Hans decided to build the lodge. The government issued CMH a lease to use the land for skiing for one year. Paying for it was another thing entirely, but again Hans turned to his guests. By offering them "skiers' loans" paid back with 6 per cent interest and a ski trip for every $5,000, enough money was raised to nearly pay for the construction. The Calgary investment firm of Barlow & Mackenzie thought the project was interesting enough to pick up the rest of the bill. Some skiers put in so much money that they were unable to use all of their ski trips, and their sons and daughters cashed in on the investment. It wasn't just wealthy people who anted up, either. Joe and Anne Jones borrowed $5,000 from their life insurance policy to invest in CMH. The enterprise was a business paid for by its customers and built almost entirely on feedback from its customers.

For the construction, Hans needed someone with an understanding of the mountains and the demands they would put on a structure, someone who could be trusted to build something effective and beautiful. It had to be designed to withstand heavy snowfall and be built quickly during the short summer while the road was free of snow. He turned to his old adventure partner, Philippe Delesalle, who by this point was well into a successful career as an architect. Delesalle remembers the moment with a chuckle and a shake of his head: "Hans just said, 'Philippe, give me a lodge' and then left on one of his promotions or something, with no direction whatsoever." Added the architect, "He knew when he asked me that I would not give him an Austrian lodge or a French lodge, but a Canadian one."

Delesalle designed the lodge with the simple ideal "to live above the snow, looking out at the mountains."

After everything the two had been through, from hunger on the icefields traverse to hypoxia on Mt. Logan, and Delesalle's expertise in things Hans knew little about, Hans put his lodge design entirely in Delesalle's hands. But when Hans was presented with plans that included indoor toilets, he balked. "What's wrong with using an outhouse?" Delesalle remembers Hans arguing.

With some trouble, Delesalle and the rest of the team eventually convinced Hans of the benefits of indoor plumbing. "We told him the kind of people who are going to come heli-skiing are not going to like using an outhouse – and eventually he agreed."

The Bugaboo lodge opened in February of 1968 and changed the name of the game. It wasn't fancy, but it was the only heli-ski lodge on the planet. Leo remembers, "When we started, luxury was the furthest thing from our minds. We thought what we were selling was outside. We had eight people sleeping in a room, snoring and farting, but we always had good food."

Lynne Seidler, who eventually married Grillmair, had got the job as cook after being interviewed by Gmoser right from his hospital bed after his crevasse fall. She was one of the first cooks in the Bugaboos and an energetic woman who helped create a die-hard work ethic in the business. Lynne remembers those first accommodations as being "army style": "There were eight bunks per room with rough cedar walls. We'd get horrible splinters making the beds, so we started wearing leather gloves to make beds. The refrigerator was a well-insulated room painted silver on the inside."

Most of the food was brought in during the fall, before the road was drifted closed, so everything was canned or dried. The selection was a far cry from the culinary excellence of modern lodges, where chefs and bakers have access to fresh ingredients every week and are able to craft meals of a complexity and aesthetic quality that would be impossible without frequent resupply. As cook, Lynne was in charge of making the supply appetizing without wasting anything. "Everything was canned except a case of apples and oranges brought in each week."

By then the sport was being called heli-skiing, and the idea of using the helicopter to connect ski tours had been scratched in favour of the burning interest in skiing as much fresh powder as the best helicopter of the day could access. Fortunately, helicopter technology was advancing rapidly and almost perfectly in sync with the yearly increase in the sport's popularity. Rudi Gertsch, one of the original CMH guides, and current owner of Purcell Helicopter Skiing out of Golden, British Columbia, says it was the state of the helicopter industry at the time that made the whole idea feasible: "The price of the helicopter is what made it all possible to begin with. It cost $55 per day to hire a helicopter, plus fuel, which was cheap, too."

Today, CMH has a dozen different areas, three private lodges for groups of 11, and nine larger lodges where 30 to 40 skiers can be found living their ski fantasy. Every area has between 150 and 350 named runs and the sheer numbers of ski tracks on the mountainsides are enough to reduce avalanche hazard by breaking up dangerous slabs of snow before they build to an unstable mass. While the ownership of CMH has changed several times, and other adventurous entrepreneurs have carved out pieces of the region's idyllic terrain for helicopter, snowcat and ski touring operations, the thrill of skiing in the Columbias is the same as it was that April in 1965 when the first heli-ski group caught an effortless ride to the top.

Kitt Redhead, a 27-year-old assistant ski guide in 2007, described skiing in the Columbias as being "like swimming in a lake your whole life, and then having someone take you to the ocean!"

Roko Koell, one of the most influential modern guides, has a way of explaining things like no one else: "In this business happiness is like peeing your pants; everyone sees it but only you feel the warmth."

The magic of the remote alpine lodge in the Columbias is far more than just access to the finest skiing on the planet. Hans was quoted in *enRoute* magazine in 1978 as saying: "The gratifying thing is that when you put a group of people together in a place like the Bugaboo lodge, for instance, there are no social barriers. They are all on the same level. They come here for one reason – to ski deep snow, to ski in wild country that is otherwise inaccessible, to be thrilled by the vistas that the helicopter offers them."

David Barry, the current CEO of CMH, has noticed the same phenomenon today: "People's badges and stripes of life don't matter when they walk through the door of the lodge. It's really refreshing for them. It's this weird, egalitarian, sexy culture where we can do things we don't experience in everyday life."

Hans saw this appeal clearly, and did everything he could to make it a chance to get away from everyday life for everyone, from the rich and famous to the worker who saved for years to live his skiing dream. More than one guide remembers Hans giving them specific instructions when royalty or well-known people were in the lodge to watch out for other skiers hounding the icon about their fame, and to politely distract them with the wonders of the mountains, a conversation about skiing, or anything to keep everyone on a holiday. This isn't hard to do; deep in the wilderness on an epic powder day, it is the most natural thing in the world to treat royalty as a fellow powder hound. When the King of Spain, Juan Carlos, was visiting, he was in an off-balance position during the heli-huddle, the intimate crouch everyone assumes while the helicopter is landing just a metre away, and one of the staff who was skiing that day saw an opportunity to give him a little extra face shot. She reached over and pushed his head into the snow. The King came up laughing, spitting snow, and loving the fact that someone had played with him. On the other end of the spectrum, a mailman from New York had saved money for years to take a once in a lifetime trip to the legendary Bugaboos. On the second day, he crashed and broke his leg. Leo Grillmair, understanding the man's heartbreak, invited him back free of charge to try again after his leg healed.

While changes in guest needs and business culture eventually introduced private rooms, wireless Internet and other comforts far from the eight-person bunk rooms of the original Bugaboo lodge, the feeling and experience have remained much the same. Keeping people together after the skiing is part of the magic. Hans was acutely aware of this and went to great lengths to avoid the hotel syndrome where everyone drifts to their rooms when the activity is over. No televisions and no telephones in the bedrooms keeps everyone in the living area of the lodge making friends and telling stories a little longer. Hans was such a believer in the shared experience that, for a while, he enforced a rule of no light bulbs stronger than 40 watts in the bedrooms so that people would be less inclined to disappear to their rooms and read a book.

It worked, this Hans Gmoser school of mountain adventure – an experience built on participation. Every moment, from the first morning bell until you pull yourself away from the warmth of the fireplace at night, is involved in some way with the skiing experience. "This is the best thing about CMH," says guide Roko Koell. "When it is mid-week (on a seven-day ski trip) people forget what day of the week it is; this is the key."

Groups that meet as strangers become lifelong friends and for decades later they book weeks together to relive the experience with the same group of people. So potent is this spell of the remote heli-ski area with the intimate lodge atmosphere that Bob Geber, currently the longest-standing CMH guide, says, "If a guest asks me about a new area, we always encourage it because we know they'll come back. They almost always do. This is the best."

Providing the complete mountain experience of the remote lodges is a complicated project. "It's about giving 130 per cent service to the guests in mountain style," explains Bobbie Burns area manager Bruce Howatt. "It's not a five-star overdone style, but like if you brought friends to your house."

Working for CMH then was – and according to many current staff, still is – just as much if not more of a life-changing experience as being a guest. When Fran Gallagher, who worked in the office in Banff, first travelled to the Bugaboos to gain some understanding of what she was selling, she had minimal ski experience and didn't know how to conserve energy on the towrope behind the Nodwell snow machine. In the middle of the trip, she noticed movement in her peripheral vision. She looked over to see a huge moose running next to her. The creature's unusual and awkward double-jointed gait, which allows moose to move better than other large animals in deep snow, gave its legs a wind-milling appearance as it churned alongside her. While demonstrating the moment during the 40th anniversary celebration of Canadian heli-skiing at the Bugaboo lodge in 2005, her head was thrown back by the speed of the snowmobile and held at an awkward sideways angle, and her eyes were the size of ski pole baskets. The moment was ingrained in her memory as if it happened yesterday.

Within a few years, the popularity of skiing in the Bugaboos forced a crucial decision: whether to expand the Bugaboos operation or open another area somewhere else. With the Bugaboo skiers utilizing one small corner of the Purcell Range, and the Purcells just one of four huge ranges that make up the Columbia and Cariboo mountains, it would have been short-sighted to arrange accommodations for enough people to make moguls in the Bugaboos while there were oceans of untouched snow in other parts of the range. By then, it was clear that the commodity of most value was fresh snow, not the quirky name or the dramatic spires, so it was an easy decision to grow into another area where new peaks could be explored, leaving the fresh snow to just 44 skiers. This influenced the eventual tenure system for allocating commercial ski terrain and became the model for CMH heli-skiing: When demand exceeds capacity, open an entirely different area. Keep it intimate. Keep everyone skiing fresh snow.

In the beginning, this was easy to do. The interior of British Columbia was desperately in need of tourism, so much so that in Wilmer, a small town south of the Bugaboos, one

WITH NO TELEVISION, PHONE OR INTERNET, AND 40W BULBS IN THEIR ROOMS, EARLY HELI-SKI GUESTS ENJOYED ONE ANOTHER'S COMPANY. TODAY, THE DEMAND FOR CONNECTIVITY HAS BROUGHT INTERNET AND MODERN COMMUNICATION INTO THE LODGES, BUT THE SCENE IS STILL MUCH THE SAME.

entrepreneur took photos of apples tied to the branches of pine trees and sent them to Britain in an advertising campaign to tempt tourists to the orchards of the Purcells.

The Columbias and the Cariboos were wide open, and every community welcomed commerce. Finding another sawmill camp in a skiing epicentre was not likely to happen, but the growing popularity of heli-skiing required a move. Hans's ideal was to find a place to build another lodge, but the business couldn't yet afford the construction and more skiers wanted the experience than the Bugaboos could accommodate.

Valemount is a town of a thousand people nestled between the Cariboo and Monashee mountains, 120 kilometres west of Jasper. The town was just big enough to have a motel, the Sarak, and half a dozen other businesses. It was an ideal location where a lot of great ski terrain could be explored until another remote lodge could be built.

The culture was that of a rugged logging town where the bar scene made the modern skier's bar antics look like teatime at grandma's house. "We saw some awful fights," remembers Kiwi Gallagher. "The skiers stayed out of it, but it was great storytelling material for them – powder skiing in backwoods BC and watching these wild loggers knock each other out."

In the spring of 1969, CMH began skiing in the Cariboos. With this move, Hans's management responsibilities meant he couldn't just stay in the Bugaboos. Leo took over management of the Bugaboos and CMH started its own competition. Now skiers had a choice of areas to heli-ski, and the terrain of the Cariboos, while lacking the granite cathedrals of the spires, offered a wider variety of ski terrain and more options for skiing when conditions were poor.

At the same time, another skier was doing the groundwork to open his own heli-ski business. Hans Gmoser and Mike Wiegele had met on a bus to Banff. Wiegele was fresh from Austria and, with poor English at the time, was on the lookout for anyone who might speak German. He recalls, "You could pick out the Austrian skier pretty quick."

Hans's down jacket and ski pants stood out against the heavy winter parkas on the rest of the passengers. Wiegele approached Hans and they became fast friends. Like any two young ski bums, they went skiing. They convalesced and rehabilitated from broken legs together. Wiegele's background in ski racing and Hans's in mountaineering made them a capable team in the mountains. Hans was best man at Wiegele's wedding, and when Hans and Margaret got married, Wiegele was the usher. They had adventures together: climbing in the Bugaboos, ski film projects, ski touring in Little Yoho, with Jim Davies's plane on the Cariboos' Canoe Glacier with ski legend Jim McKonkey, and numerous attempts at a ski traverse from Panorama to Rogers Pass.

In the mid-sixties, Wiegele worked as a ski instructor at Lake Louise, but he had dreams of building a ski area and running his own operation. He explains: "I was tired of management who didn't know the difference between a rock and a snowflake. I was looking for independence. Opportunity."

Mike heli-skied for the first time with Hans in the Bugaboos, and as a natural entrepreneur, it didn't take him long to scratch his dream of lift towers in favour of rotor blades. At the same time, CMH was outgrowing the Bugaboos.

Wiegele started his business in 1970, barely a year after CMH first offered Cariboos heli-skiing. Both operations were based out of the Sarak Motel. A standoff of Western-movie proportions unfolded around the Sarak. Considering how much terrain there was to choose from, the conflict reached the ridiculous.

An article appeared in a German newspaper stating Wiegele's was the first heli-ski business, infuriating Hans and prompting other articles in response. According to Wiegele, Hans originally said he wasn't interested in skiing in the Cariboos. When Wiegele was at the printers' one day to order his first brochure and saw the CMH brochure advertising Cariboo skiing he was furious. Mike felt this was a breach of their close friendship, and the atmosphere in Valemount grew tense and fraught with machismo to the extreme. Both men were protecting their interests, but their friendship was a casualty.

Wiegele remembers everyone behaving "like a bunch of teenagers." He laughs frequently while recounting the memory: "We'd have people get ready as fast as possible. You could see their (CMH's) rotor going, you could see our rotor going, and I'd be telling the pilot Fly! Fly! He'd be telling me to shut up and let the machine warm up." While the conflict is legendary in the ski industry, the two operators also helped each other. There were no long-range radios at the time, so the other's helicopter was the first on the scene if there was a need for assistance.

Guests arrived with reservations for a seat with CMH, only to be recruited away by Wiegele. Heated words were exchanged on numerous occasions, but the conflict always stopped short of violence. Guides forgot backpacks in their haste to get the helicopter into the air. Helicopters took shortcuts to get to a landing more quickly, and once, two helicopters approached the same landing from either side of a ridge. At the last instant before a collision, the pilots managed to pull away in different directions and avoid a deadly and potentially industry-destroying crash. Skiers would arrive at the top of a run to find it tracked out by the competition. There was no regulation of heli-skiing, and things escalated to a point where both Hans and Mike were writing letters to the government asking for intervention. It was a dangerous time of young egos and wild mountains, but luckily no accidents occurred as a direct result of the conflict.

The guides managed to maintain a keen professionalism even within the lawless business that had zero government regulation at the time. To this day, what is good for one heli-ski operator is good for the others and vice versa. Realizing this, Martin Heuberger, one of Wiegele's lead guides who eventually moved back to Austria and today sells CMH trips as a ski travel agent, and Hermann Frank, one of the CMH guides and the area manager at the time, met behind their bosses' backs to plan the day to avoid conflict and maximize skiing quality. Even with such cooperation, it was difficult to share plans, because nothing was named in the unexplored wilderness of the Cariboos. And when the guides tried to use names, each team had different names for the same mountain feature or the same names for different features. Jeff Boyd, a guide and doctor, suggested the groups share their maps to ease the communication issue and facilitate rescues.

The lumbering machine of government was too slow to remedy the situation, as area-based tenures – government permits issued to a single heli-ski operator to use a particular sector of the mountains – weren't issued until the early eighties, so the guides had to sort it out themselves. Sepp Renner recalls the scene as relatively amicable: "During the day there was tension, but at night at the bar we all got along. It was me and Hermann Frank who convinced Mike to go to Blue River."

In 1973 Wiegele decided he liked the look of the Monashee and Cariboo mountains on either side of Blue River, a short drive south of Valemount. "I hired a plane to fly over Blue River," he recalled, "and when I saw the mountains from the air, it was like a book opening up in front of me." Wiegele moved out of Valemount and never looked back. In 1974 CMH completed the Cariboo lodge, 18 kilometres up the Canoe River from town.

By this point, the friendship between Hans and Mike had been changed forever. While Wiegele carved out a huge tenure in the Cariboos and Monashees, developed ski guiding in Blue River and created his own ski guide training program, the Canadian Ski Guide Association, Hans developed the profession of mountain guiding in North America, forging relationships among the various guide services, international guiding standards committees and land managers, and helped create the association now called Helicat Canada to give helicopter and cat-skiing operations a common voice. Even today, with Canada's commonly accepted stature in the International Federation of Mountain Guide Associations (IFMGA) as the international leader in ski guiding, Wiegele maintains a fierce independence and prefers to keep a comfortable distance from the rest of the Canadian skiing industry while managing the second biggest heli-ski outfit in the country from an expansive log heli-ski village in Blue River. Regarding the rift between the two industry leaders, Wiegele explains, "We were always friends, but we were just too proud to express it."

Even in the end, their paths were closely parallel. They both are inductees in the Canadian Skiing Hall of Fame, and within two months after Hans's fatal bicycle crash in 2006, Wiegele was riding his bike down the road from Mt. Robson when he ran into a boulder and tumbled headlong at high speed into a talus field, narrowly missing jagged boulders and escaping with his life and a couple of broken ribs. In describing the near miss he says, "If I had fallen just a little to one side or the other . . . " and his voice trails off into silence.

Two CMH guides started the next heli-ski operations. In 1974 Rudi Gertsch and Peter Schlunegger, schoolmates from Wengen in Switzerland and two of the original Bugaboos guides, decided they wanted to open a heli-ski business of their own. For a year, they worked together in Revelstoke before Gertsch moved to Golden.

The sudden appearance of competition was a hard thing for Hans to stomach after years of being the unrivalled king of the Columbias. Near Revelstoke, Bob Geber was running CMH operations in the same area where Schlunegger was running his groups. Geber remembers the time, laughing: "Peter would go flag a landing with his flags and I'd go pull them and put in CMH flags. Then Peter would go pull our flags and put in his own again. There was a time when I had claimed the biggest heli-ski tenure ever, but eventually we agreed to share it."

All four operators were jockeying for position in the mountains. "We got to this point where we had all pushed really hard," remembers Gertsch. "So we all sat down and said, 'We're all guides.' Somebody has to do something."

It was the beginning of what became the countrywide association of Helicat Canada, but for the first meeting Hans refused to attend. Gertsch explains, "He thought we were all ganging up on him. For the second meeting I tried really hard to convince Hans it was a good thing. He came. In those days we weren't competitors – we were guides."

Gertsch had gotten married in 1972 and was tired of working away from home. He explains his reason for opening a new business as part family needs and part a change in the business: "I tried to convince Hans there were places we could do heli-skiing and stay in town, but Hans was convinced of the value of staying and skiing for a whole week from a remote lodge. The CMH shareholders were putting pressure on us. They wanted more numbers and wanted us to ski with bigger groups. At one point, Hans got tired of them pressuring him to ski with bigger groups, so he hired a Sikorsky and took 36 shareholders skiing in the same group. It was chaos. After that, they let him keep the small groups."

Putting more skiers in each lodge would have used up the fresh snow too quickly and decreased the intimate atmosphere of the lodges, but the shareholders wanted more business to get return on their investment, so the pressure was on to expand into different areas. With profit a requirement, and four heli-ski operators in lively competition, the age of innocence of heli-skiing was officially over. Gertsch explains it simply: "The shareholders changed it. Hans had no choice."

An avalanche fatality in 1974 accentuated the change. The lofty black and white spires of the Bugaboos and "that effortless kind of powder where the skis just go wherever you look" remain the same, but the magical years of heli-skiing with total abandon in an endless mountain range were over.

3
RAPTURE OF THE DEEP

Again we come to the end of a great ski trail. Such a ski trail is many trails, and neither of those trails is ever the same. Those trails are not bound to any lift line or fenced in by trees. They are a free expression of sheer delight by people who carve them into the snow. To them it doesn't matter whether they ski good or bad because these trails will be gone again tomorrow, covered by the ever-shifting snows of the high mountains.

— Hans Gmoser, film narration for *Ski Trails*

The first time most of us experience the thrill of skiing, it is on a groomed slope or packed trail with the snow whizzing past. It's an undeniable rush, the only contact with the snow being the unfeeling bases of our skis. Then, at some point, we ski in softer snow, where the sensation of movement creeps over our boot tops and a few more of our nerve endings come in contact with the passing snow, adding another dimension to the feel of speed and excitement in skiing and forever making us look to the weather report before a ski trip to see if we'd be lucky enough to score a powder day. Even a few centimetres of fresh snow are enough to change the skiing sensation from moving over snow, to moving through the snow. It's as good as it gets. Or is it?

At some point, in a ski bar or around the table, with a group of excited faces stained tan in the shape of goggles, we hear the words champagne powder and bottomless snow float past. We begin to fantasize about what it would be like to ski snow so dry and light that it is more like the essence of snow than the element itself. We dream about snow so deep that touching the bottom with a ski or pole is like trying to touch the bottom of the swimming pool at the deep end. It is a phenomenon that exists in-bounds at a ski area only during the biggest storm cycles – in which case the area is often closed anyway. While skiing in bottomless fluff, every square millimetre of the surface of your body can feel the snow flowing past. All the senses are heightened during the experience. Snow hisses past the ears, eyes strain for visibility, wet skin and sweat flavour the tongue as your skis lose contact with anything supportive, and instead of carving and sliding, skiing takes on a sensation of flying. "It's like someone's holding you up by the hat!" says Mike Welch, the manager of Galena, smiling like a kid on Christmas morning.

Finding such snow is the problem. Before heli-skiing, venturing into the backcountry and skiing up the hill first was the only way to consistently experience these conditions, but this requires more effort and mountain savvy than is reasonable for the average downhill skier. Even considering the difficulties and danger, every year the number of backcountry skiers increases dramatically as more people join the quest for virgin powder. Heli-skiing captured the fascination of the world's skiers not because of the remote mountains, the comfortable and remote accommodations, the fast machines or the badge of ski connoisseur it indelibly leaves on those who try it, but because it offers an easy way to ski vast quantities of this dreamy snow in its most natural form. Take a base of bottomless snow and add a frosting of champagne powder and fast, effortless access to rip thousands of vertical metres every few hours, and you have the recipe for a ski experience worthy of obsession, possession and addiction.

The root of the addiction is the fresh track. Skiing through fresh snow is ultimately a destructive process. During a snowstorm, billions of geometrically perfect snowflakes pile one on top of the other like the most delicate house of cards ever made. The foam on a cappuccino or the head on your favourite ale is typically about 20 per cent liquid, while powder snow can be as little as 3 per cent liquid and is often about 5 to 7 per cent in the Columbia mountains. While skiing in the lightest powder, the stuff ski guides call cold smoke, the force of passing through it with such violence, relative to the fragile structure, creates enough displacement through the snow to cause snow crystals to lift from the surface well ahead of the skier.

EVERY SQUARE MILLIMETRE OF THE
SURFACE OF YOUR BODY CAN FEEL
THE SNOW FLOWING PAST.

Pile up enough of this kind of snow, and skiing takes on an entirely different dimension and would be considered a different sport if it were not for the similar equipment and technique; the sensation is utterly unlike skiing on a firm surface. The trouble is that each skier leaves behind massive devastation on a microscopic scale. Crystals are pulverized, the house of cards crumbles to its foundations and, on all but the most epic days when tracks fall in on themselves as they're created, a skier who crosses the track gets a very different sensation than the first skier. Skiing the chowder left behind by a thousand greedy powder hounds can still be fun, but it is nothing like the feeling of the high-velocity dance with the untouched perfection of freshly fallen snow.

One headline in the Montreal *Gazette* called powder skiing "writing your name on the face of the gods." It is a heady feeling to make such a dramatic mark on the face of the Earth in the name of fun and have it matter not a whit. Surfers send plumes of water into the sky and carve their parabolas across the face of a wave, but their tracks only last a few seconds; while skiers take a flawless surface and carve it like a sculptor shapes stone into a personal three-dimensional expression of fun and skill. Leaving tracks in the snow silently says, "I did that. I was there. I have an effect on things. I am real." In a world where we strain to make order from chaos, powder skiing is a chance to shred something to ribbons with the effect lasting only as long as the calm weather before the next storm.

Heli-skiing contains elements of the most popular addictions, and it's not just the white powder. "Once you're hooked on heli-skiing, anything else is just a little less interesting," one skier explained.

It's an experience, like a narcotic high, that only exists while it's happening. Nothing can be taken away from it and the user starts to dread the end before it's even over. The difference is that it doesn't kill brain cells, and some skiers claim it saved their lives. Roy Ostberg, a heli-ski fanatic who spends several weeks each season both heli-skiing and ski touring, says: "It's cheap compared to the medical bills I would have had by now if I hadn't changed my life because of skiing. I was overweight and headed down an ugly road. Then I discovered heli-skiing, started training and taking care of myself and turned my life around." When compared to most other addictions that tend to push families and friends apart, heli-skiing brings families and friends closer together. Skier Diane Soucheray explains it simply, "This is where my father turned into my buddy."

Even world-class athletes are awed to the point of distraction by the magic of heli-skiing. After tasting great conditions on the Red Baron run in Galena, 20-time Wimbledon winner Martina Navratilova skied up to her guide, Mike Welch, and said: "I'd have given up tennis ten years earlier had I known about this!"

A German skier named Steffanie spent a week heli-skiing in the Adamants and promptly fell in love with the deep powder of the Columbias. She explained, "I was scared at first, but after the second day I was completely addicted."

After returning home to Munich, she sold her business, left her husband and moved to Canmore to be closer to the source of her newfound passion. Ironically, the next time she went heli-skiing she broke both legs in a high-speed crash, but she rehabilitated in Canada without rescinding her commitment to live in the Rockies.

Even the guides, who ski every day, acknowledge the addiction. "CMH pays me $250 a day to serve dinner. I do the skiing for free," says Bernie Wiatzka, a Galena guide, giggling and smiling from ear to ear.

"Powder," says Roko Koell, the gleam of a pusher in his eye, "is a powerful drug. The perfect powder I had twice in all these years. Subconsciously it is what I am striving for all the time. Once, I was on Tango in the Monashees in 1989 after it had snowed for seven weeks straight. Even before reaching speed you couldn't see. Before starting I'd look down the hill and guess I had 75 turns before reaching the trees, then I'd ski blind for 75 turns and stop. When we stopped it took two minutes for the snow to settle enough so we could see again! The only way to guide was to yell. You couldn't see the others – you couldn't even see yourself!"

For skiing, this kind of snow is euphoria, but for guiding, it's nerve-wracking. Bruce Howatt remembers a day in the Bobbie Burns when the snow was so deep that he and the other guides were afraid someone would drown. "When a skier would fall, they'd just disappear," he recalls, laughing, "but somehow, everyone did alright."

When conditions are good, skiers push themselves to the limits of connective tissue and financial solvency to keep skiing. I heard one guest on a powder day say, "I'm on my 12th Advil of the day and I'm doing great."

At the bottom of a powder run in Kootenay, Bill Morck, a skier from Colorado who was planning to try heli-skiing just once, said, "All I can say is my kids better get scholarships," and gazed absently into the distance with a strange sheepish grin on his face.

That same day, another skier said, "I don't want to, but I could die now. That was a lifetime day."

One Saturday, after a big snow in the Monashees, a skier was trying to convince a friend to stay another week instead of returning home to their family: "You can always have another kid, but the skiing is never going to be this good again!"

The addicts accept their fluffy vice happily. Many groups return year after year to the same lodge, the same runs, and have the same mind-blowing ski-fest every time and are now introducing their children and great-grandchildren to the stuff. High-powered businessmen make an exception to their puritanical work ethic for their ski trips with CMH. "Our whole year revolves around this trip," a clothing magnate said about the company's annual group visit. "If business needs to be done during this time – forget about it."

Heli-skiing also has elements of the gambling addiction: getting the best week of the year is a rush of luck and makes it easy to play again, while getting the worst week of the year just makes you want to try again at whatever cost. What are the odds of winning? According to Thierry Cardon, "If you come ten times, two will be exceptional, worth the cost of all ten. Six weeks will be good, worth the price of admission, but not exceptional. Two will be total shit – not worth paying for. But if you're not willing to gamble because of the possible bad weeks, you'll never get the exceptional."

During the sixties, the wisdom was that, 70 per cent of the time, the skiing in the Bugaboos is better than anywhere else on Earth. The other 30 per cent was truly awful. One journalist called the bad skiing "a nightmare of Alfred Hitchcock proportions. Or perhaps Hans Gmoser proportions."

Long dry periods are not too bad, as the glaciers take on a Styrofoam consistency that carves well under ski edges, and the scenery alone during high pressure systems is worth the trip. Windstorms turn the high country into an unskiable maelstrom, but as long as the helicopter can fly, there are usually protected powder stashes to be found. Big dumps are a mixed blessing; sometimes they ground the helicopter, but the anticipation of what awaits after the skies clear makes the downtime buzz with anticipation.

The worst is a weather phenomenon called the Pineapple Express. It is so bad that guides don't even like to mention it by name; they call it "the P-word," as if Mother Nature were an illiterate child who will get a bad idea if they say the wrong word. It truly wrecks the skiing. Warm, wet systems can pour off the Pacific from the southwest at any time of the year, dumping centimetres of rain on the highest peaks and turning fields of glorious powder into repulsive slush within a matter of hours. A cold front on the tail of the Pineapple Express freezes the surface into a sheet of solid ice that shatters like glass under a landing helicopter. The resulting shards can be picked up and peered through like a windowpane. Skiing on such a surface is a bone-rattling experience and, while fascinating in the challenge and beauty of interacting with the glistening medium, it's a world apart from the dreamy softness of powder skiing glorified by magazines and heli-ski marketing campaigns.

Then there is the truly diabolical breakable crust. Skiers tell stories of experts who can carve perfect turns in any snow, but according to ski guides, such a skier is a myth.

At some point, there is a breakable crust that will send anyone tumbling. That point is where the surface almost supports a skier's weight but fails catastrophically at the slightest movement. It's akin to skating on a pond of ice that is too thin: no amount of skill can save you. Luckily, a helicopter is a great tool for minimizing the exposure to such snow, but all it takes is a few metres to humiliate even the most seasoned experts.

The third element of the addiction in this sport is the combination of freedom and responsibility inspired by wilderness skiing. Making decisions about where to ski and how fast to go are inherent in any skiing experience, but the big-mountain element makes the price of a mistake that much greater. There is nothing a guide can do to prevent a reckless skier from tumbling into a tree well or a big crevasse or falling off a cliff or over a fragile cornice if such a skier throws their own personal judgment to the wind, ignores the guide's instructions and skis with total abandon. As a result, the vast majority of people ski their best while heli-skiing, and each individual contributes to the overall safety record of the sport, a record that is surprisingly good considering the numbers of people skiing in the rugged mountain terrain of the Columbias every day all winter long with opportunities for self-destruction on every run. Heli-skiing with a big, experienced operation is statistically the safest way to ski backcountry powder. Nevertheless, the impression of risk in the rugged environment capped with huge cornices, draped with avalanche debris and dotted with minefields of tree wells is enough to raise the consciousness of the average person far above the level required in daily life in the modern world, where danger has been eliminated or disguised by layer after layer of routine and infrastructure. This awareness is refreshing and awakens something vital within us that we crave awfully until the next time we can leave our padded, signposted and regulated world and get back into the mountains.

Skiers play a game of timing in hopes of getting those exceptional weeks and avoiding the "nightmare of Hans Gmoser proportions," but the truth is that either extreme can happen at any time, and every part of the season has something worth experiencing. During early season, the days are short and the snow is cold and dry. For Mike Welch, manager of CMH Galena, December is his favourite month: "The snow is bottomless. Twenty centimetres fall every night. The days are short. It's kind of dark all day. I love the whole ambience! We come home wet. Our gloves are soaked. Our zippers are frozen. I just love it!"

Most guests prefer mid-season because of the fear that a dry autumn could limit the skiing, but often the early season has the lightest powder of the year. Also, the snowpack is often simpler to evaluate for avalanche hazard because it is relatively similar no matter which direction a ski run faces, so the guides have more fun because their primary job of keeping everyone safe is a lot easier. This means unlimited options for skiing. Later in the season, changing weather wreaks havoc on various aspects, leaving a slightly different snowpack on every slope. In the spring, sun bakes the snow layers into a single, stable mass, but the intense rays quickly turn the surface into a slushy bog. In December, the daily tours often touch down on runs facing every direction on the compass, while during the rest of the year, each day's program is more often limited in one way or another by snow stability or quality.

High season is January through March, when most of the spaces in CMH sell out a year in advance. Hans defined excellent skiing as "all day long from top to bottom, the face shots stop just shy of the chin." For this kind of skiing, the consistently deep snowpack in even the driest years make mid-season the best gamble for scoring a week of powder skiing. However, it is also the season most at risk of having days of poor or impossible skiing because of the dreaded P-word. In mid-winter it takes a heavy snow to heal the wound, but by springtime the warmer days quickly turn the disaster of a Pineapple Express into a bonanza of velvety corn skiing.

These days, spring skiing is almost a forgotten word in heli-skiing, but originally, heli-skiing was only offered in the spring. In 1966 the CMH heli-ski season didn't start until March 20. Longer days, buried crevasses and a generally more stable snowpack made for more options and gave the groups time to ski home at the end of the day. As demand and confidence in the system grew, the guides extended the season into December, but spring skiing still has its merits and Hans was always perplexed as to why more people don't want to ski late in the season. For many years, CMH ran heli-ski weeks through late May until the demand changed to the point where most skiers wanted mid-winter bookings and effectively changed the season of the sport.

Besides the obvious advantage of après ski beverages in the sun on the lodge deck, there is also the stuff some guides call the best snow of all: corn. Corn snow forms during cycles of hot days and cold nights when the surface freezes into an icy slab at night, and the strong rays from the spring sun loosen the surface into a layer of small kernels of forgiving snow, creating a medium that is effortless to ski at adrenaline-pumping speeds. After a few short hours however, corn snow turns to repulsive mush that grabs skis like quicksand. A day of ski touring in the spring often ends with a challenging thrash through soggy snow to get to a less solar aspect, or a short day to avoid afternoon avalanches released by the sun. The temporary nature of good corn snow makes the helicopter the ultimate corn-harvesting tool. On a corn day, the lead guide will plan the trip to hit all the right aspects, following the sun, starting on east-facing slopes in the morning and then moving to south, west and finally north at the end of the day. Corn snow is easier to ski than the most perfectly groomed piste, and the skis seem to turn with no more energy than a thought. The ideal spring week includes both powder and corn skiing as the high- and low-pressure systems battle for the season.

Both terrible and fantastic skiing is possible at any time, and any skiing is better than a day in the office. The worst scenario is what happened to one poor soul after he arrived in Valemount: as he stepped off the bus at the helipad for the flight into the Cariboos he slipped on a patch of ice and blew out his knee. He turned around and limped back onto the bus for a truly sad ride back to Calgary.

Skiing quality in the Columbias is so often fantastic that it quickly makes ski snobs out of many skiers. Like a junkie with high tolerance for their drug of choice, many powder skiers become quickly bored with less than perfect snow, irritable about delays in the skiing program, and only high doses of the white powder will put them back in a good mood.

Stefan Blochum, a German guide who has worked in the Gothics for several seasons, remembers finally getting to ski the legendary Run of the Century. It was perfect powder, and at the bottom he was thoroughly excited and waited for his group to show some appreciation. The only words spoken were from one guy who said, "I noticed the light was better half an hour ago." Stefan remembers, "I almost choked."

For most skiers, it would have been the experience of a lifetime, but for the junkies in the group, it wasn't even a buzz. This kind of skier in the throes of powder withdrawal often puts unrealistic demands on guides. During a week of particularly icy conditions, one skier from Aspen irritably told a guide, "In Colorado, this would dry out and turn to powder overnight!"

Frustrated, the guide replied, "Let's put a block of ice in the freezer overnight and see if we have a nice pile of powder in the morning!"

At other times, it can be raining to the mountain tops during the worst Pineapple Express of the year and someone will lean over to a guide during dinner and say, "A good guide could find us some powder snow on a high, north-facing bowl."

One skier brought his family, including two small kids, to the Monashees and I was fortunate to ski with them through trees cloaked so heavily with snow that not a single branch or pine needle was visible. Guides call the formations "snow ghosts" and they take on ghoulish shapes and create a fantasyland for adults and children alike. Watching the kids revel in the experience was refreshing, while seeing the father wrestle with his inner snow junkie was shocking. At times he complained to the guide about delays in the skiing that were simply due to his own children struggling with tough terrain and deep snow. In the end, the kids skied great and everyone had fun, but just before leaving the Monashees the father turned to me and said, "It was great to get the kids out there, but some of the time I just couldn't control the powder pig in me."

Hans and Leo had started guiding ski tours in 1955, and many of the original heli-skiers were long-time backcountry skiers Hans recruited to give helicopter access a try. The first heli-skiing was a ski mountaineering experience, albeit in really deep snow. Skiers signed up for an adventure in the woods and paid little attention to how steep or deep the skiing was going to be. The CMH marketing reflected the same philosophy. The 1970 brochure advertises "helicopter ski touring" and makes no mention of the ski quality, but has a terse paragraph on the experience that still holds true today: "Words are quite inadequate to describe this skiing experience. Those who have been there know what we're talking about. To those who have not been there, we can highly recommend it."

The rest of the brochure is matter-of-fact logistics that seems to suggest Hans wasn't even interested in trying to convince those who needed convincing. If you couldn't see for yourself that it was a skier's dream to use a helicopter for a ski lift in a massive and remote mountain range, you were not the kind of skier he was looking for. Helicopter ski touring took up three pages of the 21-page brochure, while human-powered ski touring was allotted six pages and the summer climbing and mountaineering program got seven.

By 1977, the brochure had grown to 33 pages, 23 of which were devoted to heli-skiing; only two promoted ski touring, and mountaineering had disappeared entirely.

Hans built every aspect of the business based on feedback from his guests, so even the promotion was representative of what guests told him they wanted to know about heli-skiing. They wanted to know what they were getting themselves into, because the brochure included exacting detail of what to expect. Hans's clients were some of the most successful business people in the world, and they taught him about promotion. Inevitably, marketing crept into the prose. The Monashees is the "steepest and the deepest," while the Bugaboos section reads, "The general consensus of our clients is, 'Unless you have skied there, you don't know what skiing is about.'" Word was out, and in typical Hans Gmoser style, the honesty of the brochure was striking: accident statistics noted one broken leg per 1,500 skier days, and two avalanche fatalities in 12 years of operation. A photo of the contents of a guide's pack showed no fewer than 60 different items, revealing everything the guides must be prepared to deal with.

The brochure contained a section on conditioning for heli-skiing and a note on skiing ability that read, with undertones of Gmoser humour, "We don't ask that you ski parallel in every kind of snow, but at least you should be able to control yourself."

The brochure also included the first program for less than expert skiers, "Introductory weeks to Heli-Skiing," which included five days of lift-service skiing and one day of heli-skiing at Radium, an area south of the Bugaboos where the Panorama ski resort and a heli-ski base allow for both varieties.

In seven years, CMH had reached maturity, and the essence of the business model has changed little in the three decades since. The company was becoming a viable business operated by skiers, and it showed: the housekeepers skied, the bartenders skied, the cooks skied, the managers skied, the office staff skied, the pilots skied, and the customers skied, with the thrill of mountain adventure the common passion that erases cultural, personal and professional boundaries.

All CMH staff and their families are encouraged to ski or hike, and every position in the company has an opportunity to get outdoors. Lodge staff go out when guests get tired in the afternoon and leave empty seats in the helicopter, while office staff get a few days of heli-skiing or hiking each year. Not every employee skis, but even the few who don't are caught up in the vibe of working in the world's greatest ski mountains with a management that encourages everyone to get out there. "Pretty much everyone I know has skied with CMH at some point." says Cindy Wiatzka, a local from Revelstoke.

Area managers find days when the whole staff can go skiing together. The vibe surrounding a staff ski day is like Christmas in a house full of six-year-olds. Indeed, there is never a more excited group of heli-skiers than a group of mostly young adults who never imagined part of their seasonal work buffet of waiting tables, cleaning rooms or washing dishes would include flying by helicopter to some remote snow-cloaked ridge with a dozen buddies, to be dropped off to go shred the kind of mountain even ski movies don't really capture.

By 1981, Hans was appealing to intermediate skiers in both marketing campaigns and editorial interviews. He told a CBC commentator, "In March and April we can take weaker skiers. The powder snow is not as deep, so it isn't as difficult to master. At the lower altitudes the sun will put a crust on the snow that gives you the feeling of skiing down a groomed slope with ball bearings under your skis. Yet, you have total control! It is very exhilarating."

Taking less skilled skiers heli-skiing changes the guide's job description dramatically, and while the instruction suited some guides perfectly, for others it was a chore. Rather than just ripping down the hill, they had to attempt to teach skiing in an uncontrolled wilderness environment to skiers who were used to buying their way into anything they wanted. Up until then, heli-ski guiding was, to a large degree, a keep up or shut up event, with some skiers being thrown out of their group for not skiing fast enough. It made guiding possible for Europeans with poor English and rough people skills. After all, the guide was not expected to make people feel good, but rather to show them the safe way down the mountain. European guides were accustomed to this approach, and a number of hardcore ones were legendary for their blunt assessment of people's skiing ability. But telling someone "You need to ski like you fuck, not like you shit" was not the most refined powder-skiing instruction to attempt to encourage a forward-leaning rather than a sitting-back position.

Ski education was always a part of the CMH world, but not as an endless continuum for everyone who wants to learn. In the mid-seventies CMH ran the "Ski School of the Canadian Rockies" out of the Banff Springs Hotel. It was essentially a regular ski school collaborating with CMH to prepare people to go heli-skiing, but the word was that you had better become an expert before you went. In Hans's 1966 "Spring Skiing" brochure – a handmade, cut and pasted, 37-page monument to his desire to share the mountains, and the publication where heli-skiing was advertised for the first time – he also offered an introductory ski mountaineering course for ski instructors. The course was designed to provide "practical and theoretical instruction in high mountain ski touring." The seven-day course was only open to qualified ski instructors and cost $120.

During the eighties there were still not enough qualified Canadian guides to fill the ranks of CMH teams, so Hans would go to Europe to recruit. On one trip to Austria he interviewed a guide who was also a level four Austrian ski instructor and coach of the Austrian women's downhill team. With zero English skills, the guide was afraid he wouldn't get the job, so he asked an English-speaking friend for help. His friend said, "No problem, we'll just make you a list of questions to memorize, and whenever it is your turn to talk, just ask Hans a question." The friend came up with a list of seemingly pertinent questions, and the young guide diligently memorized each one.

When it was time for the interview, Hans and the guide spoke in German about the details of the guide's experience. Then, at some point, Hans switched to English to test the guide's linguistic skills. Hans asked questions, and the guide replied with his own – with no idea of what Hans was asking. At the end of the interview, Hans switched back to German and told the guide he had a job for the next season. The guide was thrilled, and patted himself on the back for the cunning strategy of getting around the English issue. They shook hands, and as the guide started to walk away, Hans said in German, "Never mind the English."

That guide was Robert "Roko" Koell, and Hans, in his eerily canny way of reading people, saw enough potential in the young guide to let a morass of butchered English slide in the interview – but he also let Roko know he saw through the façade of bogus questions. Upon arrival in Canada, Hans enrolled Roko in an English course in Calgary before the beginning of ski season and assigned him to the Monashees. It was heaven for the former downhill racer.

The guide team in the Monashees at the time– Erich Unterberger, Nick Stocklhauser, and Willy Trinker, and now Roko – was a group of speed freaks obsessed with vertical as much or more than their guests were. The guide with the most vertical for the day got the honour of carrying the title of Captain Vertical for the evening. With a lodge full of strong skiers pushing the guides, and a group of ex-racers gunning for Captain Vertical status, the scene was ripe for some of the fastest commercial heli-ski runs ever made. All manner of tricks were used to maximize vertical and get the best skiing. Typically, four groups ski in generally the same order all day, but in the days of Captain Vertical, sometimes the guide for group four would call for a high pickup in order to pass the other groups and get in number one position. Other times, on a high-speed run, a guide would arrive at the helicopter with only two guests, and rather than wait, would take the ride and catch the group on the next lap.

One day, Roko was put in charge of Andy Epstein and friends, a group of veteran heli-skiers infamous for always needling the guide to ski harder. Roko was aware of this and was wearing his 225 cm downhill racing skis for the day. On top of the run Elevator he decided to give the clients what they wanted. Willy Trinker's record for skiing Elevator's 1300 vertical metres was seven minutes. Roko's English wasn't yet good enough to tell the group what he was going to do, so he just took off, and two and a half minutes later he stopped at the pickup to wait for the group. He kept the speed up all day, and on the last run the group was so wasted that Roko had to grab one skier's leg with his hands and push it manually into the binding for him because the client did not have enough strength left in his leg to engage the mechanism.

With groups like Epstein's pushing even top-level ski guides to take them to their limit, Roko saw the need for many guides to improve their skiing – and Roko can't help but teach. One day, he was skiing with a group of guides at Lake Louise when the area's downhill course was set. The guides knew the race officials, so they ran the course at the edge of control and safety. "We're lucky no one got hurt," remembers Roko laughing.

The guides saw their shortcomings, and everyone felt more instruction would help. Ski guides train to be conservative and solid rather than to push their bodies, and they typically come from a background of mountaineering rather than ski racing or instruction, so their technique, though stable while wearing a pack in all kinds of funky conditions, is not refined by professional instruction or coaching. Roko organized a guides ski instruction day to teach guides refined ski technique, as well as ski instruction methods to help weaker heli-skiers.

Plastic four-buckle ski boots had been around for nearly a decade, but "some guides showed up in leather ski boots!" remembers Roko, chuckling. "We dug some plastic boots out of the CMH basement, and I talked the office into giving me the company credit card for the day. That night I threw a huge party for the guides and ran up an $800 tab on booze. They never gave me another card." But the lifetime ski ability improvement concept stuck, and the CMH Powder Performance program began. It was not a marketing ploy, but rather a philosophical change in the idea of why people ski: even good skiers want to get better.

Roko remembers, "In the beginning I had no support for the Powder Performance program, but Mark Kingsbury was the first to go for it. Mark talked to Hans and Hans really liked it."

"Roko changed the way we think about skiing," said more than one veteran guide during the 2006 guide training at Sunshine ski area, where Roko continues to run a program for the CMH guides. The idea is simple: the guides study ski technique and ski instruction, then in turn pass on instruction to any guest who wants to improve. Roko begins his program for guides with instruction for teaching powder neophytes how to enjoy themselves more quickly, and progresses through the levels to the point where the guides are struggling to keep up and refine their own technique. Roko's continuing education for skiers became an unprecedented, all-inclusive learning curve for anyone who wants to learn to ski better, and he's the perfect man for the job. You'll never meet anyone more enthusiastic about other people's skiing than Roko Koell. He designed the Powder Intro course for first-time heli-skiers who don't have the skills to keep up with the average guest groups, and the Powder Masters course for guests with too many years of turning skis under their knees who want to ski slower and learn ways to minimize impact on their bodies to extend their ski careers. In the future, more ski technique programs may emerge from the original Powder Performance concept, but for now skiers are simply encouraged to ask a guide if they want tips on skiing better.

Fat skis and good instruction allow intermediate skiers to quickly reach a point where they can keep up with an average heli-ski group. Powder snow is usually a very forgiving medium, and most people take a number of spectacular but harmless falls while learning. An article in *Skisport* magazine described the experience of learning to ski powder in 1977, and it all still holds true today: "In powder, if you ski slow, you end up flailing all over the place and using an incredible amount of energy to make the skis perform. The trick is to relax and let your self go. Even when you fall it's like tumbling into a bottomless pit filled with feathers. You come up spitting snow and gasping for breath, and looking around for your goggles, ski poles and other equipment. But nothing hurts."

After the requisite cartwheels in the feather pit, sooner or later everyone who tries hard enough experiences a euphoric moment when it all comes together and the crashes are replaced by the unbeatable sensation of floating through a substance made of 95 per cent air. Theresa Brand, a writer for the Montreal *Gazette*, was moved to the soul by the breakthrough: "All I could think about was survival (at first). I remembered something about risk exercise and how good it is for one's mind and soul. Indeed. Suddenly I got the knack of it. I was floating. The tips of my skis were up and I had begun to feel what it was all about – oneness with the elements, with the universe. The majestic peaks were smiling on me."

On the other end of the spectrum, expert skiers find that the fatter skis and collective knowledge of the mountains among guides and pilots continuously redefine anyone's definition of excellent skiing. John Byrnes describes a run in Galena that captures the experience even experts have when their eyes are open as wide as any beginner's:

> Andi opens the door, but instead of walking away to unload the skis, he stands in the open door until he sees that he has everyone's attention. Shouting would do no good with the machine still running, so he points right and shakes his head emphatically, NO! He points left and shakes his head again. He points straight down with both hands and nods slowly. We can read his lips: "RIGHT HERE!'
>
> We're on this knife-edge ridge just wide enough for a few skiers. Major drops on either side; what the guides call "terminal air." Andi says this isn't really a landing and stay away from the sides! After a short zip down the ridge, we swing left and look down on the most amazing section of technical terrain I've ever seen. Really steep, trees, staircases, small cliffs, ridges and convolutions in over-the-shoulder powder.

After learning to ski powder, the age-old tendency to quantify an experience raises its ugly head. With all the mountain complexities, differences in perspective and abilities, and elemental enjoyment that comes from skiing in the backcountry, when modern humans decide to communicate an experience it always comes down to numbers. Some sports, like baseball, easily succumb to description by statistics. Other sports, like heli-skiing, do not. The one metric that seems to have stuck while trying to describe the immeasurable world of skiing with a helicopter lift is the amount of vertical elevation skied – in a day, a week, a year, a lifetime. This one inarguable, objective measurement is so compelling that it inspired the world's first frequent flyer program: the million-foot club. American Airlines claims credit for the first commercial airline frequent flier program, but legend has it that an American Airlines executive went heli-skiing and saw the CMH program and decided to reward his customers in some way for repeat business.

Anyone who skis a million vertical feet with CMH is given a ski suit and lifetime bragging rights. The night after a skier hits a million, an impromptu ceremony welcomes the new member of the million-foot club. Like snowflakes, no two ceremonies are ever the same, but most conclude in the dining room after dinner with a few staff of the opposite sex replacing the million-footer's clothes with the new suit.

At 100,000 feet per week guaranteed, it would take ten weeks to get a million vertical feet, although it is possible to do it in half that time with the right group and the right conditions. That means at the current rate of heli-skiing, a million-foot suit costs between fifty and a hundred thousand dollars. The first million-foot suit was a cheesy blue blazer of seventies fashion. Hans was usually spot-on with his perception of what his guests wanted, but a blazer for million-footers was an exception. Something to wear while skiing made more sense, and at the time, Bogner ski suits were hitting the slopes with force and bringing sexiness to the ski world for the first time in history. The next year, the million-foot suit was an oh-so-seventies Bogner ski suit. Since then, the million-foot suits have followed the fashion of the day through the fart-in-your-own-face one-piece era to today's minimalist, versatile technical pants and jackets.

These suits have made their way into virtually every ski area on the planet, and for the person standing in a lift line, the suit tells the story of endless face shots in mind-blowing terrain, of having seen the stunning scenery, felt the tight companionship and family atmosphere at the lodges, and of belonging to the fraternity of wilderness skiers. Some skiers, however, prefer to take a credit towards a heli-hiking trip with CMH rather than take a ski suit. For them, the suits are more of a statement of elitism than an award. Olav Ruud is a skier with several million feet who spends his time between Canmore and northern Italy. He skis the Monashees in a beat-up anorak and says, "Every time I see the suits in a ski area they look so snobbish. The only time I am comfortable in the suit is here, so I just take the heli-hiking credit instead." Like letter jackets for varsity high-school athletes, the suits can make a statement of either utter cool or elitist attitude.

With 3,400 people in the million-foot club, just watch the lift lines at Vail or St. Moritz, and at some point two skiers in million-foot suits will see each other, strike up a conversation about heli-skiing and become instant friends. The suit in no way captures the experience, but since the rest of the obsession is the intangible, indescribable experience of skiing fairy-tale mountains in dreamy snow that only exists while it is happening, the suits are cherished, tangible trophies hanging in positions of honour in aficionados' closets.

While hanging out in the world of CMH, it's easy to get caught up in the quest for numbers. Chasing a million vertical feet with teams of millionaires is to belong to one of the most exclusive, challenging and envied sporting clubs anywhere. Gery Unterasinger, a lead guide at the Bobbie Burns, observed that "for people's first few trips, they get obsessed with chasing vertical, but then they realize it's more about having good days and having fun at the right pace."

But there are people who are so distracted by the quest for maximum vertical that they miss out on some of the best parts of heli-skiing. In a 1998 issue of *Snow Country* magazine, an editor wrote:

> A few years ago, a friend returned from a week at CMH, the largest heli-ski operation in British Columbia, in a grumbling mood. The weather had been good, the snow was fine, the guides were excellent, the scenery was spectacular and the drinks and meals at the lodge plentiful. So, I asked, what was the matter? It turned out he was put off by an obnoxious breed of heli-skier that has become all too common, the big-game bagger of vertical. Clad with a well-used Avocet altimeter, a surplus of adrenaline and a good month's worth of anticipation, the character is often the central antagonist in the tales of others returning from heli-ski trips.
>
> My friend, a lover of mountains and the full breadth of experience they offer, was especially put off by this new breed's lack of reverence for

the beauty around him and his inability to stop and enjoy it. Worse, woe to the laggard who might be cutting into the day's volume of vertical. In a place you'd expect civility to reign, a remote mountain lodge far from work and phones, he simply trades his compulsive work habits for equally compulsive play habits.

The editor then quotes a heli-ski operation manager as saying, "With all the danger of avalanches we face and the absolute need for us to protect our clients, we still have customers who get furious if they can't go out on days when bad weather clearly puts their lives in danger or when the snow is especially prone to sliding." He then added, "They just don't get it."

And they don't. A guide for Mike Wiegele once stopped to dig a pit to check stability, and a testy Canadian got so irate with the forsaken vertical that, according to the other skiers there, it almost came to blows.

The editorial later mentions another writer being warned not to be there during mid-season. "The Europeans," she said, "especially the Germans, are all business at that time and have no tolerance for anyone holding them up."

Not surprisingly, impatience and obsession have little to do with nationality and more to do with personality. In an article in the *Christian Science Monitor*, Rainer Degimann-Schwartz wrote:

> We Europeans were always surprised to discover in conversation with our American counterparts that as far as they were concerned, neither the length nor the steepness of the slope counted. Rather, they calculated each day's summary in terms of the vertical feet covered, counting, adding, multiplying.

A group of Australians made anyone who caused the group to miss a lift buy Dom Perignon that night. One season, they drained the entire year's champagne stash at the Galena lodge before Christmas. While the motivation for vertical takes on many disguises, it sounds like regardless of which side of the pond you're on, it's fun to ski fast all day long with whatever kind of lift you use, and it is easy to get carried away with endless speed and fresh snow. Add a group of successful Type A personalities to the mix and you have a recipe for monomaniacal focus.

Hans once said,

> You could dig a pit in the ground with the right pitch and vertical, cover it with the right snow, and most of these people wouldn't miss the mountains at all! Most of our helicopter skiers are really only interested in the act of downhill skiing, the quality of the snow, and many of them, after years and years of skiing with us still have not learned to pay proper respect to the mountains.

Hans viewed the mountain experience as an adventure, a single product, not one to be piecemealed à la carte where you select the part you want to buy. To him, powder snow, breakable crust, blue ice, loose rock, solid granite, thick forest and the unpredictable nature of the mountain elements were inseparable parts of the experience. He intended the million-foot award to be a thank-you to the people who enjoyed CMH enough to keep coming back and to acknowledge them for making the business possible, not as a marketing tool or a motivation to collect vertical like some sort of ego currency. It is phenomenal how fast a group of even average skiers can rack up vertical with fat skis and a fat helicopter. A lot of times the day's difference between the fastest group and the slowest group is laughably small, so the biggest difference between chasing vertical and savouring the mountain experience is purely psychological.

The world record for vertical skied in a day is 294,380 feet – 10 laps from the summit of Mt. Everest to sea level – but it wasn't much fun. At the end of the day, after skiing the same 3,590-foot run 82 times, Mark Bennett, a heli-skier who became infatuated with the record, couldn't walk and couldn't sleep. He told a reporter for *Snow Country*, "Every time I closed my eyes I saw ski tracks rushing at me. I was nauseous. It was like falling into a nightmare."

In 1963, the same year Hans led the first heli-ski runs through the breakable crust of Goat Glacier, several Americans were experimenting with the first snowboards. Tom Sims made a snowboard out of plywood in his eighth-grade shop class. In a separate brainstorm in 1965, Sherman Poppen was watching his daughter attempt to ride her sled standing up and was struck with the idea to bolt two skis together and tie a string to the tip for steerage. The Snurfer was born. Over the next ten years, he sold half a million Snurfers and held competitions that inspired improvement on the design.

Jake Burton Carpenter added a binding to the Snurfer concept, which made the steering strap obsolete and started Burton Snowboards in 1977. A 1980s CMH promotional film featured "Ted Shred," a surfer who brought a surfboard to the Bugaboos equipped like a modern tow-in big-wave board with neoprene straps. Ted also used the Snurfer idea of a tip strap for steering and, for the first of many times, made skiers look silly with their little wiggles as he ripped by them, straight-lining on his board and kicking up a plume of snow that could be seen from outer space.

A combination of factors has kept snowboarding from booming in the heli-ski business, although for pure downhill speed and control in crud and powder the snowboard is arguably the superior tool. The difficulty of heli-skiing with snowboards is complex. For expert snowboarders, there is no trouble and they'll blow away any group of skiers in the backcountry – as long as the terrain doesn't flatten out, causing the fluid, effortless, high speed motion of snowboarding to change to the awkward limp of an amputee with a bad prosthesis. Heli-skiing happens in the backcountry, where crossing frozen lakes, slogging through rolling hillocks, and doing uphill traverses can be necessary to reach pickups or avoid dangerous slopes. For these reasons, snowboarders were discouraged from going heli-skiing until the demand exceeded the resistance and guides learned how to show snowboarders the time of their lives.

FAT SKIS EXTEND THE HEALTH OF SKIERS, LET AVERAGE SKIERS EXPERIENCE DEEP POWDER, AND LET YOU GET AWAY WITH A LOT SLOPPIER TECHNIQUE.

Nowadays, the guides know the limitations and strengths of snowboards and are able to accommodate boarders by choosing runs and giving directions that minimize struggling and frustration. During the pre-season training, CMH hires a snowboard instructor and takes the guides riding as part of their training so they can relate to the fun and challenge of the game. However, the mountains make it hard for everyone at some point and some snowboarders complain bitterly as soon as they have problems, unaware that at times the skiers will be having problems and snowboarders will still be shredding. Whether you're on one board or two, at some point the backcountry kicks your ass. In 2006, Canadian Scott Newsome did what was once considered unthinkable: he passed the assistant ski guide exam on a split snowboard – separating it and using skins on the uphills, parallel skiing on the two halves for short downhills, and clipping the two pieces together and snowboarding for the big descents. The lines are blurring, and the difference between snowboarding and skiing today is really only a matter of choice and experience. Many guides and guests today have both skis and snowboards at the lodge, and each morning they choose their weapons based entirely on the snow conditions.

The cross-pollination began in the late eighties when Atomic, inspired by the flotation and performance of snowboards in deep powder, introduced the Fat Boy ski and forever changed the face of skiing. CMH was one of the first to embrace the concept, but the guests and guides weren't so quick to ditch their beloved old skis. At first CMH kept a few fat skis at the lodges for guests who were having trouble with deep powder, but everyone thought real skiers used skinny skis. One by one, guides and guests tried the Fat Boys for a day – and never wanted to go back. By 1991, fat skis had become standard heli-ski equipment, and any pride wrapped up in the traditional skis was replaced by the utter confidence and security the greater flotation afforded a skier in the deepest powder.

For the heli-ski industry, it was a windfall. Fat skis made off-piste (outside of ski resort) skiing a lot easier, which meant less-skilled skiers could shred big vertical and have the time of their lives. Fat skis are also much easier on the body, which, like Viagra for the powder hound, meant older heli-skiers and guides could keep it up a lot longer. Roko, who watches septuagenarians and octogenarians in the Powder Masters program come back year after year for 100,000-foot weeks of skiing, says, "Fat skis gave heli-skiers another 15 years." Skiers could go heli-skiing both earlier and later in their careers, the potential client base for heli-ski outfits grew significantly, and guide work became a lot easier thanks to an idea that was born on the waves.

Ironically, the piggybacking of ideas went the other way in the nineties when surfers were catching bigger and bigger waves to the point where their equipment became the limiting factor. Big waves travel fast and the airflow against their faces creates small waves, called chop, that make it extremely hard for traditional surfers to keep their feet on their boards – think skiing moguls with no bindings. A group of Hawaiian surfers went snowboarding, and had an epiphany that changed their sport as much as snowboarding changed skiing: if we can ride these huge mountains on these short little boards with bindings, why can't we do the same on big waves?

They put straps on short boards and, using jet-skis to catch some of the fastest and biggest waves anywhere on the ocean, are able to ride huge, rough waves where traditional surfers wouldn't last a second. Now, big-wave surfers are looking to deep ocean breaks and weather buoy data to find waves with faces nearing a hundred feet tall.

What will be next in the quest to rip powder? Legendary skier and assistant Cariboos manager Dave Gauley launched the first CMH Steep Camp in the Cariboos during April of 2008 when the stable spring conditions were most likely to allow steeper and more technical alpine features to be skied safely. John Mellis, the Cariboos manager, explained some of the possible variations the Steep Camp might reveal: "I hope we can find a place where we can rappel over a cornice to start a ski run. We can chop out a platform for people to put on their skis and then ski an exciting line with a good runout in case someone falls."

Snowboard icon Devon Walsh is visiting Galena to rip with riders who want to share the snow with a pro. In the future, both more advanced and more basic heli-ski experiences are likely. Also, new ways of playing in the snow are being explored. One day, a guide was unloading skis at the top of a peak and found a funky contraption with handlebars in his ski basket. Someone else had loaded the basket at the lodge, so it was the first time he'd seen the thing. With the helicopter waiting, he decided to just unload it and decide what to do about it later. It was a ski bike, and it belonged to one of the guests waiting anxiously on the other side of the machine to try his new tool in the deep snow and big terrain of the Columbias.

The guide didn't know what to do about it so he radioed the area manager for advice. The area manager passed the buck to the Banff office, which checked to see if a ski bike was covered by insurance and found there was no reason not to let it ride. The reply went back through the chain of communication to the group waiting on the mountaintop. The skiers locked into their skis, the biker got on his bike, and everyone pointed their tips towards the valley bottom and had a great run. The rest of the day went seamlessly, with the biker having no problem enjoying the fresh powder just as much as the skiers.

Recently, a group of veteran snowboarders in BC pulled the bindings off their boards, attached a steering cord to the tip, and took the game one step closer to surfing by getting rid of the rigid attachment of a binding. Watching them rip powder you'd never guess they were just standing on their boards. The free feel of riding on powder with no binding – "noboarding" – inspired some of them to proclaim they'll never use bindings again.

Today, maybe the only real issue is the helicopter's ski basket. It is designed for a dozen pairs of skis and neither a dozen high-back snowboard bindings nor that many ski bikes will fit in the current design. Changing the design is not trivial: any new design has to be approved by Transport Canada to make sure it does not interfere with the aerodynamics or landing abilities of the helicopter. By the 2008/09 season, the changes will be integrated and full groups of snowboarders will be able to ride together in comfort. Getting the tools up there is the only real difference; once everyone is on top of the mountain, it doesn't really matter what you ride.

SKI GUIDE DAVE GAULEY, WHO
BROUGHT THE "STEEP CAMP"
CONCEPT TO CMH, IS SHOWN HERE
TAKING STRONG SKIERS INTO STEEP
AND CHALLENGING TERRAIN.

In the end, whether it is a snow rider's first or 100th week of deep powder, the experience cannot be held onto. It slips like water through the fingers, leaving a haunting memory for the trip home that doesn't really go away until the next time.

4

FULL CIRCLE

A single footprint is a big impact – if you happen to be the flower that gets stepped on.

— Hans Gmoser

Each gust of wind pushes the suspension bridge back and forth beneath my feet. My boots are planted firmly on solid wood planks, my hands are on steel cables and I'm attached to a cable with a climbing harness. But even knowing I'm anchored like a sail in a hurricane, I'm acutely aware of the exposure below and adjust my balance intently with each movement of the span. The experience is more a Lord of the Rings than a Bay Bridge kind of affair; a perfect Hollywood set for a battle between wizards or maybe a causeway for elves. It's a hundred feet to the solid rock on the other side and almost the same to go back where I came from. Beneath me a rock face sweeps into the deep valley a vertical kilometre below, and in the distance the forested valleys and prickly peaks of the Columbias stretch past the horizon. To my left, a blinding white glacier catches my eye. I stop, balanced between two planks with nothing but air between my feet and take in the view from this unique perch.

In 30 years of mountain adventures from the Himalaya to the Andes, I have never been in such a place. Looking past my feet, I see the multicoloured layers of rock in the folded earth form a quilt of bizarre patterns where the glacier ends. I turn my head to look over my shoulder towards the spire we just climbed on our traverse of Nimbus Tower. It is far more slender than it appeared while we were climbing on it, the summit a razor point against the deep blue sky. Looking up from the swaying bridge is dizzying, and clouds move behind the spire, complicating my mind's attempts to compensate for my unstable footing. Another gust of wind brings my attention quickly back to the airy path in front of me. I am thankful for the climbing harness and tether attaching me to a cable running above the bridge. Nothing short of an errant helicopter could actually send me tumbling from the exposed position, but it sure feels tenuous. Step by careful step I walk closer to the other end of the bridge. A question runs through my mind, "And this is heli-hiking?"

The bridge is made of cables attached to a spider web of anchors and expansion bolts drilled into the rock. It is part of a trail of rungs and safety cables that make the ascent possible for anyone who can climb a ladder. The exposed passage is called a *via ferrata*, a European invention that has yet to catch on in North America, although a few exist here, including the popular cable route to the summit of Yosemite's Half Dome. Via ferrata is Italian for "iron road," and in the Alps they are as common as parking lots in the Rockies. The online encyclopedia Wikipedia explains their purpose as allowing "otherwise isolated routes to be joined to create longer routes, which are accessible to people with a wide range of climbing abilities. Walkers and climbers can follow via ferratas without needing to use their own ropes and belays, and without the risks associated with unprotected scrambling and climbing."

Via ferratas open access to the kind of terrain usually reserved for technical climbers, and in the rugged terrain of the Columbia Mountains they are a practical next step to connect valleys, bypass glaciers, surmount cliff bands and reach summits that otherwise would be unappealing to climb with traditional means and impossible to reach for hikers. The first two via ferratas in the Columbias were built by the CMH Bobbie Burns guides, and their thrills are just beginning to be experienced by hikers. The first, on a lonely ridge below Mt. Syphax, was completed in 2005. It connects a traditional climb from a glacier to the summit with an exciting knife-edge ridge that only expert climbers would dare traverse without the metal rungs and safety cables – and even for experts, some sections of the rock are too fractured to be a worthwhile rock-climbing objective. The second is the Nimbus Tower traverse, finished in 2007, and it includes the sphincter-tightening 60-metre suspension bridge.

Like heli-skiing in the early days, the project is an isolated labour of love by the guides. No one is telling them what to do or how to do it. It is not a marketing scheme or a brand statement – it is a way of taking people into a part of the mountains they wouldn't get to otherwise. Just like the Bugaboos in the sixties, the Bobbie Burns in the new millennium is redefining the nature of mountain sport. Hikers who finish the via ferratas experience something they've never heard of, seen photos of, or imagined. With the position and exposure of a technical climb but the ease of climbing a ladder, in an environment with the remoteness of a National Geographic expedition but the ease of access of a long weekend away from home, the via ferratas of the Columbias are destined to inspire wide eyes, future stories and controversy.

For many North American outdoor enthusiasts, the idea of drilling metal ladders into the rock, festooning a stone spire with cables and creating a pathway out of vertical rock is anathema. If anyone tried to install a via ferrata in a national park anywhere on the continent, there would be outrage. Interestingly, the ladder up Yosemite's Half Dome was installed first by a blacksmith and then rebuilt by none other than the Sierra Club, one of the world's most respected environmental organizations. The use of our wilderness hangs on a pendulum swinging between access and conservation, and the future use of wilderness will require careful consideration of both elements.

The via ferratas of the Columbias are not in national parks and are located in the heart of a mountain range where few, if any, other hikers, backpackers, backcountry skiers or climbers will ever see them. They allow access to peaks made of such loose rock that even the most adventurous climbers would choose another route. If placed with consideration, a number of breathtaking via ferratas could be installed in the Columbias that would affect the aesthetic of the range not at all. Just like huts, trails, roads, climbing anchors and other human installations, if via ferratas are placed with abandon, they will be little more than permanent litter on our beloved mountains, but if placed with care they will only enhance the wilderness experience.

While heli-skiing is the most famous aspect of the legacy of Hans Gmoser, the summer program more closely fits his original vision of using the helicopter as a means to extend alpine tours into the most remote terrain western Canada has to offer. During the winter, the helicopter is used hourly or more as a ski lift for shuttling skiers into as many powder turns as possible over the course of a day. In the summer, the machine is merely a way of getting out there – albeit an incredibly exciting, scenic and versatile way. Often the helicopter will be used once in the morning to access the high cirques above the thick bush, pesky mosquitoes, monster bears and even bigger and more irritable moose. The hikers and climbers are left in silence for the day and their chosen adventure. When they have explored everything time, weather and curiosity allows, or hiked to a state of contented exhaustion, the guide calls in the helicopter for a quick return to the lodge.

One hiker commented, "That's the magic of it – one minute you're in the alpine world and the next you're sitting on the deck with a cocktail in your hand."

The potential of the jet-powered equalizer is still being realized, and recently the term heli-hiking has become a bit of a misnomer. The summer use of the helicopter and the remote lodges ranges from world-class rock climbing on one extreme to short strolls through a flower garden on the other, or as one hiker explained, "I just found a spot I liked, sat down, and drew pictures in my tablet while the others went hiking."

An artist finding a view to get the creative juices flowing and a hard-core climber finding a first ascent to get the endorphins flowing are at opposite ends of the spectrum of mountain pursuits, but both accomplish the same thing: full immersion in a wild world and an experience giving the individual a time away from the hectic and complicated world of jobs, family needs, automobiles, deadlines and stress. One hiker summed it up: "Heli-hiking, heli-eating, heli-hot-tubbing; it's a heli of a good time. It's a very sad day to depart from this majestic mountain lodge and return to the reality of the everyday world."

By using technology, information and experience, more and more people are finding the rewards of this kind of unmeasured time in an alpine environment where, if they were left naked and alone, death would find them in a matter of hours or days. It is a world where we are not at the top of the food chain, a world where we are forced to be humble and respectful, and a world where the ephemeral value of the wilderness is clear.

For a time, only the hardiest adventurers explored the wildest mountains of North America; then trains, highways, trails, logging roads and shared information allowed fit adventurers to achieve the lofty heights and to walk across the lush tundra ecosystem and return home with a greater respect for the natural world. More recently, roads have been bulldozed into some of the most spectacular alpine terrain in North America. Mt. Evans and Pikes Peak in Colorado are particularly dramatic examples, with roads slicing through tundra to reach 4000-metre summits. These roads invite questions: do the roads take people into the wilderness, or does the wilderness retreat from the road, making the two utterly irreconcilable? Can a person gain respect for the natural world by seeing it through the window of a car? According to the Hans Gmoser school of wilderness, the answer is no, the mountains must be touched, smelled, felt and even tasted, as well as seen. Getting out of the car and off the road is necessary to experience and learn from wilderness. The obvious question, then, which surely enters the reader's mind even before finishing this sentence, is: can people experience the natural world by flying a helicopter into it?

According to the Hans Gmoser school of thought, the answer is yes, as long as they get out of the machine. Just a sightseeing tour, spent peering from the window of a plane or helicopter, is little better than watching a video of the mountains rolling past – albeit in a thrilling amusement park ride. During the winter, the hectic pace of heli-skiing's powder mania and the trend of chasing vertical footage distracted people's attention from the natural world and took heli-skiing further from Hans's original vision of sharing the complete mountain experience. Ironically, it was the pressure of business that inspired a return to the more meditative touring element of heli-sport.

Hans became indebted to bankers as his business grew, and increasing the number of guests was essential to the project's survival. Winter was lucrative, but just because the snow melted didn't mean the bills stopped coming. Margaret Bezzola, the original house-manager of the Bobbie Burns lodge, remembers: "Hans would never have enough money to pay for (jet fuel) for the winter, so every summer he would have to take out a loan to pay for the next season's fuel." There were times when the cook only put one tea bag in a huge pot of water to save the pennies needed to flavour the pot properly. Kiwi remembers the atmosphere of the difficult times. "Investors were pulling their hair out that the only way the business would keep going was because the bankers liked Hans."

Back in civilization, heli-skiing is a business like any other, and Hans and his team had a number of near disasters in the bankers' world as well as in the mountain world. First, it was the cost of building the lodges, each one putting the business on the edge of bankruptcy. Next, it was finding something to do when the deep snows melted. Like the ptarmigan, the alpine bird that every spring replaces a coat of thick white winter feathers with dark ones to blend with the summer tundra, the project needed to change dramatically with the seasons.

In the Hans Gmoser school, participation is essential to experiencing and respecting the natural world. Skiing was a natural reason to use a helicopter to increase access for people who wouldn't go there otherwise, but what to do in the summer? CMH already had lodges and staff, so all that was lacking was the right activity to get people out there. As usual, there was no clear, grand vision, so in the beginning the guides tried everything they could think of. Early attempts to create a summer program ranged from the nearly disastrous to the hilarious. Summer offerings included horseback riding, canoeing in Bugaboo Creek and even tennis on a court installed at the Bugaboo lodge. Much fun was had and millions of mosquitoes enjoyed litres of fresh blood, but nothing really caught on.

One of the more promising summer programs was the Young Explorers Club, an impromptu camp for teenagers led by the ski guides in the mountains around the Bugaboo lodge. However, the ski guides were far from expert summer camp instructors. Rudi Krannebitter once went ahead to prepare camp and set up a group of tents – in the wrong valley. Canoeing in Bugaboo Creek was fun, but as Krannebitter put it, "Sepp (Renner) and Rudi (Gertsch) didn't know what end of the canoe was front. They weren't water people but they had to pretend they knew what they were doing in front of a group of teenagers."

Recently, Renner met a middle-aged man who told him, "I know you, we blew up some outhouses together." At first, Sepp was incredulous, but then he realized the man was a former Young Explorer. On one of the camping trips, the Explorers found a box of dynamite and blasting caps in an old mining claim, and while the guides were not skilled at boating, they knew how to blow things up from their work building the lodges and doing avalanche control. The campers wired up the dynamite and proceeded to pulverize everything they could find, including the outhouse of the mining claim. While this was not the solution for summer solvency for CMH, it left some lasting memories for a number of Canadian teenagers. Renner laughs with the memory: "Those kids loved it, but imagine when they went home and their parents asked them what they did at camp. 'We learned to blow up outhouses.'"

Explosives were not a standard part of the syllabus, but no two camps were ever the same. The two-week programs involved backpacking, canoeing and mountaineering in wilderness so remote the kids were forced to become woodsmen and find comfort in the rugged high country.

A particularly memorable adventure began with Hans and Sepp taking a group canoeing on the Spillimacheen River. Hans claimed to know the best put-in, and when the group pulled up to the edge of the river, Renner looked out over the water and said, "Those are some pretty big waves. Are you sure this is it?"

Hans was confident, as usual, and simply said, "This is it."

They got everyone organized and cast off down the river. In no time, they ran into much bigger water than they expected. Renner tells the story with wide eyes. "We went around a corner and all I could see were haystacks of water! All six canoes flipped! We swam to shore, did a head count, and one kid was missing. We ran around in a panic but found the girl hanging from an avalanche alder at the edge of the river."

They lost two of the canoes, and Renner "gave Hans hell for that one."

"It was a hell of a good program," says Renner. "Nobody does these trips anymore. It's too bad. There is too much risk. We're turning into a nation of wimps because we can't do anything risky anymore."

Using helicopters to access the wilderness in the summertime never even crossed the guides' minds. They were skiers, and in their minds, using helicopters to reach the heart of the mountain experience was the pinnacle of elitist pursuits for skiers and skiers alone. It required athletic prowess to steer long and unwieldy skis through the deep snow, and a deep pocketbook to match. Heli-skiing gave the aficionado the cachet of golfing St. Andrews along with the physical superiority of an Ironman finisher. Heli-sport was for the fit, the young and the bold – or so everyone thought.

Over the years, old ladies matched the young and cocky skiers for metres skied in a week, beginners learned to ski deep in the Columbias, and slowly people realized the true power of the helicopter was, quite simply, access. It is still expensive and, with rising energy costs, is becoming even more so. The days when using a helicopter to play in the mountains conferred automatic elite status are long gone. The game has gone full circle, and Hans's original goal of using the helicopter to show more people the rewards and lessons of the mountains has been realized, with skiing only one aspect of it.

One man had a vision to use the helicopter as a tool to bring tour groups of retirees into the mountains. In 1925 Arthur Tauck began leading escorted travel tours in New England. He passed on his business to his son, Arthur Tauck Jr., who saw the potential in changing the flavour of adventure travel from one of hardship to one of comfort.

A GROUP OF YOUNG EXPLORERS NEARING TREELINE BELOW THE BUGABOO SPIRES.

By removing the logistics from the minds of the travellers and teaming up with hotels, restaurants, transportation services and resorts, he changed the world of tourism. In the fifties, Tauck Jr. introduced the world to tour packages combining air and bus travel to visit America's national parks while the rest of the tourism industry was still using trains. His business flourished, and during a holiday to the Bugaboos to try the exotic sport of heli-skiing, Tauck saw an ever more diverse method of showing people the world.

He called Hans immediately, but Hans was still wrapped up in the illusion of the elitism of heli-skiing. According to Hans, after Tauck's original phone call, he forgot about the offer entirely. Luckily, Tauck was convinced of his idea, and after Hans failed to return his call, he tried again. This time he explained his vision more succinctly: "Look, Hans, all you have to do is take people into the mountains with the helicopter and let them walk around for a while, and then bring them back to the lodge."

According to Hans, "It was like a light bulb went off in my head."

The next year, in 1978, Tauck included a stop at the Cariboos lodge in his Canadian tour. Soon the Cariboos were booked with Tauck's guests and the Bugaboos started including the new activity, called heli-hiking, in their program. Thousands of older travellers have now seen the most remote flower gardens, sparkling tarns, age-old glaciers, pumping waterfalls and splendid isolation of the Columbias during a Tauck

DISCOVERING THE SUBLIME WORLD
OF TUNDRA ON GRIZZLY RIDGE
BETWEEN THE BUGABOOS
AND THE BOBBIE BURNS.

heli-hiking tour. Soon, individuals not involved in a Tauck tour were also booking heli-hiking trips, often with two or three generations enjoying an alpine adventure together.

Heli-skiing captured the imagination of the world by representing the speed, the perception of danger, flying snow and the agility and coordination of the skiers. From cigarette and beer ads to ski films, clothing commercials and tourism promotions, heli-skiing had the instant appeal that caught the attention of the world, and from Hollywood to Munich it became the stuff of film producers' and marketers' dreams. Summer heli-sport, on the other hand, is a much more subtle experience and is possible for anyone with a big enough bank account.

To understand the experience for hikers, imagine the waterfalls of Yosemite or Switzerland. Instead of flowing from a forest perched on the edge of a cliff, the water-falls burst from the very guts of glaciers perched on dizzying precipices. And instead of standing in a smoggy valley with another 20,000 people every day, it is just you and a maximum of 44 hikers split into smaller groups in an area the size of many large na-tional parks. The Cariboos tenure, with 1073 square kilometres, is one square kilometre bigger than Colorado's Rocky Mountain National Park. The Adamants encompass 1498 square kilometres, over 200 square kilometres bigger than Wyoming's Grand Teton National Park. The Monashees tenure is about 150 square kilometres smaller than the entire Hawaiian island of Maui, and the Bobbie Burns, one of the smallest of the CMH heli-hiking areas, is the twice the size of France's Vanoise National Park near Mont Blanc. The best photographer or film producer in the world cannot capture the feeling of being the only human beings in such vast and spectacular areas.

Imagine the most stunning valleys in the Alps or California's Sierra Nevada, but instead of walking along a dusty trail used by hundreds of people each day, you follow game trails made by goats, bear, caribou, moose and wolves – humans are the minority species on these trails.

Imagine the wildflowers at the peak of the season in the Tetons or Colorado's San Juans, but multiply their numbers by the difference in annual precipitation: the Tetons average 40 centimetres of precipitation annually, while Mt. Revelstoke, a peak in the geographic centre of the heli-hiking areas, receives 127 centimetres of precipitation, three times the Tetons quota. Add long summer days of the 50-degree latitude and the growing season is a bonanza of photosynthesis for all things green and blossoming. The wildflowers and tundra in the Columbias boggle the mind. Bushes as tall as a man are draped with colour, while underfoot a carpet of life grows so thick and vivacious as to support the passing of human and animal feet, then simply bounce back to its original healthy state.

Imagine spending a day trekking through a series of glacier-carved cirques, the glaciers sitting at the top of the valleys, still immense in their retreat but mere snowdrifts compared to the mighty ice monsters that carved the mountains. The glaciers feed rivers and streams that empty into turquoise-coloured tarns sitting at the end of the moraines – the piles of rubble left by the bulldozer action of the glaciers when they began to recede after their last period of growth. It's a glimpse into the natural machinery that shapes our world. The glaciers churn the stone into dirt, which mixes with rain and decaying plants to form rich soil where flowers can grow. Birds bring seeds from the forests, spreading vivid colours slowly across the once lifeless moraines left as the ice recedes. The caribou move through seeking nourishment in the lush flora, and the wolves follow. Bears eat everything and seek places with an abundance of life, finding the Columbias suit them just fine.

In the tourist centres of public lands in North America, the beauty of these processes is often guarded by heavily built trails and paved lookouts, signposted into lifeless facts. When you're left in the middle of it, without a sign of human passage anywhere, the picture becomes clear in a way no tour guide could ever describe. It is an intuitive understanding, independent of statistics or names of flowers and ages of the rock, that makes all of our endeavours, struggles and interactions with the world somehow as clear as a fresh gloss of ice across a limpid alpine pond.

This is where Hans Gmoser told his clients not to throw orange peels because they don't biodegrade as quickly as other fruit and vegetable waste. This is where the strong are brought to tears by beauty, and young men find the confidence to propose marriage. The helicopter allows an experience without the athletic prerequisite that getting there otherwise would require, and then flies away to let the clarity soak in unhindered by the physical demands of backpacking or the mechanical element of heli-skiing and ski touring – the other options for experiencing these mountains.

Imagine the experience is akin to going on a scenic flight over the Himalaya before taking a scenic walk through the most elaborate arboreal display in the Americas outside of the Amazon. This is where a wheelchair user was lifted out of the helicopter to spend the day on a scenic perch while her family went hiking. She soaked in the experience, tears pouring from her eyes at the opportunity to experience raw wilderness for what was likely the last time in her life. This is where a grandfather taught his grandson to skip rocks across ponds surrounded by sheets of shale broken into a million perfect skipping stones. This is where white-haired couples in their eighties and nineties walk together along high ridges above a sea of clouds hiding the deep valleys below.

This is also where a group of backpackers once stomped the words "We Hate You, Hans Gmoser" into the snow after being buzzed several days in a row by a helicopter full of heli-hikers. In the summer, logging roads give non-motorized hikers, at least once they leave their cars, access to some of the heli-hiking terrain, so the heli-hiking guides are tuned in to other backcountry users in the area. Popular backpacking routes are avoided entirely, but the mere concept of helicopter-driven mountain sport is enough to raise some people's hackles.

After my first experience with CMH, a heli-climbing trip in the Adamants, I wrote an article for *Climbing* magazine describing the novelty of bagging first ascents during daily excursions from the comforts of the lodge. In the next month's issue, a letter to the editor described the whole idea as "execrable" and a new low standard of wilderness use. It's a delicate balance between showing people the wilderness and taking care of it. It's for this reason that CMH hired Dave Butler, a biologist and forestry expert, to monitor the programs and stay in tune with government changes and public perception.

An article in *SKI* magazine describes the diversity of heli-hikers:

> Taking quick stock of this mismatched crowd standing awestruck on a grassy mountain ledge at 7500 feet, I wonder, "How did we get here?' There's a 70-something grandfather, a fit heli-skier, a famous chef, an overweight businessman, an elderly lady and a family of five. You'd never guess that in just a couple of hours this wildly diverse group will scramble to the summit and stand together on a lofty peak in the remote Cariboo Mountains of British Columbia.

With the helicopter access, people who never imagined themselves as alpine fanatics can be enthusiasts, devoting as little or as much of their lives as they want to the natural world of the high tundra, the dark blue skies, the tenacious little flowers, the crisp air that somehow flows easier in and out of the lungs, and the forays into the wilderness where it feels like you and your fellow hikers are the only people on Planet Earth. Alpinists discovered this a long time ago and used planes and helicopters to access the most remote peaks, but before Arthur Tauck convinced Hans to take people into the mountains with a helicopter, only the young, the bold, the fit and people with a lot of free time could go out there and live it.

While the spectacular arena is why most people sign up in the first place, as with heli-skiing, it's only part of the magic. Emmy Blechmann, a hiker from Idaho, said, "You know what is the most exciting part of this whole thing? The helicopter. It is so thrilling to get off the bus after a long trip and suddenly be flying over the treetops and into these amazing mountains you've been looking at from the bus windows all day!"

She continues, in response to the mountain hospitality, "I've been all over the world, to the fanciest retreats and resorts that cost way more than this, and this is the best I've ever been treated – better than anywhere else."

Indeed, there is no environment on earth where you can make friends faster than in the mountains. This is true regardless of the season. Something about the isolation, the way the old hills make a person feel young, mortal and lucky to have a chance to explore.

The guide's job is to give people with vastly different abilities, ages and strengths an ideal experience. During the ski season, gravity helps to help keep people together, but in the summer there are marathon runners, overweight executives and patient seniors visiting at the same time. The solution is to have more guides with smaller groups so people can do their own thing at their own pace.

One of the lodge staff observed, "On the first night the (dining) room is pretty quiet. On the second night there's a lot of conversation. And on the third night it is downright noisy in here. People show up as strangers and leave as friends. It's really inspiring."

The summer program today is about where heli-skiing was in 1969. The guides and staff are inventing it as they go, accommodating the changing desires of the kinds of people who want helicopter access. Younger guests are inspiring more adventurous and demanding routes, while family groups often want less mileage and more opportunity to relax together.

Some hikers have become as enthralled with the experience as heli-skiers. To honour their devotion to the game, the lodge staff gives an award, called the Alpinist Award, to anyone who has spent 15 days heli-hiking. When Barb Ostberg received her award – a hiking kit including a jacket, pack and water bottle – she blushed and said humbly, "The last person in the world who should be called an alpinist is me."

For people like Ostberg, the helicopter is the only way she'll ever find herself, many kilometres from the nearest road, walking along an alpine ridge towards a remote summit in anticipation of the view from the top – a vista rivalling the infamous perspective from the summit of Mt. Everest, with peaks and glaciers stretching to the horizon in every direction. For her, it is Everest, a place where she can strive for a lofty perch and feel the pulse of this rugged planet, a place where she can focus on taking the next step in tune with the rocks, ice and life around her, a place where she can forget about the rest of the world for a moment.

Some of the most sublime acreages on the planet are frequented by heli-hikers. These places have never been on *Outside* magazine's hot 100 lists, photos of these places have never been in *National Geographic*, and Outdoor Life Network has never made a show about them. Yet, they rival all of the places featured in these famous publications and productions. With a road nearby, there would be walkways built with signs marking the best views, overlooks built on rock outcrops with pay-per-view telescopes, and a Relais-et-Chateaux-worthy hotel and restaurant would be built on the tundra nearby. Instead, they remain unnamed, except unofficially by a few guides who needed some nomenclature to communicate with each other, and unknown except for the memory and photo albums of a handful of lucky people who fly there each summer while heli-hiking.

One of the areas is a natural golf course, aptly called the Ninth Hole, perched at the edge of a precipice overlooking the terminus of the North Canoe Glacier in the Cariboos. The glacier ends where the ice reaches the edge of a skyscraper-sized cliff, and while part of the ice has tenaciously clung to one side of the rock, creating a cascade of frozen chaos with ice pillars and blocks the size of houses defying gravity, the other half has fallen away, leaving bare rock below the ice. Waterfalls burst from the ice, pumping the very lifeblood of the glacier over the stone at a phenomenal rate. The waterfalls have no name but would be world famous if anyone knew about them. Walking up to an unnamed, unknown waterfall in a setting that could be the eighth wonder of the world is an experience typically reserved for only the most audacious explorers.

Unicorn Basin in the Adamants is an otherworldly meadow with lush flower gardens and speckles of tiny ponds reflecting black spires and white glaciers hanging over the ridges above. It is the sort of drainage that inspires fantasy writers to describe the birthplace of rainbows or unicorns. Underfoot the foliage is so lush that the sturdy growth prevents a hikers foot from reaching the ground. The basin is named after Unicorn Mountain, an 800-metre-tall, horn-shaped black spire perched atop the cirque. Unicorn Basin is located on the rugged side of one of the most glaciated and precipitous areas in the Columbias, the headwaters of Austerity Creek. No logging roads penetrate the valley, and the massive black bulk of Mt. Remillard and the great granite cathedrals of the Gothics hide the area, enhancing its isolation.

One of the most unique spots frequented by heli-hikers is a rocky and often windy place named Anthea's Anatomy by typically irreverent heli-skiers. Had this spot been found by explorers, it would likely have been called something more like Eagle's View. It is a high moraine left by the bulldozer of the Conrad Icefield, the biggest icefield in the Columbias, when it receded. A series of tundra-covered ledges at the edge of a cliff make for idyllic viewing platforms to gaze across the ice from a perspective most often reserved for birds. Looking down onto the old ice, criss-crossed with crevasses, you can see each winter's snowfall preserved in the ice, telling its story like the rings in a tree. Dark layers mark each summer, where dust from winds and ash from forest fires were blown onto the ice, and lighter layers mark each winter's snow accumulation. Recently, hot summers have melted the previous winter's snow entirely, leaving no story in the ice at all except for the tale of what's not there: the snow that has disappeared down the rivers draining into the mighty Columbia and on to the Pacific. It is one of those rare places where you need no understanding of science or precision instruments to see climate change even relative to a human lifetime.

In the Bugaboos, an area of uncountable beauties, there is a place of almost unnatural artistic balance between a meadow cut by sparkling streams accented by brightly coloured flowers, a ridge bristling with the symmetrical forms of pine trees, and the castle-like bulk of the Howser Towers standing against the ever-changing mountain sky. The small but vibrant flowers, some no bigger than a grain of wheat, can be seen in the same view with the lifeless granite wall of the Howsers rising a vertical kilometre high and two kilometres wide just beyond the pine trees. It is a scene where our sense of scale is titillated with the visual anomaly of something very small standing proud against something very big. The area is unassumingly called Kick Off, and it is a ski run in the winter that overlooks the unsurpassed grandeur of the East Creek drainage, an area seen only by heli-hikers, heli-skiers and a handful of adventurous climbers who enjoy the remote challenge of exploring the famous west face of the Howser Towers.

As unique as it is to have an area the size of a national park all to yourself, the helicopter does a disservice to the reputation of the experience. Who needs a helicopter to go hiking? Almost anyone can drive their car to a trailhead and go for a perfectly lovely hike. We don't call it auto-hiking just because we use a car to get to the hiking areas. The helicopter is such an unusual, exciting and expensive means of transportation that it overshadows the experience of spending time in these places. While heli-hiking has been happening since 1978, its potential was largely ignored by traditional backcountry users until recently.

My first experience with heli-hiking was as a photographer. Instantly I recognized the value of the helicopter as a tool for finding a perfect location without having to carry a backbreaking load of glass for hours. It gave me time to shoot, free from the worry of making it back to the trailhead by dark. I could spend hours in the alien world of macro lenses: chasing the sun as it caught the delicate golden petals of a glacier lily,

A TEAM OF HELI-MOUNTAINEERS IN
THE ADAMANTS ASCEND THE EASY
YET THRILLING GLACIER EN ROUTE TO
THE SUMMIT OF MT. REMILLARD.

trying not to dislodge drops of dew while manoeuvring a tripod to shoot them clinging to the hairs on the delicate purple petals of an anemone, shooting air bubbles just beneath the ice at the toe of a glacier, and trying in vain to catch a bee as it feeds on the vibrant red heart of an Indian paintbrush.

With a camera kit I would never carry into such a location, the compositions are infinite. With a big telephoto lens I could juxtapose a lush field of wildflowers against the blue-grey of a glacier's snout, slow the shutter to let a river blur into silky patterns below a craggy peak, pose hikers next to an ancient glacier in front of a gaping crevasse, frame lofty spires against a billowing thunderhead – all the while knowing there's a helicopter waiting to lift us to safety before the storm hits.

Even with a simple point and shoot camera, the opportunity for phenomenal photos is everywhere. More than one person arrived on a heli-hiking trip as a casual amateur photographer and left as a committed shutterbug. Everywhere you look, a postcard or cover photo meets the eye. The hard part is making it look as good in the photo as it appears while standing there immersed in beauty.

For hard-core hikers, the potential is just beginning to be realized. The 20 kilometres of the gently rolling Grizzly Ridge between the Bugaboos and Bobbie Burns would be a world-class trail run or a long day hike past the jagged teeth of the entire Bugaboo and Vowell ranges. The 15-kilometre-long rim of Alpina Basin in the Adamants is like a huge margarita glass, with ice rather than salt lining the rim, and tundra, lakes and gurgling streams where the tequila and lime would be. The Adamants' manager, Erich Unterberger, and a particularly motivated hiker from Boulder, Colorado, traversed the entire rim in a single day. It entails easy snow walking and a view of Sir Sanford's grey and icy hulk on one side and the sea of glacier on the other. This kind of heli-sport could be a wave of the future, but for now the majority of hikers are still more interested in relaxing hikes through jungles of wildflowers to reach a lunch spot above a tarn rippling with the reflection of lofty peaks and crumbling glaciers.

Climbers are also experimenting with the helicopter access from the lodges built for heli-skiing. A heli-mountaineering program has been growing slowly, but few mountaineers have realized the true potential. Most climbing areas today are recorded in guidebooks with such detail that it removes much of the adventure from the experience. Maps of each climb are drawn in detail, giving away many of the secrets of the rock, to the point where climbers know exactly what equipment to pack, how long the climb will take, even what size cracks to expect and how difficult each passage will be.

Because of the pure adventure involved and the chance to go where no human has ever been, first ascents are the proverbial feather in the cap for climbers. In places where most climbers live, every summit has been climbed, and first ascents can only be found, if at all, in between cracks and faces that have already been climbed. To do a first ascent is the ultimate climbing experience and is one of the rare times in this modern world where we can be true explorers of geography, touching a piece of our planet that has never been touched, seeing a view that has never been seen, spending a day as no human ever has. It is a chance to play Ernest Shackleton in a microcosm where success is not certain, difficulty is unpredictable and finishing is a chance to make history.

After a first ascent, the climbs are recorded in guidebooks and by alpine clubs. The Bugaboos and the Bobbie Burns lodges both have world-class mountaineering programs, but the Adamants is the climber's bonanza and the potential is just beginning to be explored. The Adamants are particularly well endowed with steep rock faces. Many are named, some have been climbed and a number have yet to be explored. Many faces have never felt the touch of a human hand, and it is every climber's dream to walk up to such a piece of rock and be the first person to ascend the wall. The golden age of heli-climbing has yet to happen. The climbers who can afford the access don't yet realize that a week in the Adamants can give them more first ascents than most climbers will do in a lifetime. For mountaineering, the Monashees is the least developed of areas, and future adventurers will find lifetimes of classic mountaineering routes on the range's spectacular peaks.

While the guides call the technical ascents heli-mountaineering, and typically focus on spectacular routes of relatively moderate difficulty, a group of rock climbers from Boulder, Colorado, wanted something more: heli-climbing. They wanted the helicopter to drop them at the base of the most remote rock faces in the Columbias for a day of climbing and a return flight to the lodge in the evening.

Heli-climbing in the Adamants began when a heli-skier from Boulder named Kyle Lefkoff saw the opportunity to do numerous first ascents while based out of the Adamants lodge, with gourmet meals on a table rather than ramen in an oatmeal-stained pot, fine wine from a glass instead of Gatorade mix from a Nalgene bottle, a hot shower in place of a cold stream, a massage replacing a long walk back to camp, and a private bedroom instead of a cramped and fetid tent. Boulder, being statistically the fittest city in the United States, was an ideal place to recruit someone for the most comfortable first-ascent blitz in the history of mountaineering. He found a willing partner in a climber named Wayne Goss. In an essay titled "A Brief History of Heli-climbing," Lefkoff wrote:

> We finally got serious in the winter of 1994, after back-to-back ten-day trips over Christmas and New Year's in the Adamants convinced me of the correct venue, and of the right guide for the job: Erich Unterberger. Erich was the assistant manager to Franz Fux in those days, and Fux ran a tight ship. But I'd never met a guide as motivated and committed to climbing his range as Erich.
>
> The next season, Wayne and I were invited to join Brooks and Ann Dodge and Art Dion on an Adamants tour. We thought this would be our perfect entrée to heli-climbing, but Ann sent us all a flower book for the trip, and a half hour call with Fux and Mark Kingsbury ("you want to climb what!?") convinced us we were barking up the wrong tree.
>
> Three years of advanced training for heli-climbing ensued ("climb, spa, drink, repeat as necessary") until Goss and I got our big break: Fux left CMH and Erich was in charge of the Adamants. We made a solemn vow: if Erich would let us climb what we all wanted, Goss and I would bring the A team to the Adamants. All the promises were kept, and in August 1999 we showed up at the lodge with a crew of legendary Boulder climbers, all with decades of first ascents around the world.
>
> It wasn't just the miles of untouched alpine granite. It wasn't just driving a 212 (helicopter) around the ranges like a Chinese rickshaw. It wasn't just rolling out of bed at 8 a.m. for a big breakfast and then roping up at the base of the wall at 9:10. And it wasn't just sending the big lines for the first time, ever. No, it was doing all this stuff that all of us lived for, and then making it back for a 4 p.m. massage and hot tub, a decent martini and a fine bottle of claret at dinner.

Lefkoff returned to the Adamants numerous times since then, developing the Silver Shadow cliffs on the sunny side of Alpina Basin into an ideal climbing area for beginners and experts alike, doing first ascents on the bigger peaks with his wife, Cindy, and introducing CMH to the potential of heli-climbing for expert rock climbers.

While heli-climbing is still relatively unknown, it has graced the pages of *Climbing* magazine, and with the number of climbers in the United States growing (from

7.5 million to 9.2 million in a single year, 2004), future generations will be looking for unexplored terrain, and the growth of heli-climbing is likely just around the corner.

The heli-mountaineering program, where small groups climb alpine peaks of more moderate difficulty, is already more popular than even the CMH marketing office knows. Many hikers end up feeling the adventurous spirit once they arrive at the lodges, and guides' enthusiasm for mountaineering inspires them to give it a try. Almost without exception, people return from a day of mountaineering and say, "I just had the best day of my life!"

The Columbia Range contains a fantastic variety of climbing and mountaineering objectives. Some peaks are cut into monolithic spires like arrowheads shaped by a meticulous warrior; others are piles of boulders chaotically thrown together like pyramids built by a lazy god trying to tempt gravity and entropy. The spires and solid walls are better for climbing, but mountains of all types are intriguing to mountaineers. Some, like Downie, the pyramid located prominently down valley from the Adamants lodge, have summits that beg to be climbed but are made of such rubble and broken rock that only a few climbers have ever stood atop them.

While hanging from a few millimetres of rock protruding from the edge of a black wall hundreds of metres above the ground, walking along a ridge with the profile of a kitchen knife, or climbing a steep glacier by swinging medieval-looking axes into the ice may not appeal to everyone, gazing from tiny summits balanced above wild valleys is an experience no one regrets.

The Adamants and the Bugaboos inarguably have the best climbing of any of the areas, but it is the Bobbie Burns team that is currently carrying Hans Gmoser's torch of exploration. It began with a dilemma of what to do when the weather shut down the helicopter for an afternoon. The Bobbie Burns guides, mostly restless young climbers – or at least former restless young climbers – felt there was more excitement to be found in the surrounding area during the summer than just heli-hiking.

The Vowell River passes in front of the lodge and enters a narrow gorge complete with powerful waterfalls and frothing whitewater. Thick bush along its shore not only makes walking nearly impossible but also blocks the view of the gorge entirely. Since ropes and harnesses are natural tools for guides, it didn't take long to decide to build a zipline across the river. Hikers wear climbing harnesses and clip into ropes strung above the rapids, and with a belay to control speed, they zip across the torrent. The roar of the rapids hammers the eardrums, drowning out all other sounds, the exposure of the cliffs dropping into whitewater confuses visual perception, the smell of the lush forest fills the nose, the sensation of speed is enhanced by the cool prickles of airborne water droplets hitting your skin while you fly over the rapids.

The guides called their new outing the Adventure Trail, and it was such a rush among the younger and more audacious hikers that many started asking to do this trail instead of going hiking in the high country. The guides built longer ziplines over the biggest waterfalls in the gorge and assembled an unprecedented zipline that runs 200 metres through one section of the canyon. With guests asking for the Adventure Trail,

AN EXPERT CLIMBER FEELING THE
EXPOSURE ON THE APTLY NAMED
IRONMAN IN THE ADAMANTS.
OPPOSITE: A COUPLE OF
NONAGENARIANS EXPLORE
THE HIGH ALPINE.

the guides saw the appeal of combining the stunning alpine locations with adventurous routes using via ferratas.

Between the via ferratas and the Adventure Trail, as well as the traditional hiking and climbing options, the Bobbie Burns summer experience is as unreal, fresh and adventurous as heli-skiing was in 1969. Other lodges are innovating, as well. The Adamants has a long zipline, a ropes course and a few rock-climbing areas that often make a poor weather day into the most memorable and thrilling part of the trip. Fitting to the spirit of Hans Gmoser, the new programs are not the result of marketing decisions but simply evolved from the idea of giving people a mountain experience beyond their wildest dreams.

5

BY TRIAL AND AIR

The turns are the manoeuvres by which the skier alters his course when running downhill and so controls not only his direction but his speed. The good skier uses them as sparingly as possible, his aim being to make a beeline down the hill whenever he safely can. It should be clearly understood that the difficulty of turning is a twofold one, being a matter partly of steering – the bringing of the skis round – and partly of the keeping of the balance. These two difficulties are to a great extent independent. In skid-turning it often happens that the greater the difficulty in one respect, the less it is in the other. The higher the speed, for instance, the more difficult it is to avoid losing one's balance, but the less difficult it usually is to get the skis to come round; so that a skid-turn at a very slow speed, though in one way it may be absurdly easy, may in another be the highest test of skill.

—Vivian Caulfeild, *Ski-ing Turns*, 1922

Consider this business model: combine a ski area, a resort hotel, a remote expedition base camp, a travel agency, a mountain guide service, a helicopter company, a wilderness mapping project, an avalanche forecasting agency, a forestry consulting group, a food and beverage service, an intermountain transportation system, and a mountain rescue and medical service. Essentially, this is the complex machine that is remote-base heli-skiing. And today, for the most part, it works like a fine Swiss timepiece.

For a couple of poor immigrant mountain bums to build this machine from a rudimentary sawmill camp was a feat of rarely matched boldness and good fortune. Hans Gmoser and Leo Grillmair recruited a team of skilled mountain guides from Austria, Germany and Switzerland and ventured into some of the snowiest mountains on earth with an eye for skiing at a time when airplane and helicopter technology was just enabling the first takeoffs and landings in mountain environments with any significant payload. Climbing and skiing made sense to the guides, but the rest of the equation had to be learned from hard work, from every mistake and close call, as well as from the perfect days when everything went smoothly. As Lloyd "Kiwi" Gallagher puts it, "CMH is the most experienced company in the business, and experience generates good judgment, but it is generally poor judgment that has led to gaining this experience."

Bryan MacPherson, a heli-ski pilot in Kootenay, has a similar view of the learning process: "In order to increase experience, you have to take risks. What's important is how you take the risks. You have to do it a little at a time to increase the experience without getting in trouble."

The state of the art of heli-sport was not planned. It was learned. Getting to where it is today was a series of eureka moments, tragedies and near misses that shed light on how things should be done. Since so many different kinds of expertise need to come together for a smooth week of heli-skiing, the learning curve and potential pitfalls were almost unlimited. Add a group of guides and guests with different languages and experiences, and the scene was ripe for hilarity and the unexpected.

The first thing Hans used to say whenever anyone credited him with the invention of heli-skiing was that a lot of other people were part of it. He wasn't just talking about his fellow guides. He was talking about pilots, house staff, office attendants, cooks, maintenance crews, early investors, the many guests and the families of all these people who gave a bit of their lives to the project. Developing heli-skiing from a cowboy joyride chasing after the ski run of all time into the organized wonder we see today was a colossal epic of learning for everyone involved.

Misadventures have shaped every aspect of the experience. Today, it seems like a precision system with every detail accounted for, but every cog in the machine was built on the trials and tribulations of many staff and guests enduring all manner of experiences and epics of grand proportions.

The first big problem was covering so much mountain terrain in such a short time with so many people. With modern helicopters, CMH lodges work with four guides and 44 skiers, or 11 skiers per guide, while ski touring guides more often work in pairs with a dozen or so skiers. In ski touring, guides had to deal with a smaller and more experienced group of skiers encountering a smaller slice of the mountains. The most important part of the heli-ski equation was managing the groups in the mountains. If the guides did it wrong, the lodging could be Shangri-La and heli-skiing would still never work. If they did it right, it wouldn't matter if the lodging was a snowcave – heli-skiing would be the ultimate ski experience. Explains Leo, "I don't know how we survived with the knowledge we had about heli-skiing, which was zero."

Wilderness skiing with larger groups was mind-boggling for guides used to the slow pace of ski touring. On one occasion, a guest was accidentally left behind after getting delayed in the woods. The marooned skier found his way to a cache and curled up in the sleeping bag in the rescue equipment, where guides found him a few hours later. This kind of error was unacceptable and potentially deadly if it had happened in the wrong place. Today, guides religiously count skiers all day long. It's nothing like traditional ski mountaineering to keep track of a group of powder-hungry tree skiers blundering pell-mell down 10,000 metres of vertical wilderness terrain over the course of a single day.

In another incident, a skier was crossing a crevasse when the snow gave way beneath his skis. The tips and tails of the skis stayed on the surface, supported by either lip of the crevasse, but the skier fell into the hole. It was in the days before ski brakes were invented, so straps were used to prevent runaway skis if they released. The straps held the full weight of the skier, and he found himself hanging upside down, staring into the blackness of the ancient ice. The guide was able to quickly extricate his hapless client, but it was as close as close calls get. "The difference between a close call and an accident," explained Hans, "is that in a close call you walk away from it."

Just the cold of the Canadian winter is a formidable problem. Veteran guide Thierry Cardon remembers being unable to ski in the Bugaboos with temperatures of –42°C, and trying to ski in –37°. He says, "After 45 minutes, everyone had frostbite."

Avalanche understanding was a huge learning curve that, while well studied today, is still being advanced. Today, while searching for instabilities in the snow, guides study everything from the minutiae of the nearly microscopic shape and size of the ice crystals and the temperature differences between the layers to the large-scale deposition of wind-transported snow and daily storm snow accumulation and settlement. Throughout the season they perform a number of different tests on columns of snow to determine interaction between layers within the snowpack. All this information is recorded and shared among snow professionals throughout the region.

Bob Geber explains what the snow stability test was like in the early days: "For the rough test we would push the ski pole basket into the snow. For the fine test we would push the handle into the snow."

Leo shakes his head and laughs hysterically when talking about the first forays into avalanche terrain using the helicopter. "We would just ski onto the slope first, and try to cut it. If it didn't go we would ski it."

During a heli-hiking trip to the Bobbie Burns lodge, Leo sat down with Joe Jones, one of the original heli-skiers, to reminisce about the early days. The conversation began with a friendly argument about how it happened – a common theme when remembering things that happened nearly half a century ago – and described a day of epic learning. Joe Jones began:

"Remember we got into the little avalanche that time?"

"With you and Dave Hoff and his wife?" Leo asked.

"Yeah. You cut the slope and set off a little slab and then told us to come on down."

"I didn't say to come on! You bastards jumped on the slope before I said go, and released the avalanche!"

"No, no!" retorted Jones. "That was the first avalanche! Dave Hoff cut into the slope a couple of hundred feet above us and set it off. All of a sudden the whole thing went like a big blast. Remember?"

"Oh yeah."

"You were standing down below watching Dave riding it like a huge wave and it came right over me. You were looking up but I ended up right by your feet."

"Oh yeah. All of a sudden I hear this voice by my feet: 'Leo, can you help me!' I remember that avalanche."

"I tell you, my adrenaline was up. Remember how Dave lost his ski?"

At this point Leo gets caught up in the memory and takes over the narration entirely. During the telling of the story, Leo's yodeller's voice is a cacophony of laughter, sighs and chortles intermingling with his tenacious Austrian accent. His eyes alternate between growing wide, rolling back in his head and grimacing:

That was my blackest day of heli-skiing. We were skiing Powder Pig and I was group four so all the groups were ahead of me. I went down a little ways and said, "Hold it here." There's this little slope out the left side and I go out there and cut this slope which I knew was going to cut loose – and then we could ski it. So I go out there and cut this avalanche and sure enough it goes. I look down and realize – oh shit, down there is Hans Gmoser! He was trying to put his ski back on! He had fallen and he looks up, goes "Oh fuck!" and takes off on one ski! He gets away, but I thought, "That's not the way to do it – bury your boss in an avalanche!"

So the next run we go up to Rooftop and I could see it's all hammered by wind, but there's this other run off the north side which is very nice. Okay, so we got to the top of that and I looked at it and I say, "Jesus, I'm not so sure."

So I say, "Why don't you guys stay here for a minute, I want to check this out."

She let me get right to the middle (of the slope) when she let go, but I managed to out-ski it out to the left and the whole avalanche went down past me. The group was standing on top and they say, "What should we do?"

I say, "Fuck, it's okay now. We go on down and ski some more." We have lunch on the north side (of the Bugaboos), then we make our way back run by run and come again to Rooftop. I didn't want to ski Rooftop because it was so hammered, but when we flew up I saw another little gully over there that leads down and there's a nice little slope down there. So we go there, it slides too, and that's when you (Jones) and Dave Hoff got caught and Dave lost his ski.

So we're looking for that ski and we couldn't find it, so I eventually say, "Look, Dave, forget about it. Take my ski and I'll ski down on one ski."

I take my ski off and throw it over to Dave, and bang! my ski hits the lost ski! After 50 minutes of searching by everyone, my ski just hits it! The metal-on-metal blang! – we knew it hit the ski. So we ski into this canyon, which was quite nice, and on the last run we are on the Black Forest.

I tell the group, "There's the Good, the Bad and the Ugly. We're going to ski the Ugly. Do you see the forked tree down there? We go to that and then make the traverse; then we ski down to the lodge."

We get to the traverse and there is one skier missing. I say, "Oh shit."

Dave says, "Don't worry, I know exactly where she is. Don't worry, go on the traverse and I'll look after her. We'll meet her on the traverse."

She was on our right, so we went across and she met us alright – she met me! Bang! She comes flying out of the trees, hits me, throws me into this tree and breaks my shoulder, delaminates my Head ski – it was like an accordion. I decided I've had enough today, so I say to the group, "Look, there's the lodge, go on down. I don't want to see anybody anymore. Fuck you." I ski down on one ski with a broken shoulder. I came back to the lodge that day like Napoleon back from Russia!

When asked about the avalanche Leo set loose on him, Hans just shook his head and casually replied, "That's not the only time Leo cut an avalanche on me."

"We had so many accidents," says Leo of the early days during the steepest learning curve of heli-skiing. Today, the safety record is significantly better in every respect. Why? There are uncountable reasons, including snow science, legal accountability, conservative business ethics and just plain experience. But one of the biggest is leadership style. The competition, like the guiding teams chasing Captain Vertical status, is gone from the guiding groups, and only good-natured ribbing remains. Those who make small mistakes buy wine for the rest of the guides as a friendly reminder to stay on their toes. Wine from the guide who forgot to put on his ski boots for a day of checking fuel caches during pre-season setup and ended up in the helicopter wearing his Sorels; wine from the guide who forgot to return the skis for the guest who went in early, cluttering the ski-basket for the rest of the day; and wine from the pilot who forgot to pick up the staff for skiing when there were spaces on the helicopter.

Guides are constantly looking for chances to tease each other as long as it doesn't affect safety – in fact, it is a subtle way to remind everyone stay on guard. Gery Unterasinger said before the morning meeting, "It's Friday the 13th and the last day of my 13th season." Upon hearing his superstitious concerns, someone doctored the weather report so the wind looked as if it was higher overnight to make Gery even more nervous. He figured out the joke quickly, but the significance was obvious. Just a slight change of the wind changes everything, but it took decades to get the understanding to where it is today.

When the Skadi, the first avalanche transceiver that sent a signal and could be located by a trained user with another unit, was invented, it too was not an overnight sensation, because of the guides' less sophisticated understanding of snow dangers. At first the CMH guides put Skadis only on the first group of skiers, figuring that if the slope avalanched, it would be on the first group. Then the guides put the beacons on the first and last skiers in each group, thinking they were the most likely to get buried. All that changed one day in the Bugaboos. All the guides felt comfortable about the stability, so they left the Skadis behind entirely rather than deal with the awkward, long devices. They proceeded to release a huge avalanche that day, nearly burying two groups, but everyone walked away unharmed. Now it is well documented that the first or the 50th skier on a slope can trigger an avalanche, and every skier who leaves the lodge is tested for a functioning transceiver every day.

The helicopter is a fantastic tool that took a bit of getting used to for the ski mountaineers who were learning how to heli-ski. It allows skiers to chase good conditions to whatever altitude is best. If the weather is deteriorating on one side of the range, in no time everyone can be on the other side enjoying clear skies. However, for any mountaineer, it is an uncomfortable feeling to be a two-day walk from the nearest shelter with nothing but a pair of skis.

At first, the guides felt that if the helicopter part of the system broke down and they were left to their own devices in the woods, they could go back to their old touring tactics and simply ski home. Since both bad weather and darkness will ground a helicopter, everyone carried skins tied around their waists so they could ski back up over the mountains and return to the lodge. In those days, ski bindings were cables that could be released near the heel to allow for a cross-country gait, so it was a realistic consideration – or so they thought. Then one day, a group ended up at the bottom of the Vowell glacier without enough time to fly back to the lodge as darkness fell.

According to Kiwi, Hans said, "No problem, I'll ski ahead and break trail over the top and you bring the group along." Hans laboured ahead for a while, breaking trail in the deep snow until he was exhausted, and then skied back to the group, who had barely started the climb. "It was then that we realized how ridiculous the idea of walking back to the lodge really was," says Kiwi, "but we thought we could ski down the valley to a cabin that didn't seem so far away." It was the last time groups carried skins while heli-skiing.

They headed down the valley, the exhausted guests doing the best they could to keep going and the guides doing their best to avoid leading the group into open water in the river. Soon, it became clear there was no way they would make it to the cabin. Without the helicopter, the terrain grew in size and the humans shrank in capability until their efforts ceased to be a means of reaching a warm place to sleep and became simply an action to keep warm blood pumping to fend off the winter chill.

Action pumps blood through the body and produces warmth until a person runs out of energy, and then the sly fingers of hypothermia reach towards the heart. Jack London's *To Build a Fire* tells the story of a man's demise in the Arctic as he tries to save his life with the seemingly simple task of building a fire. It is not so easy to find dry, dead wood with several metres of snow on the ground. Moving kept the strong skiers warm longer, but the weaker ones slowly chilled and walked even slower, allowing the cold to sneak in through their extremities. As exhaustion increased and the pace decreased, the guides found a large snag, a dead tree entangled with living trees holding it out of the snow. The guides made the life-saving decision to stop before everyone was spent, and lit the snag on fire. The pillar of fire then became a beacon of life for the rest of the night. In the morning, the group continued on down the valley to a place where the helicopter could pick them up.

Twenty years later, another night fell upon a group from the Bobbie Burns lodge, but this time a storm caused the adventure. Three groups were skiing near the Duncan River Valley, one of the most inaccessible valleys in the Columbias and a grizzly-infested wonderland that separates the Purcells from the Selkirks. The pass to return to the lodge was closing out quickly, but the first group, led by guide Kobi Wyss, was able to catch a flight over the pass.

After that flight, visibility became so poor that the pilot was afraid to continue with a full machine but was unable to find a reasonable landing. Kobi and the pilot found a spot where they could hover close enough to the ground that everyone could climb out, and Kobi was able to unload the ski basket while the pilot held his hover in the quickly strengthening storm. Alone, the pilot had the maximum manoeuvrability of the powerful Bell 212 engine, and even with almost zero visibility he was able to feel his way just above the treetops to clear flying below the clouds at the valley bottom. The skiers descended through thick forest to meet the helicopter beneath the cloud ceiling, and after an easy pickup they flew back to the lodge.

The Bobbie Burns crew tried to recruit the Bugaboos helicopter to help, but the storm had already enveloped the Bugaboo Valley in thick cloud and falling snow. The Bobbie Burns machine was able to get over the pass to pick up the second group but was unable to return. To avoid a replay of the dicey hovering drop-off, the pilot flew up the Duncan River to near Rogers Pass and then down the Columbia to return to the Bobbie Burns lodge – a detour of a couple hundred kilometres. By the time he could return for guide Colani Bezzola's group, it was too late.

The remaining skiers were stranded at the base of Creamer, separated from the lodge by the Conrad Icefield and the formidable 3000-metre peaks of Tetragon and Thorington. Walking home was not even a consideration. Below the ski run, a thick forest in the Giegerich Creek drainage promised protection from the wind and fuel for a fire. Luckily, the storm was not too fierce and the group was able to build a roaring fire under some big trees. Colani recalls the story with the sparkle in his eyes of someone telling of a favourite memory: "The group did really well, but there was one guy who took until about midnight to realize the helicopter was not coming back until morning. He kind of folded – he couldn't imagine we would survive the night.

"I was cutting wood (the guides carry folding saws to cut branches and bushes if they threaten the rotors of the helicopter at a pickup) and the other guys were carrying it back to the fire. After a while we had a big enough fire that people were pretty comfortable. The feet were the only problem, so we built a 'midnight slalom' so we could ski a bit."

The night passed slowly, as all unplanned bivouacs do. Some skiers passed the time by dragging their skis up the hill to take turns in the midnight slalom, the gates fashioned from tree branches and the flickering light from the fire lighting the impromptu course. In between runs, they snuggled around the roaring fire under the shelter of a couple of big cedar and hemlock trees, the only human beings in the entire Duncan River drainage.

True to the spirit of heli-skiing, in the morning, the helicopter picked them up and took them back to the lodge for a hot breakfast before going back out to ski all day in fresh snow. The next year the group returned with T-shirts printed with "heli-camping" in honour of the lasting memory.

Even with the current lodges of friendly comfort and fast helicopters, fat skis, real-time weather reports and more accurate forecasts, CMH heli-skiing is still an unpredictable mountain experience. Thierry Cardon puts it bluntly: "In business, we always hear that the customer is king. But out here the customer is not king, the guide is not king, the mountain is the fucking king!"

No amount of technology, paperwork or protocol will ever change the true authority – the mountains themselves. Dealing with the mountains has reached such a refined point that even the personalities of the lead guides are juggled to put the guide in front who can best handle the current conditions. Guide Daniel Zimmerman observed: "Analytical lead guides are better at running a smooth, efficient, blue-sky day. Intuitive leaders are better at running a day with changing conditions, poor stability and bad weather. It took me years to see the difference, but it is huge. Different leadership styles do better in different conditions."

Today the system is so well defined that for a guide to go ski a run that has never been skied is a significant departure from the norm, unlike back in Leo's day. However, while he may have to buy a few bottles of wine for getting out of line, if the new run is any good it may end up on the run list. The adventure goes on.

Even with all the experience and preparation, almost every day a story is made, a memory that will be shared for years and add to the multicoloured cloth of the collective experience. Some are unpredictable in the extreme, like the skier who arrived with a prosthetic leg but told no one about his detachable limb. He skied well enough, so no one suspected he was physically any different from the other skiers, but halfway through the day he went for one of those yard-sale wipeouts where everything that can detach from the skier goes in different directions, and rather than breaking out of the binding, his leg pulled out of its joint. The rest of the group was standing below when, out of the snow cloud caused by his tumble, a ski came flying towards them with what appeared to be a boot and a leg still attached! For a moment everyone was sure they were witnessing a crash so severe as to separate the man's leg from his body.

Other stories are inspiring, like the blind man whose father skied behind him and gave instructions as they ripped down the mountain like any other pair of skiers. Some days, when the light is so flat that a skier could run into a car-sized snowball without seeing it, the rest of the group is not much better than blind anyway. These are the days when the first guide down the hill is almost seasick from the disorienting feeling of skiing with nothing but whiteness in front of the goggles. Add some funky snow and even the best skiers with two functioning eyes are learning how to ski all over again.

By Trial and Air 105

Guides take such conditions with a sense of humour whenever they can. One day, after a Pineapple Express and a solid freeze left the surface a sheet of ice so hard a ski pole could hardly penetrate, and the conditions were ripe for injury, one guide said sarcastically, "Maybe we can get people to wear leg splints today to save us some time."

Even Hans's promotional films were steeped in this sort of irreverent humour and the underlying lesson: you're responsible for yourself out there. In the film *Ski Trails*, he says: "You are free to ski wherever you feel like skiing, today here, tomorrow there, the whole country is yours. You can ski every bit of it. Jump over every rock you feel like jumping over and if you should happen to jump too far you just hope someone finds your body – so the wife can collect the life insurance."

Nowadays, CMH measures footage on every run, recording it for the bragging rights of the skiers, and guest satisfaction is second only to snow stability. This is a far cry from the early days. "The concept of guest services was different then," remembers Cardon. "We used to sidestep up to the lodge after skiing Homerun at the end of the day and verbally abuse the guests for being slow on the hill."

After one guest skied too close to a crevasse, Bob Geber scolded him for risking his life. The skier, who happened to be Prime Minister Pierre Trudeau, turned and said, "Bob, you would never make it in politics."

Drinking at lunch was standard behaviour. After all, in Europe there are still slope-side bars where skiers can sip schnapps without even taking off their skis.

This all sounds unacceptable in today's litigation-crazed and service-oriented culture, but if you consider the history of the guides, it makes more sense. Not long before moving to Canada, Cardon had skied the north face of Mont Blanc in leather Galibier climbing boots with cable bindings. He came from an era of toughness where men could ski with a buzz if they wanted – and still leave everyone in the dust skinning uphill at the end of the day. In the early days, guides would often push the groups as hard as they could, trying to pass other groups and hooting and hollering when they succeeded; guides even switched in the middle of the day, with a second set of guides leading for the afternoon while the first one rested. Hans called his stable of guides at the time "the Swiss Mafia."

While Hans and Leo were intuitive mountaineers, in the beginning they lacked fundamental business knowledge. "One day I was skiing with a banker from Seattle," remembers Leo, "when the banker said 'I have a suggestion about pricing.' I started to explain all the expenses, and the banker interrupted me: 'No, no. You don't understand. I'm a banker. I did the math and I know you're not making any profit. You need to be charging double!' I said if we do that we'll halve our numbers! And the banker replied, 'Isn't that what you want?'"

Leo thought about it and decided charging at least a little more was essential to the survival of the business. People wanted to heli-ski, and this drove Hans to expand. Marion Kingsbury was working in reservations and remembers the moment in the late eighties when Hans decided to open more areas. "I went to Hans in tears saying we had all these people who want to ski and we have no space. It was like, bingo! we were opening Galena and the Gothics. He didn't even ask permission first. We started selling the areas and applied for tenure and built the lodges later!"

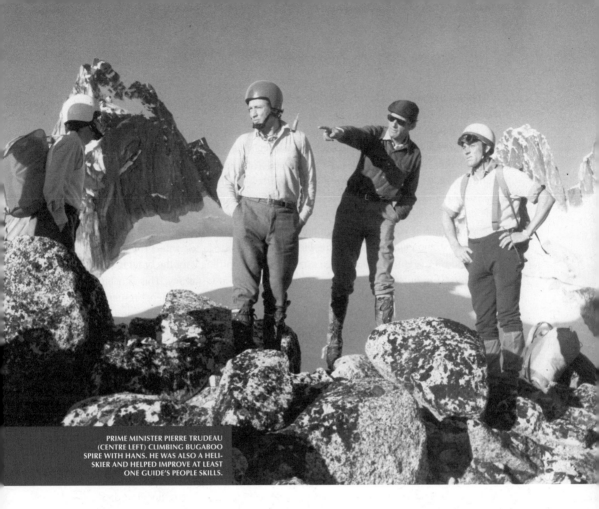

PRIME MINISTER PIERRE TRUDEAU
(CENTRE LEFT) CLIMBING BUGABOO
SPIRE WITH HANS. HE WAS ALSO A HELI-
SKIER AND HELPED IMPROVE AT LEAST
ONE GUIDE'S PEOPLE SKILLS.

To open Galena with the pressure on to make it work, the guides had eight hours one day during the touchiest stability of the season to learn the area before the first skiers arrived. On that particular day, the Day-Glo guide suit became mandatory after Mark Kingsbury got caught in an avalanche in a one-piece white ski suit. They found him, but after that no one was allowed to ski in white. Bernard Ehman remembers, "We could tell right away (guiding) the terrain was going to be challenging."

There was no guide training; guides just showed up and went skiing. Kobi Wyss remembers his first day guiding with CMH: "Hans told me to just follow the tracks. They dropped me off (with his group) on top of this peak in a complete whiteout. The snow was rock hard and there was no sign of a track anywhere. I just started skiing slowly and somehow it all worked out."

Today, a guide very familiar with the area leads the first group, and the other three groups follow on either side of the first group's tracks, but at first it was more of a free for all, with each guide taking his group wherever he wanted. Bob Geber took a wrong turn in the Monashees and ended up on the bank of the Columbia River, far from the pickup, in an area where the forest is too thick to walk through. With only one option left to get to a place where the helicopter could land, he and his group took off their skis and stepped into the river. With their boots slowly filling with icy water, they waded through the shallows to reach the pickup.

Hans's theory of guide training in those days was: "It is like with many other things in life. If you survive the first day, then you have made it."

For the most part, the guides did whatever they could get away with. There were no rules, no precedents, and they had well-stocked lodges and a helicopter with a master pilot to conspire with. Peter Lustenberger remembers some outings not likely to happen again: "We went skiing with a couple of pilots while the guests were having breakfast. One pilot would fly and the other would ski, then they would switch for the next run.

"Another day we went heli-fishing and came back to the lodge with a bunch of fish we weren't supposed to have because we didn't have fishing licences, and the RCMP (Royal Canadian Mounted Police) was there! So we took the RCMP and their family on a heli-tour and everything was okay. We got away with a lot back then."

Sometimes, this impromptu heli-hooky didn't work out so well. Not so long ago, there was a gap in the summer schedule, and the manager decided to give the staff a treat. They rounded up a bunch of ski gear and took the helicopter for a bit of summer heli-skiing. It was all fun and games until a girl fell on the hard summer snow and hurt her hip. There was no place to land nearby, and the manager didn't want to initiate a rescue in the middle of summer when they weren't supposed to be skiing at all, so a particularly strong skier picked up the girl and skied the rest of the run with her in his arms.

Pat Aldous, CEO of CMH's exclusive helicopter operator, Alpine Helicopters, until 2007, observed, "Mountain guides and helicopter pilots are an interesting workforce. They have huge responsibility, are strong-minded and like to do their own thing. It's a lot of fun."

The anarchy days of heli-skiing slowly ended with the learning, the close calls and the fear of litigation, but the fundamental freedom of skiing in the mountains is still there.

Sometimes it wasn't the mountains, but rather guest complaints or suggestions that caused changes. And Hans, building every aspect of the business based on guest feedback, made many of the changes. Eventually, the Swiss Mafia were long gone, but the mountains still rule.

Not all guest suggestions were implemented, and not all guest perspectives are right. Some guests stand in the middle of a forest and ask if they are on a glacier. Some check for cell phone coverage deep in remotest canyons in the Columbias. So their suggestions must be taken with consideration of their experience in the mountains – or lack thereof. In extreme cases, a couple of notorious guests have been banned from CMH – one for complaining bitterly if he was skiing on anything except his three favourite runs in the Monashees and abusing the staff to no end, and another for beating a fellow guest with his poles after he skied too close to his track and later pulling a knife on a Japanese guest for hitting on his gorgeous blonde daughter.

Dealing with these kinds of guests begins with frustration and ends with refusal to take them skiing. In between, different guides had different ways of handling the troublemakers. Rudi Gertsch remembers one notorious group who was always pushing the guide to make it better and harder. While skiing with them in Mica Creek in the

Monashees, Gertsch noticed a gnarly line interspersed with cliffs. "There's a line for some tough skiers."

"Aren't we tough?" said the group leader, egging Gertsch to take them down the heinous line.

Gertsch decided to give the group what they deserved, so he grabbed a climbing rope and went for it. They started jumping over the cliffs and eventually the drops got too big to ski over. There was no way to go back up so they started rappelling. Gertsch remembers, smiling, "Those guys thought they were going to die. Hans never got mad at me for that run. I think he was happy to see those guys put in their place."

Hans himself was not above giving an overly demanding group a bit of karmic payback in the form of suffering. After a group had been skiing past him and not listening to directions, Hans skied right past the pickup spot into the forest and bushwhacked for the lodge, which took hours. "I remember watching Hans walking in first, in a bad mood," says Gertsch, "and the rest of the group slowly trickling in afterward, completely wasted."

The run was never skied again, but it has a name: Gmoser's Revenge.

If there were a university degree in operating a remote heli-skiing area, it would have to be called Logistical Engineering. From the transportation, the timing of skiing, pickups and fuel conservation, to the smallest detail of making landing flags easy to place and redesigning the helicopter basket to accommodate a full group of snowboards, the logistics are staggering.

To begin with, the guides and staff have to manage transporting skiers across the entire Rocky Mountain Range from the nearest airport, usually Calgary, through the rugged winter mountains and then fly them in to the lodges. While these days snowdrifted logging roads are bypassed with a usually effortless 15-minute flight, there is still plenty of adventure to reach the mountaintops, where the advertised fun really begins. In the beginning, there were no rules, tenures or systems for heli-skiing, so everything had to be invented literally on the fly.

Efficiency is considered to the smallest detail. During the summer months, fuel trucks travel up logging roads to replenish tanks in the remotest parts of each area's tenure so the helicopter can refuel without a long flight back to the lodge. Lodges use each other's fuel tanks if it reduces flight time. During the off-season, each cache is maintained and refilled, but then they are prone to bullets from excited hunters and rabble-rousers. When the snow falls and it is time to set up for the ski season, the guides must dig out each cache and prepare the fuel lines and the rescue equipment. Each cache is built like a small hut on stilts that looks like an oversized birdhouse and is equipped with a drip catchment system to keep the ground and snow around the fuel tank free of spillage. Even the small avalanches off the roofs of the rescue caches can slam into fuel lines, making the next refuel difficult or impossible. Even the minutest details, if missed, can result in big problems.

Systems for recording snowpack went from the lead guides scratching their heads and trying to remember what happened last month, to a computer database storing every snowfall and wind event from the first snowflake to the last ski run of the season. Even with such technology at their fingertips, many guides keep their own records in notebooks in case the computer crashes or is otherwise not usable. They record the information required in case of legal issues reluctantly, as it is not always pertinent to the areas where they ski, but the rest of the information they gather they trust with their lives. A cold night, a warm day, an unusual wind are all things that make or ruin the fun of heli-skiing for everyone involved and change the guide's job from the ski professional's dream to the ski professional's nightmare.

Each area's setup at the beginning of each season is preparation for everything that can go wrong, and an opportunity to stack the cards in a way that gives the best chance of everything going right.

Most areas spend a week preparing for the season. Guides flag mineshafts, rock crevasses and some hidden cliffs in the middle of popular runs, although the vast majority of hazards are left unmarked. It is impossible to mark a heli-ski tenure like a ski resort and, quite frankly, who would want to see red tape across every rock and drop?

Every year, the guides meet for a pre-season training week that combines new concepts and reiteration of old learning. Greg Yavorski, the McBride area manager, explained the changing element of each year's guide training: "It's not so much that our training is always in flux, but we do a lot of experimenting so we can be sure to be at the forefront when the time comes to change."

One of the most enlightening parts of the training is the dissection of close calls by guides who were involved in the incidents. It is easy to tell, by the body language of the guides, which parts they view as the same old same old and which parts they consider the meat of the training. During the incident dissections, the guides sit forward in their chairs, hanging on every word that passes from the lips of their fellow guide who is sharing an experience and the learning that came from it.

Tree-well incidents have been far more deadly than avalanches in recent years. While avalanches are something the guides can manage by simply avoiding certain slopes on certain days, the tree well is a potentially lethal trap that is the responsibility of the individual skier. When snow falls around a tree, the branches prevent the snow from collecting against its trunk, so a hole forms around the tree, often about the size of a skier's torso. Falling into a tree well head first pins the skier's arms at their sides and snow falls in around their face. Death from asphyxiation can follow if the skier is not rescued quickly. Much time is spent reviewing tree-well accidents, discussing ways to teach skiers how to avoid the dangers, and going over the scenario of finding a skier lost in a tree well on a large, tracked-up slope where it is not possible to simply follow a single set of tracks leading to the trapped skier.

Leadership and personality issues are examined, guide health is monitored through physical examinations, ski instruction is broken down from the beginner to the expert, recent breakthroughs and protocols in avalanche rescues are shared, and outside specialists in snow science and stressful workplaces are brought in. Essentially, the guide training is a chance to share recent learning from professionals all over the world so that each guide can start the season with the most cutting-edge techniques and the most up-to-date knowledge fresh in mind.

The logistical engineering is a source of endless frustration and fascination for the guides and staff. Guide Daniel Zimmerman explained it as his primary motivation: "The main reason I'm still here is the group dynamics, decision-making and leadership styles, and the instant feedback, both positive and negative. I love it."

However perfected heli-skiing has become, there will always be plenty of opportunity for skiers who don't listen, or insist on doing their own thing, to get in trouble. It is one of the joys and dangers of the sport: you can do whatever you want – and if you do it at the wrong time, you'll pay the consequences. Barbara Guild wrote an article in *Skiing* magazine describing just such an experience. She explains that the guide specifically

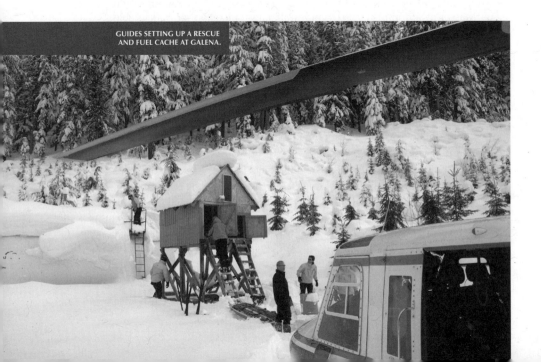

GUIDES SETTING UP A RESCUE
AND FUEL CACHE AT GALENA.

warned her not to go too far left, but then she started skiing and the seductive powder called her into trouble like a siren's song:

> I spot an opening in the trees and dive for it. Before anyone else can get it I make a series of turns in the untracked snow. Exhilarated, I squeal with delight! Then another slope appears. I go for it, through a perfect stand of trees all my own. Then an irresistible spot opens toward the left. Oblivious to the dangers I take off down it. The whoops and hollers of the other skiers fade into the distance. I am entranced by the untouched snow and never look back. The quiet entrances me. More smooth fluff beckons me.

Guild finds herself perched on the edge of a cliff, in a steep gully that is a waterfall in the summertime, and futilely tries to climb back up the slope she just skied down. She calls for help, her cries absorbed by the snowy forest around her. Attempts to climb back up result in only sliding lower in the soft snow. In desperation, she tries sideslipping through a weakness in the cliff below:

> Soon after I start, the slope lets go of the snow that tenuously clung to it, and my slow sideslipping becomes rapid. I reach for anything I can grab, as rocks and twigs and logs zoom by me. I am shunted into a steep chute, much like coal being dumped into a hopper. I manage to keep my skis below me. Finally I come to rest on a high, craggy knob next to a vertical wall. I balance on this perch, scarcely the width of my ski boots, the tips and tails of my skis cantilevering into space, knowing if I slip I will fall farther than I can see. I am afraid to move, to even pull a Kleenex from my pocket to wipe my nose, which needs it. Again I yell for help, but the only sound is the rumble of falling debris from far below. What am I going to do?
>
> I am in the midst of branches so thick they form a roof above me. Masses of underbrush intertwine with clumps of ice and snow. A jumble of immense, sharp-edged boulders slippery with algae rise around me and spill into the steep gully below me. Matted parasitic moss hangs like goblin's beards from dead twigs. The dense forest muffles sound and diffuses light. Now the rumble, caused by my struggling slide, has subsided, leaving an eerie stillness.
>
> Suddenly, the cold, black forest overwhelms me. My eyes get blurry and before I know it tears stream down my cheeks. I break into sobs. Oh, dear Lord, I am really in a jam. I got myself into this. Now I need help to get out of it. I know humility is not one of my outstanding characteristics, but I would be on my knees if I could be there without slipping.

Eventually, somehow, Guild claws her way into the valley bottom and finds an opening near a creek where she hopes the watchful eyes in the helicopter will be able to see her. During her wait, praying for rescue, she ponders her mistake:

Without the slightest notion of going wrong, I was enticed by the pleasures of the moment. How innocently I kept going, never once looking back, until it was too late – far too late to do anything about it. The huge obstruction on my right had separated the two distinct draws, but it was hidden by the trees. The group followed Sepp (the guide) down the right one; I was sucked into the one on the left. Why, oh why, didn't I heed his warning?

Eventually Guild is rescued, and she concludes her story with an attempt to paint it as a heroic act of survival. Hans read the article, and the next time he saw her, he expressed his displeasure about the story. Guild explained, "I think he thought the story made it look like the guides weren't doing their job."

In fact, the best guide on the planet can't keep skiers from heading off a cliff if they don't listen to directions. One of the thrilling things about backcountry skiing, with a helicopter or otherwise, is a feeling of self-reliance as well as responsibility. Everyone out there has to watch out for their own safety as well as the group's. If a skier decides to cut out onto a face above a group and releases an avalanche onto the other skiers, the results will be catastrophic. Experienced heli-skiers learn that their actions affect everyone. In a world of fences, defining your own boundaries is a great lesson and a powerful feeling. Not defining your boundaries, and getting out of line, may have zero consequences, it may result in a lecture from a guide or another guest or a narrow escape like Guild's – and it may result in the worst day of your life: the last one. Years later, Guild mentions that there is now a name for the run she did: Stupid.

6

THE WHITE DRAGON

The thing about heli-skiing is that things can go from really, really good to really, really bad really, really quickly.

—Roger Atkins, CMH guide

An avalanche is as shocking a transformation as you'll ever see in the natural world. One second there is an utterly still slope of downy-soft powder and the next, a storm of irresistible movement and lethal violence. Watching an avalanche happen is as shocking as if a calm lake suddenly produced a tsunami or a blue sky gave birth to a tornado.

In the quintessential slab avalanche, the kind most frequently encountered by skiers, the perimeter of the slide is the first thing to appear, with jagged cracks running chaotically around the edge. The avalanche starts in slow motion but quickly gains speed and recruits every flake of snow within its perimeter into the monster. Within five seconds, the beast can be moving at 100 kilometres per hour – faster acceleration than an Audi S4. The delicate snowflakes are quickly demolished by the violence, changing cappuccino fluff into thick concrete in a matter of seconds. The ensuing force is irresistible. Entire villages have been razed, train cars thrown from their tracks and road graders twisted like soda cans.

The destructive power of the avalanche is on par with the world's greatest natural forces. In the First World War, avalanches caused significant loss of life during the fighting in the Alps. On both sides, soldiers learned the snow was more powerful than their guns, and by bombing snowfields above enemy troops, they started lethal slides that roared down on entire platoons, killing hundreds of people with the efficiency of weapons that didn't even exist at the time. One report claimed at least 10,000 Austrian and Italian troops were killed by avalanches during a two-day period and quoted one officer as saying, "The mountains in winter are more dangerous than the Italians."

In 1970 an earthquake released the biggest avalanche in history from the slopes of Huascaran, a 6768-metre peak in the Cordillera Blanca of Peru. In a matter of minutes, the monster was 10 miles long, a mile wide, and contained over 50 million cubic metres of snow – enough snow to fill the 102-storey Empire State Building in New York City ten times over. During its 4000-metre descent, the slide picked up mud, rocks and water as it demolished the moraine dams of two alpine lakes, hit a top speed of 280 kilometres per hour and travelled 25 kilometres – including a rapid climb over a 280-metre ridge – before dropping with the violence of a nuclear warhead onto the unsuspecting town of Yungay. Later, a pilot surveying the damage from the air commented, "Yungay no longer exists."

So complete was the destruction of Yungay, and the chance of survival non-existent for the 20,000 people buried under the snow and rubble, that the Peruvian government prohibited any digging into the debris and declared the former town a national cemetery. In an eerie twist to the story, the only people in town who survived the tragedy were three little girls playing, against their parent's wishes, in a cemetery on a small hill. A new town with the same name has been built in a slightly different location, but to this day the old town of Yungay is buried entirely under the rubble left behind when the snows of Huascaran melted, the victims entombed for eternity in the very spot where they drew their last breath.

Granted, an earthquake is an unusual trigger, but even the dry slab avalanches most common in ski environments can travel at speeds around 100 kilometres per hour. Just air moving at a similar speed is considered a gale force wind on the sailor's Beaufort scale and is enough to knock a man off his feet. To imagine the force of getting hit with an avalanche moving at full speed, think about what it would feel like to stand in front of a snowplow travelling at highway velocity. A skier caught when the snow begins to slide might survive the ride, but anyone standing far enough below the avalanche to allow the moving snow to reach top speed before impact would likely be killed instantly.

In modern day North America, avalanches are a threat mostly encountered by backcountry users, but roads and railways also cross avalanche paths and inevitably are hit by large slides, sometimes resulting in mangled automobiles and derailed trains. The population most at risk of getting caught has slowly changed in the past 50 years. Mountaineers topped the list of fatalities during the sixties and seventies. Backcountry skiers took it hardest through the eighties, and snowmobilers were snuffed most often during the nineties. Since 1950, most avalanche incidents involved people engaged in some sort of voluntary recreation, but ever since man first devised infrastructure to live in mountain areas during the winter, avalanches have been a killer.

Each year, about 150 people die in avalanches in countries where such statistics are tracked, but many of the poorest regions of the world are in rugged alpine country where many farmers, nomads, herdsmen and traders meet their makers in a cloud of white death without being reported. Without the soaring popularity of mountain recreation, avalanches would be just another force of nature that claims lives with seemingly chaotic abandon.

When people are killed by an avalanche while driving across a mountain range during a blizzard, no one says "What were they thinking?!" and the media don't swarm like flies on a fresh one to find out who made mistakes and who is to blame – it is simply a tragedy. Dying while going about our normal routine, regardless of how mundane and unhealthy the routine may be, is viewed by our culture as somehow acceptable, but dying while recreating is often viewed as irresponsible.

Thanks to mountaineering, then skiing and now snowmobiling, the avalanche is part of our recreation culture, a risk perceived as being more akin to a trampling by a bull in Pamplona than getting hit by lightning while building a house. When something goes wrong in everyday life, people say "What a tragedy!" or "I can't believe it!" or "They were in the wrong place at the wrong time!" But when something goes wrong in recreation, the reaction can be "They were asking for it!" or "It's not really surprising!" or "They shouldn't have been there in the first place!"

For those who find recreation an essential part of their lives, their sport shapes their personas and replaces something lacking in our temperate and risk-controlled modern lives. Some ride waves knowing that a curious shark might eviscerate them; some climb cliffs knowing that an errant boulder might flatten them; some hike in the high country knowing that a lightning bolt might barbecue them; some float rivers knowing that a whitewater hole might drown them; some sail the oceans knowing that a rogue wave might smash them; and some ski powder knowing that an avalanche might crush them.

In microcosm, powder skiing itself is riding an avalanche. Every snow crystal in contact with a skier moving downhill bashes into other crystals creating small tremors that spread out like a bow wave around the skier. The weight of the skier and the moving snow compresses deeper crystals in the snowpack and the snowpack changes subtly with each passing skier far to either side of the visible track. The sensation of skiing in control through a medium that is moving down the hill makes deep powder skiing a thrill on par with any experience human beings have ever invented. When enough snow gets moving to carry its own momentum, it is called a sluff. The powder clouds created by sluffs are impressive, and they can carry a skier over a cliff or into a tree well. For ski guides, the smaller avalanches can be more of a concern than the big ones. It is easy enough to avoid the big slide paths during dangerous avalanche cycles, but the smaller slides can be equally deadly and harder to manage. Even a sluff can push a skier into a tree well, riverbed or other terrain trap where the snow can pile up and quickly asphyxiate the strongest person if the rest of the skiers are not paying attention and continue skiing rather than help their buried friend.

While the avalanches lurking on ski slopes are relatively small on the scale of the world's biggest slides, they are powerful enough that many avalanche fatalities in North America are not from asphyxiation under the snow, but rather from trauma caused by the forces within the avalanche and collisions with rocks and trees before the snow stops moving. The sensational element of avalanches makes off-piste skiers seem like daredevils compared to the seemingly benign resort skier, but even skiing in-bounds at a ski area has some exposure to avalanche risk. On a warm spring day in 2005, a steep mogul run named Pallavicini in Colorado's Arapahoe Basin ski area lost adhesion to the mountainside beneath it as the snow melted, and the entire slab cut loose under the weight of a skier who was in the wrong place at the wrong time. The ensuing slab avalanche crushed him to death in an open ski resort. Thanks to the work of ski patrols and snow professionals, less than 0.1 per cent of avalanche fatalities in North American happen in-bounds in a ski area. Now, avalanche forecasting services are giving backcountry skiers, mountaineers and snowmobilers information that, if they adjust their plans accordingly, makes travel in avalanche country a reasonably safe form of recreation.

For humans, avalanches are a purely destructive force, but even avalanches are part of the life cycle. Every spring, the grizzlies of the Columbia mountains awake from hibernation with a mighty hunger only to find the valley bottoms still full of snow, preventing access to the grubs, roots, herbs, berries and insects that make up most of their diet, so they climb into the high country looking for edibles. Springtime heli-skiers see tracks of the bears high on the mountainsides tracing the animals' movements between avalanche debris fields where they can find uprooted trees and bushes with exposed and nourishing root systems – or carcasses of goats and caribou that have succumbed to a slide and are nicely refrigerated until the spring thaw.

The trouble is that the terrain where skiers find the most fun, and where caribou and goats find wintering grounds, is the same terrain where avalanches happen with the most frequency. Many of the veteran CMH guides and guests have stories that make the blood of any skier run cold. Veteran heli-skier Ken Ferrin was caught in a slide and remembers, "The hiss of the snow crystals moving against each other was followed by sudden silence as everything came to a stop. I was thinking about my family and that this might be it." Ferrin was uncovered quickly and was unhurt.

Cariboos guide Bob Sawyer once watched a massive avalanche roar over him during a run with a group of guides. "I looked up as a huge lens of snow started moving above me. I ducked under a fallen tree, and as it roared over me, it sounded like two freight trains passing at the same time, and I could hear trees snapping around me."

The early days of CMH heli-skiing in the Bugaboos were a race between the guides' learning and a potential avalanche disaster that would have ended the heli-ski industry almost before it began. The guides' ignorance about snow stability was indeed bliss, and luckily the first few seasons were blessed with consistent snowfall and relatively stable conditions. Lloyd "Kiwi" Gallagher remembers the avalanche knowledge during the mid-sixties and shakes his head, saying, "If we'd had poor stability during those first few winters, we'd all be dead."

The sixth sense of a ski guide is still a potent and respected weapon against the white monster, but in those days it was the only weapon. Heli-skiing spit in the face of avalanche wisdom of the time. In 1970 the European guiding standard for avoiding avalanches was never to ski during a storm nor for a couple of days after a storm ended. During a big winter in the Columbias, this could mean waiting until April. In the Bugaboos, from the beginning, heli-skiing happened any day the helicopter could fly, and the sport introduced the greater ski world to the idea that it is during and just after a storm when the magic of deep powder skiing really happens – along with the majority of avalanches.

There were days when the mountains were just falling down and the ski groups avoided disaster by the narrowest of margins. Guide Thierry Cardon remembers a day in the Bugaboos when he was guiding behind a group led by Ernst Buehler. Thierry skied onto a slope and the warning bells started ringing in his ears. He stopped his group on a little knoll and traversed across the slope to test it while his group waited in a safe place. From right in front of his skis, a fracture shot ahead of him through three big gullies, effectively putting the entire valley into motion and creating a slab avalanche two metres thick and a kilometre wide. As the snow under Thierry's skis began to drag him inexorably towards the ride of his life, a little tree popped out of the snow where it had been hiding, bent under the weight of the snowpack until the slab's release uncovered it. Thierry grabbed the sprig with one hand with the conviction of a man whose life depended on it, and pushed the talk button on his radio with the other hand to tell Ernst, "Get out of the way, the whole mountain is coming down!"

"I don't know how I held on to the tree – it was a massive force," Thierry recalls with a distant gaze in his typically focused countenance. Somehow, he clung to the tree as car-sized blocks of snow accelerated past him. As far as Thierry knew, both his and Ernst's groups were being devoured. When the force had passed, Thierry stood up and turned around to see his group standing wide-eyed on the knoll, safely perched on the one patch of snow on the entire mountainside that did not succumb to the massive slide. Ernst's voice came over the radio asking if everyone was okay. His group had cut into the trees earlier than usual and was well out of harm's way when the avalanche thundered past.

It was a lucky day. Ernst's group would have been buried if he hadn't decided to ski a slightly different line, and Thierry's group was only saved by the behaviour of the slab that day. In some conditions, just being on a knoll or ridge doesn't mean you're safe. Slabs of snow can have enough tensile strength to pull snow from the opposite side of a ridge like a massive blanket being pulled over the top. On another day with particularly nasty slab formation, Thierry and fellow guide Pierre Lemire were checking snow conditions atop the Black Forest above the Bugaboo lodge. The two guides knew conditions were unstable, but they decided to poke around a little to see if they could find something safe enough to ski with the groups. As they stood on the ridge, they debated what should be done. Coming to no particular consensus, Pierre decided to ski. Just before he started, Thierry asked, "Do you have your Skadi turned on?"

Pierre checked, and his Skadi was not transmitting. He turned it on and jumped in. Within a few turns, a fracture line ran 270 degrees around the cirque and the ensuing slide ran to the valley bottom. The slab had enough cohesion to pull Thierry into the beast as if he was standing on a table when someone pulled off the tablecloth. He remembers being sucked helplessly into the slide and as it picked up speed: "It was that uncomfortable, 'clothes dryer spinning a rag doll' feeling."

When everything came to a stop hundreds of metres lower, with mountains of debris everywhere, Thierry found himself lying unhurt on the surface. Using his transceiver, he quickly found Pierre, who was blue and unconscious but still alive. The helicopter responded immediately, and soon they were on the way to the hospital. After a few minutes in the air, Pierre regained consciousness and seemed unhurt. With a house full of guests, and skiing to be done, they turned the machine around and went back to the lodge. Pierre guided the next day. With no precedent or policy for handling accidents, they accepted near misses stoically. Thierry explains, "After these close calls we'd just go back out and keep skiing. The show must go on."

Had Pierre not checked his Skadi on top of Black Forest that day, he would have almost certainly been killed. The little devices have saved many lives over the last three decades, and have increased the chance of surviving an avalanche by a significant margin.

Long-time heli-ski guide Brian Keefer has been on the lucky end of a few mind-bending rides and managed to come out unscathed. Once while tumbling along in a slide he was knocked out briefly, and when he regained consciousness, the first thing that came into focus was his avalanche transceiver lying on the snow in front of him. He had placed it in a zipped pocket rather than strapping it to his torso, and only the random motion of the moving snow that left him on top rather than underneath saved his life. It's not surprising that during his holidays, Brian is now more likely to be found working a point break in Baja than ski touring near home.

Helicopters are sometimes used for avalanche control, either as a vehicle from which to throw bombs onto an unstable feature or, on occasion, to release a nearby slide by landing. The helicopter has occasionally released slides unintentionally as well.

Once, as a guide was loading skis into the basket, a large fracture appeared under his feet. The helicopter was on stable ground, but the guide slipped over the vertical wall of snow, or crown, left where the slab pulled away. He clambered back onto flat ground unhurt.

Another time, an avalanche released from above during a pickup and roared towards the helicopter and the waiting group. The helicopter lifted off, leaving the group on the ground, but the guide managed to climb into the ski basket. The slide lost its momentum before reaching the group, and the guide sheepishly climbed out of the basket.

One of the serendipitous developments that happened alongside the fledgling heli-ski industry was a focused study on snow science and avalanche mitigation for ski areas and highways. While the Swiss had the most advanced understanding of snow stability – almost their entire country is in avalanche-prone mountains – it was an American, Ed LaChapelle, who brought the study of snow science to North America.

LaChapelle studied at the Swiss Avalanche Institute in the fifties and brought his learning to Alta, Utah. With its unusually deep and frequent snow, Alta was a proving ground for both avalanche work and powder skiing technique at the same time Hans and Leo were learning the hard way in the Rockies and Columbias. In the early sixties, LaChapelle wrote the first comprehensive avalanche handbook for the US Forest Service and then rewrote it in simpler terms to produce *The ABC of Avalanche Safety*. The latter was the first publicly available avalanche handbook and is a resource still sold today after a number of revisions and reprints.

In the late sixties, LaChapelle began a project that had little to do with snow science or avalanche forecasting but everything to do with increasing one's chances of surviving a burial. He built a radio transmitter about the size of a deck of cards that could be carried in a jacket pocket and, in case of burial, could be found with a small transistor radio. While experimenting with his invention, he talked to another skier, John Lawton, who happened to be an electrical engineer. Lawton suggested using an audio-frequency induction field because the strength of the signal diminishes more quickly than a radio signal, making the signal more sensitive to the location of the transmitter. Lawton ran with the concept and eventually took the Skadi avalanche transceiver, named for the Viking goddess of winter, to market in 1971. That very season, the first life was saved with a Skadi after an avalanche in the Bugaboos by the quick work of one Leo Grillmair. LaChapelle's work helped make backcountry skiing a safer and more popular pursuit. He skied right up until his last breath, dying of a heart attack at 80 years old while carving powder at Monarch ski area in Colorado in 2007.

For good reason, many mountain professionals in the seventies were skeptical of avalanche transceivers or beacons. If people could be recovered after a complete burial, would they be more willing to step onto a hazardous slope? For ski guides, there was no question as to the usefulness of the devices, and heli-ski operations jumped on the technology the moment it became available. Today, with directional sensitivity and digital displays, beacons are easier to operate by less-practised users – although Leo Grillmair claims to be faster with a Skadi than anyone with any modern unit. Ken France, the manager of Kootenay, remembers when the current model, the Barryvox, came into use. "It was kind of a rude wake-up call when we got the new digital beacons," he remembers. "People who had been skiing with us for years came up after our practice search and said 'Cool! That was the first time I've found one of those things!' We were all like . . . whoa."

In 1976 Hans gave a presentation on heli-skiing and avalanches at an avalanche workshop sponsored by the Associate Committee on Geotechnical Research, Fisheries and Environment Canada, the British Columbia Department of·Highways and the University of Calgary. It was the beginning of a symbiotic relationship between snow scientists and ski guides whereby the scientists shared their breakthroughs with the guides and the guides put them into practice in the field and returned with recommendations, results and new information. Hans's presentation at the 1976 workshop forever established heli-ski guides as some of the foremost practical experts on avalanche issues. It began: "After having guided and conducted high mountain alpine ski tours for 12 consecutive seasons, I recognized one overriding difference when I seriously got involved in helicopter skiing in 1965: the exposure to avalanches is considerably greater in heli-skiing than in ski touring."

Hans went on to explain the differences between the two disciplines and summarize the systems CMH used to deal with the hazard:

> The groups were small, their expectations were very reasonable, and hence they were easy to control if conditions did get marginal. Further, on the climb or approach, you had sufficient time for observation. The climbs up the mountain took anywhere from two to five hours. With each push of the ski forward into the unbroken snow, with each plant of the pole, you got a message, and you had time to digest it. You could look around in all directions, you could listen, you could feel the temperature and the wind.
>
> On almost every count the opposite holds true in skiing by helicopter. Because of the rapid uphill transportation, one or two runs a day is not enough. So even though you can find one or two runs you feel comfortable about, you are called upon to produce more. The expectations of these skiers are very high, and tend to be more so if your operations have been restricted by bad weather for a few days. When the weather clears you have 40 eager skiers making demands. They want to ski some new slopes. Now that there is a lot of fresh snow they want to ski where the snow is deepest, and on the steepest slopes! Most of these people are very eager downhill skiers, and seldom impressed with the inherent dangers of the surrounding mountain country.
>
> In addition, there is very little time for observation. The flight up takes only minutes and although, with experience, you can draw some conclusions as to the nature of the snow by inspecting it by air, this kind of observation could not possibly compare with feeling the snow every inch of the way up a slope. So, with a minimum of observations, the heli-ski

guide has to make some very difficult decisions. Often, he is called upon
to make these decisions many times a day.

Hans and the CMH guides took every opportunity to attend avalanche education
seminars and to talk with experts like LaChapelle. The popularity of heli-skiing was
skyrocketing, and with the greater numbers of skiers, the exposure to avalanches
increased accordingly. Between 1965 and 1976, CMH hosted a total of 58,000 skier-
days. During the 1978/79 season, there were 25,000 skier days – almost half of the
total of CMH's first decade in a single winter. Several accidents involving various heli-
ski operators and multiple victims brought pressure on the industry to scrutinize their
practices thoroughly. In the 1980 avalanche workshop in Vancouver, Hans explained
the recent changes in the industry:

> Prior to the 1977 accident (resulting in three fatalities in the Bugaboos),
> the problem of minimizing the avalanche hazard while still providing ex-
> citing skiing had already received our attention. In retrospect, the proce-
> dures developed, while useful, were not adequate. The normal, intuitive
> field experience of the guides and the on-the-spot decision-making, while
> certainly very valuable, were no longer enough.

By this point, CMH was thirsty for avalanche education even as it was leading the
industry in practical experience. Each year, CMH brought LaChapelle or snow science
expert Peter Schaerer to guide training to introduce the guides to the most recent
breakthroughs and practices, and enrolled guides in courses offered by the British
Columbia Institute of Technology and Canada's National Research Council. Hans
noticed a shift in guiding due to the inevitable close calls – and worse – that had
happened. While in the past, guides had been operating almost entirely as individuals
making decisions based on their own vast experience, the accidents were a call for
the industry to combine the individuals into a single, much more powerful decision-
making entity. For CMH, it was the beginning of the modern era of avalanche hazard
mitigation. Hans put it simply: "The emphasis is that scientific observation is indeed a
very important part of avalanche hazard evaluation, even for a qualified and practising
mountain guide."

To determine what went wrong when skiers were involved in avalanches, Hans
enlisted LaChapelle, with his scientific approach to avalanche analysis, and had him
review close calls and accidents to uncover any commonalities among incidents. What
LaChapelle found was that the lust for the fresh track pushed the groups into the danger
zone. Summarized Hans, "In each case, the accident happened when a guide, in trying
to find untracked snow for his group, was pushed way out to the side of one run."

He concluded, "This study showed that the guides were perhaps too eager to
always provide unbroken snow for their groups; that each guide, apart from skiing in
the same general area as the other groups, operated pretty well on his own; and that
there was no formal decision-making process in outlining the day's skiing program."

To better manage groups in the complicated and vast terrain of CMH tenures, the guides began to build the system in use today. Thierry Cardon was instrumental in developing the daily "run list." Thierry explained his vision for the run list: "Avalanches would happen when we would get out there and ski something we wouldn't have skied if we had made the decision before leaving the lodge." Thierry knew that the difference between a safe slope and a dangerous one is subtle, and that it is easy to get caught up in the pressure from the skiers and the pursuit of the fresh track. By giving every guide veto power before leaving the lodge, the guides had a tool for utilizing the collective experience and intuition of the team.

The list is a catalogue of all or most of the commonly skied runs in an area, and each morning before leaving the lodge the guides review the conditions and the estimated change overnight and collectively decide which runs are green, yellow or red. Green means the guide can choose to ski if he still feels good about it after seeing and touching it. Yellow means the run can be skied if a certain hazard is not present – like a cornice that needs to fall off before the run is safe. Red means the run cannot be skied that particular day under any circumstance. Most days, the run list looks like a Christmas tree with red and green scattered across the page.

Photographs of each ski run accompany the run list to create a tool for reviewing the day's plan visually before leaving the lodge. The photos were placed in a loose-leaf binder with transparent overlays on each photo showing the ski lines, as well as hazards such as cornices and hidden cliffs, and the potential avalanche activity on the run. Today the entire system is digitized. According to Hans the run list and photo collection "largely eliminates a problem of the earlier days where often a guide would find himself on a run where, in retrospect, under the conditions, he would have preferred not to be, but he had no other choice than to try to get his group down safely."

Recording weather and snowpack observations became a bigger part of the ever-changing effort to monitor hazard. Starting in the late seventies, each area was equipped with two weather stations, one at the base and one on a suitable summit, as well as snow stakes in various places, to keep track of each storm and the winter's snow totals. Each area keeps a study plot fenced off to prevent skiers from affecting the snowpack, and every two weeks, guides dig deep pits and record the layering profile of the snowpack as the winter progresses. This system is still in place today. While snow scientists are still adamant about the value of study plots, empirical observations have shown that they often have little bearing on the actual stability of the slopes where the skiing happens. Mountains create extraordinarily complicated weather, and two valleys, sometimes just a few hundred metres apart, can have dramatically different wind and snow in any given storm. Even on the same run, snow profiles can show entirely different results.

A complete snow profile is a time-intensive project. Even with a couple of guides to dig and take observations, a thorough snow profile takes over an hour. First, the guide digs a pit as deep as the lowest layers of concern, then the cross-section of the snow is examined for differences in density, temperature and bonding by using probing, thermometers and various shear tests. The results are diligently recorded using acronyms, symbols and the language of snow science that is indecipherable to the average skier.

The whole process is not practical or even possible with a herd of powder pigs frothing at the bit behind the guide, so guides sometimes do abbreviated snow profiles, just digging far enough to evaluate layers of greatest concern. But by no means does this imply guides only evaluate the snow when they have a shovel in their hands. The way snow skis, the way the wind has rippled its surface, the reaction within a snow mushroom when they ski through it, the sound snow makes when they walk away from the landing pad to take a leak, the changes from morning to evening and every aspect of the guide's own personal radar are all recorded and considered.

At the 1980 workshop, Hans also reported collaboration with Environment Canada's Pacific Weather Centre to obtain conditions from three different elevations measured at four different locations around British Columbia in 12-hour intervals. At the time, getting the weather report required a phone call from each lodge to one of several regional weather offices. The system was rudimentary compared with today's real-time Internet information exchange among highway departments, ski patrols, backcountry ski huts, heli- and cat-ski outfits and weather computers, but any access to up-to-date weather forecasting was a huge step for the remote heli-ski lodges, where for 15 years a weather report meant looking out the window – a technique still frequently used for its reliability and relevance.

Hans was a fan of science, but at the same time he saw its limitations in the real world of ski guiding. He observed, "Among our group of 42 guides we have, on one hand, highly experienced people who view all this paperwork with great suspicion, feel very uncomfortable with it and thus get very little or anything out of it. On the other hand, we have people who chart and record snow and weather observations with admirable diligence, do the most detailed snow profiles, but have little sense of and feel for the terrain."

While the number of guides has grown since then to over a hundred, and all of them see value in recording snow observations, there is an eternal debate over how much snow science can really predict something as chaotic as an avalanche. Hans concluded his 1980 presentation with a prediction that raised the hackles of the individualist guides of the day:

> We may, however, be headed in the direction of today's commercial airline pilot who no longer controls the machine, but rather becomes an extension of the machine with programmed actions. While heli-skiing will be some time in reaching this point, the direction is already very clear. More and more the emphasis is shifting to the scientific observation, the gathering of records, and the ensuing programmed responses. The day will come when, each morning, the heli-skiing guide will add the latest computer printouts to the stack of papers and manuals in his rucksack and then proceed with his group to the predetermined run, follow the

GUIDE ERNST BUEHLER EXAMINES
SNOW CRYSTALS, LOOKING FOR A TINY
SURFACE HOAR LAYER THAT COULD
CAUSE INSTABILITY IN THE SNOWPACK.

predetermined lines to the predetermined pickup place and repeat this until, upon receiving a certain signal from skiing control centre, he knows it is time to head home.

While prophetic, this was not Hans's personal way of handling the mountain world. Nancy DaDalt, from the marketing department of the CMH office in Banff, remembers a meeting where a group was debating the intricacies of snow science and data collection. Hans was looking steadily more irritated as the debate continued. Eventually he banged his fist on the table and yelled, "Damn it! You have to go out and smell it and taste it and see it and touch it!"

While some of Hans's predictions have come to pass – for instance, the predetermined, computer-generated run list for the day – the concept of a skiing control centre calling the shots is as far-fetched today as it was 25 years ago. In fact, recent trends in snow safety are tipping back towards individuals in the field rather than towards an Orwellian skiing control centre. If such a centre were to dictate that skiing was only allowed on slopes of 25 degrees or less with no danger from above, the risk of avalanches could almost be eliminated entirely, but so would the heli-ski industry. People who can afford heli-skiing live in an ultra-safe world, and the taste of danger is invigorating and makes many of them feel more alive than they ever have before.

Jan Burks, a switchboard operator for CMH, was always surprised how many people wanted to go skiing after a high-profile accident somewhere in the industry. "Did the danger make it more exciting or what?" she wondered.

A number of magazine articles attempted to explain the intrigue with risk. Roberta Walker wrote in *Maclean's* magazine that the risk "adds a taste of that most exotic of all spices."

Tom Briggs wrote in *Business World*: "Gmoser is forthright about the risks: he says flatly, 'We are probing a new frontier of skiing and there are bound to be hazards.' He acknowledges that it is up to him and his skilled guides to cut those risks to a minimum. Nevertheless, without those risks, there wouldn't be the same sense of adventure in this, the greatest skiing the world has to offer."

The unrivalled fun of powder skiing in the big mountains, and the inseparable risk of a catastrophic avalanche is the yin and yang of the experience. There have been a number of fatal accidents in the heli-ski industry, but the defining incident for CMH happened on March 12, 1991, when a spectacular day of heli-skiing was drawing to a close in the Bugaboos. The snow was fantastic and conditions were the sort that allow the biggest features to be skied: good visibility and deep powder on top of a relatively stable snowpack. A couple of seemingly well-bonded layers hid deep in the snowpack, but all observations from earlier in the season had concluded that the layers were of no concern. After half the group had returned to the lodge, due to tired legs from three days of non-stop powder skiing, the rest flew to the top of a steep north-facing avalanche path to finish their day on an exciting 2,500-foot run called Baystreet.

Like many big runs, Baystreet begins with smaller bowls that converge into one chute about halfway down the slope. Guide Dean Walton led the first group into the run and, following advice from lead guide Leo Grillmair, stayed along the right edge of the rightmost bowl. The skiers found the light powder and spectacular terrain that makes heli-skiing in British Columbia an experience to live for. At the bottom, Walton radioed back to Jocelyn Lang, the guide of the last group and the assistant manager of the Bugaboos area, to expect excellent conditions along the right side of the run. Lang led her group slowly through a rocky shoulder to access the run and gave them specific directions on how to ski the pitch.

To minimize danger, even when conditions are good, most guides give concise instructions on how to ski each run – especially big, steep, exposed runs like Baystreet. Lang instructed her guests to ski to the right of the tracks left by the first group and to stop before an island of trees in order to keep everyone in sight for the main part of the run. Lang skied to the trees and stopped to watch the rest of the group. After about half the group made their way down, a German skier cut wide to the left of the other tracks and a second skier followed. Five years later, in a Vancouver courtroom, Lang recalled realizing the skier must not have understood her instructions, which were in English, and she yelled at them to ski back towards the group.

It's impossible to know if it was the language barrier or the burning desire to ski a fresh line, but when the skiers cut wide of the group's tracks, an imperceptible tremor ran through the slope as an old layer of crystals lost their tenuous adhesion to one another and set the slope in motion. According to court hearings, Lang remembers hearing no sound, but only sensing the sudden movement of the ground beneath her feet. Far above, the slope released, building into a large avalanche before slamming into the hapless skiers. The skiers were only ten metres from the relative safety of the trees, and they struggled to escape. One of the two skiers left standing on solid ground

15 or 20 metres from the maelstrom described the mass of the avalanche that bore down on the rest of the group as an "enormous tidal wave of snow."

A minute later, nine skiers were buried at the bottom of the slope. Jocelyn Lang was the sole survivor of the hideous ride, left relatively unhurt on the surface of the snow facing up the mountain that had just devoured her group, killing everyone caught in the slide except Lang, who was left with minor injuries to her body but massive injuries to her heart and soul. Even the typically objective court report of the incident called her survival a "miracle."

The pain that ended when the snow stopped moving shifted quickly to the victims' families, and the entire heli-ski industry shuddered with the worst accident in the sport's 25-year history. The media bore down on the Bugaboos like angry wasps to sensationalize the tragedy. By the following day, the helicopter traffic was thick in the air surrounding the Bugaboo lodge, forcing the authorities to close the area to all aircraft except rescue helicopters. While the media scoured the area for controversy and gore, the families of the victims entered the limbo of mourning.

A couple of years passed while the heli-ski industry and the victims' families processed the tragedy. Eventually, the wife of one of the victims decided CMH had been negligent, and a year-long lawsuit ensued, a case that crossed the boundary of the particular tragedy and became an inquest into the entire sport of heli-skiing. In each stage of the case, the judge followed a similar chain of reasoning: first the CMH guides and systems were judged against the industry standards, with expert witnesses brought in to examine the complex decision-making involved in ski guiding. In every aspect, it was determined that the guides' standards that day, and the CMH standards in general, were equal to the best in the industry. So then the industry standards were brought into consideration. The judge wrote in the case summary: "The next question is – is there a basis for finding the industry standard negligent? One might be – does the standard affront the court's general experience, sense of logic and common sense? Or, is there some broader standard against which this industry standard can be found wanting?"

It was determined that the industry standard was acceptable, the signed waiver stood up in court and the backcountry ski guiding industry breathed a collective sigh of relief. Bugaboo guides no longer ski Baystreet, not in a retroactive attempt to avoid a repeat incident, but in honour of those who died there.

It is a testament to CMH and other large-scale heli-ski businesses that skiing with the big operations is statistically the safest way to ski backcountry powder. Individual backcountry users and smaller helicopter and cat-skiing teams have traditionally not had the same number of experienced guides collectively making decisions and gathering information. Now, with InfoEx and Internet access to observations and forecasts, all professional backcountry users have similar information available, but every evening a conference call among CMH areas gives them the widest range of observations of any guide service.

At CMH, a custom database is the backbone of the system. It is the brainchild of Roger Atkins, a heli-ski guide, physicist and expat American, and one of the most respected guides in the world of avalanche studies. He began a quest for accurate avalanche forecasting while working in Utah for the Alta ski patrol. Atkins built a database called Snowbase, a name still used today for the system used by CMH to track animal sightings and changes in the snowpack, and to catalog runs, hikes and other information useful for making sound decisions. In the beginning, Atkins's program used analytical layer modelling and statistical comparisons over time to predict avalanches on a particular slope. For a single ski run or an area like Alta, which is both blessed and plagued by big snows and big avalanches, it was an extremely useful tool. Walter Bruns and Colani Bezzola, always looking for the next step in snow safety, caught wind of Atkins's Snowbase and invited him to a guide training in the Adamants to share his findings. At the time, Atkins was searching for the Holy Grail for avalanche professionals: a way to model avalanche activity and in effect be able to forecast avalanches. "The ultimate goal was to bring avalanche forecasting into the guiding world," says Atkins.

Almost inevitably, CMH hired Atkins to develop such a program, but it was nearly impossible to help heli-ski guides operating in huge areas from extremely inaccessible locations with no Internet and only patchy phone and fax contact. To begin with, the CMH headquarters in Banff distributed a weekly fax of pertinent weather and avalanche information. In a serendipitous development akin to the helicopter improvements in the late sixties, computer technology in the eighties reached a point where real-time exchange of information was possible for the guiding profession. Atkins remembers, "I was public enemy number one at first, when guides started to have to use computers as part of their job."

In its current incarnation, also managed by Atkins and Bezzola, Snowbase helps the guides collect and use the massive data sets of daily temperature, snowfall, wind, snowpack evaluation, skier impact on the snow layers, and expert opinion. For the vast heli-ski tenures, run photos connected to the run list were added to the program and are now the most useful part of the system, according to Atkins. Guides are able to review the terrain they will be skiing in just minutes or hours before committing to the runs, rather than rely on old memories and other guides' verbal descriptions.

As for Atkins's original vision for using a computer to forecast avalanches, it has proven unrealistic for the vast backcountry of the Columbia Mountains. Atkins quickly realized the program was far better as an information gathering tool.

A snow scientist from Vancouver, Pascal Hägeli, came to the same conclusion after attempting to create a forecasting tool for the backcountry that would "create a model telling people where avalanches will be." To conduct the project, Hägeli used datasets from Atkins's Snowbase and evaluated the potential to create a modelling program. In a phone conversation with the author, Hägeli explained, "Avalanches are a complex phenomenon. Because of spatial and time variables we are far from being able to model them over a large area. From my perspective, guides have a much better ability to extrapolate based on their experience than we (scientists) can with modelling. We are far from the point of a guide as far as modelling where avalanches will occur over the next 24 hours."

And it is the next 24 hours that mountain guides and other avalanche terrain professionals obsess over. Every day, no fewer than 50 different areas in the interior ranges of western Canada report on an information exchange called InfoEx, a system for sharing snowpack and weather observations among professionals operating in avalanche country, including highway departments, backcountry ski lodges, ski resorts, cat-ski operators and heli-ski companies.

As of 2007, Thierry Cardon was spearheading an effort to make historical observations of ski runs an easy and useful part of the system. When a first-year guide clicks on a photo of a run, observations from 30-year veterans will pop up on the screen. Atkins's Snowbase already has the capability of cataloguing the information, but collecting the information from the memories of the guides is no small task. The future breakthroughs in avalanche avoidance will likely be built around the utilization of historical observations of particular slopes.

Anyone with avalanche forecasting as part of their profession takes things seriously. Ski guides, however, are the only avalanche professionals who bet their lives on their decisions every single time. Ski patrols, road crews and avalanche/snowpack consultants know people's lives hinge on their judgment, but it's a whole different kind of commitment when a ski guide drops onto a huge mountain face with a group of skiers hammering the hill behind him.

Like a school-bus driver who takes off her seatbelt on an unusually dangerous drive with a busload of kids, more than one guide has turned off his or her own beacon on extremely unstable days when any slope that could slide would slide, when cracks are shooting out from under the skis on every rollover, when only a few of the hundreds of runs in the tenure are safe enough to ski, in order to sharpen the edge of self-preservation in the name of the group's safety. This is a counterintuitive concept for those of us who would want every chance at survival if we were buried. However, for the guides, who become accustomed to the routine of making life or death decisions, turning off the transmission from the personal beacon turns off the routine and raises the guide's instincts and assessment to a fever pitch. One guide explained the reasoning this way: "It makes it like skiing alone, where there is no chance of help if you make the wrong decision."

Based on the growing popularity of off-piste skiing with and without helicopters, many skiers are willing to take the risk, provided the risk is small. Here is where the guide's job gets tricky. It is possible to avoid avalanche risk altogether, but doing so limits the skiing to such low-angled terrain that on deep powder days heli-skiing would feel like crosscountry skiing in heavy gear. The pressure to find exciting skiing while minimizing the risk squeezes the guides like a vise.

Roko Koell laments, "I see a tendency now to try to turn the mountains into a big amusement park, but a hyper-controlled environment is not possible."

Thierry Cardon agrees: "There is one thing business-based management will never get: you cannot have two forces like 'steeper and deeper' and 'increased safety' at the same time. There is a fine line between having it safe and having it exciting – the line I've been balancing on for 30 years. I'm constantly fighting between people who want to have it more safe, and people who want to ski more aggressive."

The common goal of avoiding fatal incidents forces cooperation among the guides, and the balancing act of collective decisions made by a group of strong individuals works incredibly well – most of the time. On a good day, guiding for CMH is like playing in an all-star game. On a bad day, nerves are strung to the breaking point and it's an all-too-real exercise in survival where every hair on the guide team's collective neck is standing on end. The entire industry rides the waves of ski conditions versus avalanche hazard. High hazard cycles put the guides in a predicament. Says Thierry, "The only way you can increase the satisfaction when conditions are poor is to increase hazard."

The innovators of the ski world are working on the next system to predict more accurately where and when avalanches are likely to happen, as well as the next tool to increase the chances of survival when someone predicts wrong. The next generation of beacons promises features that no one really wants to ever have to use. Vital signs sensors will identify a beacon on a corpse so searchers can move in to save victims still alive under the snow. A controversial feature is being tested that will give each beacon a code. This way, it will be clear how many people are buried, but it will also invite playing favourites in the triage of a multi-burial incident. Who wouldn't recover wife or brother before a stranger they met only yesterday?

Recent technological innovations offer tools that may one day improve the chances of surviving a slide. Avalungs are a simple tube-and-filter system that skiers can wear on their chest or integrated into a backpack. In case of burial, if the skier manages to survive the ride and keeps the mouthpiece from getting ripped out of his mouth and has enough space to breathe when the snow stops moving, the device will filter fresh air out of the snow and a valve expels stale carbon-dioxide-rich exhalations away from the intake filter and prevents a seal forming around the mouth as warm air melts the nearby snow before refreezing in a small bubble of ice. In tests, the Avalung allows people to stay alive for hours under the snow, and at least one survivor of an avalanche in Europe credits the device with saving his life. In North America, where most avalanche fatalities occur from trauma during the slide, Avalungs have yet to be fully embraced by the ski guiding community.

Airbags that inflate like a parachute if a skier pulls the cord work well to keep the victim floating on the surface, and new designs protect a skier's head from impact. Filling a helicopter with people wearing inflatable airbags presents another hazard – the accidental inflation of the airbag, which would interfere with the pilot's vision and controls. For this reason, airbags are not allowed inside a helicopter but can be carried in the ski basket. While not required, some heli-skiers bring along either Avalungs or airbags in the hope that the technology will increase their chances of surviving an avalanche.

But no amount of technology will completely remove the danger from avalanche. Beacons, airbags, Avalungs and technology are not nearly as effective as staying out of an avalanche in the first place. Bob Geber summed it up when a guest asked him, "In case of an avalanche, what position would you take?"

Geber responded, "There's only one position you can take: bend over and kiss your ass goodbye."

7

THE FIRST TRACK

A few points the guide should keep in mind:
First, he should show no fear.
Second, he should be courteous to all and always give special attention
to the weakest member of the party.
Third, he should be witty and able to make up a white lie if necessary
on short notice and tell it in a convincing manner.
Fourth, he should know when to show authority and, if the situation
demands it, be able to give a good scolding to whosoever demands it.

— Conrad Kain, early Canadian guide

"Where's the pickup?" asks a skier.
"At the end of my track," replies the guide, pushing off into the void.

In its essence, this is ski guiding. When the helicopter is gone, along with the white noise of travel, expense and the complications of life, the only thing left is the naked black and white of alpine winter where even the green of the trees seems to retreat into monochrome, as if colour itself were a waste of warmth. The guide's track is the only remnant of humanity, a serpentine beacon leading the way to fun, friendship, challenge and adventure. To depart from the track, however, means the veil of recreation suddenly lifts, revealing the unfeeling fangs of mountain winter. What minutes earlier was a benign and beautiful mountainside becomes a living, hunting predator waiting for a wayward skier to step on the wrong slope, ride a sluff off a cliff, flirt with the wrong tree well or simply fall in a tangle of alder where movement becomes impossible and the armies of cold can then march slowly and inexorably into the small space of a human being. Diving among sharks without a cage would be far safer than skiing where your ski guide warns you not to go.

Considering the options, it's easy to trust ski guides. Not only do they point the way to the goods, they throw themselves in first every time. This ensures their decision-making comes from the core of their own self-preservation. Many professions call the shots from the sidelines. Doctors, engineers, mechanics, builders, judges, politicians, businesspeople and a host of others make important decisions about matters of life and death, but few pay the ultimate price if something goes wrong.

From a guide's perspective, the trust put on their shoulders is staggering. Dropping onto a potential avalanche slope the size of a small town, a few seconds in front of 11 other skiers ripping down the mountain, is enough to raise the hackles of even the most steel-nerved alpinist. Sepp Renner remembers, "My first season guiding heli-skiers I felt like a fox being chased by an excited pack of dogs. I was always looking over my shoulder and skiing as fast as I could to stay ahead."

Anyone who has skied with Sepp knows his perspective had nothing to do with his skiing ability. Rather, it is due to the forced mental adjustment needed to go from individual free skiing, racing or zen-paced ski touring to leading the charge down some of the biggest ski terrain on the planet at high speed with a group of rabid powder hounds he may have met only the night before.

While the systems of modern heli-skiing approach NASA-esque complexity, the reality of riding nearly frictionless boards down a snow-covered mountain defies absolute control and requires a form of leadership more akin to leading a jazz band than docking a space station. The heli-ski guide is inarguably the most technologically advanced of the various genres of mountain guides, but regardless of all the bells and whistles at their fingertips, the profession remains the same. The hazard mitigation, the interpersonal element, the environment they call the office, and the risk-to-reward ratio all ensure that, regardless how systematically proficient heli-skiing becomes, those who carve that first track will always need to be mountain guides.

Mountain guiding as we know it had its humble beginnings almost 300 years ago among the farming communities of the Alps. The 1700s were the autumn of the Age of Enlightenment, the era of Galileo and Newton and the first popular acceptance of science and reason. With gravity defined, gravity sports weren't far behind, and with the oceans navigated and the great lands mapped, popular opinion held that great discoveries were rapidly growing fewer and farther between. The mountains were a natural next step to satisfy the human thirst for exploration, and intellectuals and thrill-seekers looked towards the lofty summits of the Alps for inspiration and self-discovery. These first climbing gentry showed up on the hill in the same exacting fashions they wore in the cafés and streets of Paris and Geneva. In their eyes, top hats and long skirts were as important as a rope for a proper day out in the Alps.

The first employment of a mountain guide is lost in time, but it likely started with an ambitious tourist deciding to climb a mountain. After getting roundly punished by loose talus fields and thick forests while trying to even begin the climb, the tourist offers a local woodsman payment to lead the way to the top of a distant peak. It must have seemed like a ridiculous request. As late as the 1700s, the mountains were still viewed as haunted places, the lairs of dragons, demons and gods. The shepherds worked higher on the mountainsides than anyone, so they were natural guides. They already knew the mountain trails, were adept and comfortable living with mountain weather and were used to leading their herd safely among the hazards of their home valleys.

Recreational climbers wanted a wild mountain adventure, but they also wanted to return safely to their homes and families. The best way to ensure a safe return was to hire a local to accompany them into the high country. The shepherd would take care of the incidental issues, such as route finding, logistics and weather-watching, and the climbers could focus on the more glamorous task of becoming the first person to stand on a summit or gaze across a vista.

This put the shepherds in a dilemma that still haunts mountain guides to this day. The shepherds were mountain people; they knew the mountains were far more powerful than they themselves could ever be. A piece of rope and a shepherd's staff were flimsy defence against avalanches, loose rock, lightning and the real demons of the mountains. People hire guides to keep them safe in an uncontrollable, dangerous environment – an ultimately impossible demand. Today, even with directionally sensitive avalanche beacons, waterproof/breathable fabrics, ultralight equipment, GPS, guidebooks, jet helicopters and multi-year guide training programs, human power has changed little relative to the raw power of the mountains.

The shepherds enjoyed the money brought by the thrill-seekers, who found the mountains provided something that tame everyday culture did not. Some shepherds welded rudimentary ice axe heads on their staffs and began to market themselves as mountain guides. Their product for sale was the childlike sense of discovery and a clear and unsullied challenge. Their office was the mountain where they had always lived. It was a natural progression, and mountain guides have been around ever since. But what a mystery it must have been to try to understand why people would pay money to get to the top of a hill!

The thirst for adventure was unquenchable, and the potential for discovery in the mountains seemed limitless – and remains so today. In 1821 the Compagnie des guides de Chamonix was formed to regulate access to the mountain slopes around Chamonix, and essentially demand a little money from anyone going into the mountains. Safety standards had little to do with the original guiding regulation.

It wasn't until 1965, the same year Hans Gmoser and his friends were busy launching the wildest guiding enterprise since the shepherds first modified their staffs, that the European guides of France, Austria and Switzerland decided to standardize practices and create the International Federation of Mountain Guides Associations (IFMGA), also known as l'Union internationale des associations de guide de montagne (UIAGM) and International Vereinigung der Bergführerverbände (IVBV). Since mountains pay no attention to the accidents of history that form national boundaries, and many climbs in the Alps start in one country and summit in another, it only made sense to internationalize guiding standards. Forty years later, there are 26 countries now recognized as members of the IFMGA. In most cases, the guides are free to work anywhere in any IFMGA-recognized country, making guiding one of the most internationally flexible professions in modern commerce and a shining example of truly free trade.

North America, with its vast mountain ranges, frontier mentality and burgeoning wealthy class, was a natural place for guiding to take root. The guiding industry in the United States, however, developed quite differently from that of Canada. For the last ten years, the American Mountain Guides Association (AMGA) has been recognized by the IFMGA for meeting international standards of guide training, but a US federal government system for selling a guiding permit, or concession, to a limited number of operators on each piece of public land still prevents international guides from freely working in most areas in the States. Denali National Park, with the highest peak in North America, allows six guide services, while Rocky Mountain National Park in Colorado allows only one. This system may eventually change, but until then guides will have to work within the antiquated system. The AMGA is currently collecting permits for guiding on public land, so any IFMGA can guide on the great peaks of the United States.

Canada, on the other hand, fit the international guiding model like an old glove. The original guides in western Canada were skilled Swiss guides imported by the Canadian Pacific Railway beginning in 1899. The wilderness of western Alberta and eastern British Columbia was seen for the first time as a commodity in its own right rather than merely a rugged barrier to progress, and having mountain guides on hand allowed the adventuresome tourists of the era to be the first human beings to stand on many of the dramatic summits dotting the Canadian Pacific line in almost uncountable numbers. As a result of this marketing program, guided groups made the first ascents of the most famous peaks in the area including Mt. Robson, Mt. Assiniboine and Mt. Sir Sandford. True to the trend of the guide playing second fiddle on a successful ascent, the *Canadian Encyclopedia* entry for Mt. Assiniboine reads: "Sir James Outram, with Swiss guides, made the first ascent in 1901."

Hans Gmoser was a by-product of the first wave of European guides. He was not a trained guide when he arrived in Canada but was inspired by the achievements of one guide in particular, fellow Austrian Conrad Kain. Kain was the first guide in North America to take groups into terrain that even today is seen as highly technical. The Kain Route on Bugaboo Spire is remembered as his most difficult, and even in our modern era of shock-absorbent ropes, high-friction shoes and detailed guidebooks, it inspires a puckered sphincter and careful use of climbing equipment not available to Kain's team. The combination of Kain's Austrian heritage and his willingness to push the standards of mountain adventure with a guided group inspired Hans greatly, and he modelled his own projects after Kain's philosophy of full-throttle adventure while guiding.

Many experienced guides today lament the loss of this philosophy and the self-imposed standards that restrict the very adventure that brought them to the mountains in the first place. The mountain guiding industry worldwide, to a large degree, has changed from one of exploration to one of entertainment. This transition has been made in the name of safety and to meet the demand of guests with limited time and with goals having little to do with mountaineering. Still, to become a full mountain guide is as demanding a training program as you'll find in any profession, and for good reason: the responsibility a guide assumes is staggering.

Betty MacRae, a neurosurgeon who has skied and climbed with CMH to achieve some of her greatest dreams, works in a field that is respected and paid at a much higher level than mountain guiding. She routinely does 12-hour brain surgeries, but after seeing mountain guides in action, she honestly says, "I think the responsibility of a guide is the same as a neurosurgeon's."

Traditionally, mountain guiding was viewed as one profession involving all the specialties we see today. Skiing, rock climbing and mountaineering were the three essential elements of the field. To say you were a guide in 1965 meant you could do it all. Today, the standards have advanced to levels unimaginable 40 years ago, but rock, ski and alpine specialists have stolen the limelight from the multi-faceted classical guides. Mountaineering as a sport has mirrored the guiding industry, splitting into finer and finer specializations.

Climbing itself is split into a mind-boggling number of subcategories. Big-wall climbers seek multi-day ascents of the planet's biggest vertical faces. Aid climbers hammer, drill or hook their way up the sheerest walls. Sport climbers obsess over smaller, extremely difficult climbs protected by predrilled expansion bolts. Traditional, or "trad," climbers use easily removable cams and other gadgets to climb cracks and features, leaving the rock in its natural state. Ice climbers find their game on delicate frozen waterfalls. The mountaineer's arena ranges from the biggest, coldest and most dangerous of the world's mountains, to sublime peaks where they can breathe the clean air and gain a vantage point looking down on the world. Alpine climbers distinguish themselves from mountaineers by taking less equipment and washing their long underwear less frequently. Boulderers leave behind the distractions of ropes and gear and stay close to the ground, using portable pads to soften the falls, while pushing the gymnastic limits of human tendon, muscle and imagination. Free soloists leave the ropes, fear and ground behind and find clarity in the certainty of death should they slip.

Skiing too has gone beyond its traditional categories of alpine and nordic. Snowboarders started the more recent specialization when they drew a line in the snow with new terminology, equipment and fashion. Slope-stylers crossed that line on skis by borrowing baggy clothes and twin tips from the snowboarders to play on the mogul fields and terrain parks in entirely new ways. Big-mountain skiers seek out technical runs on the biggest faces. Ski mountaineers combine disciplines to take skiing into the rarefied air of the Himalaya, Peru and Alaska and onto terrain better suited for crampons and ice axes than skis. Jibbers spend their days in the terrain park and their sport doesn't really begin until the boards leave the ground. Kite skiers now traverse the vast expanses of the Midwest and Baffin Island at spectacular speeds and have introduced fast skiing to the flattest terrain.

Modern guides can come from any of these specialties, and training programs are continuously redesigned to more effectively take aspirants of varying specialties and teach them the broader range of skills needed to be a guide. Today, it is possible for someone to become a rock-climbing guide without ever putting on a pair of skis, and ski guides can skip the climbing element almost entirely – but not quite. Even the most specialized ski guides still need basic alpine climbing techniques to execute a crevasse or cliff rescue in the unruly terrain of ski country. To become a full guide in any IFMGA-recognized country requires demonstrating proficiency on snow, rock and alpine terrain. Each of the three elements requires several seasons of practice to perform at the minimum standard to even begin guide training. After an aspirant becomes a proficient skier and climber, the process typically takes four to eight years of diligent work and commitment to guide training.

Outdoor programs at a few universities in Canada and the United States are now offering programs to prepare students to become mountain guides. At first glance, it seems like a good idea. Why not make guiding a path to follow beginning in mainstream education? In many ways, these programs are an indicator of the success and health of the industry and could help the profession become more accepted as a respectable career choice for young mountaineers and skiers. However, the concept is unsettling to some experienced guides, which is not lost on mainstream media. One journalist described guides as "snow counterparts of what sailors call sea wolves. They are men with a sixth sense about snow and can veritably smell out danger; all have spent their lives in mountaineering and in snow lands."

The rigorous and lengthy training program is mandatory to work in most countries and to get liability insurance, and is well suited for a university program. But the training is just the tip of the iceberg in becoming a guide. Most important, a guide must first make the choice to spend a large portion of his or her life immersed in the element where they will work. Most guides first fall in love with skiing or climbing, become quite proficient at one or both, and then decide to become guides. The potential danger of institutionalized guide education is voiced clearly by Rudi Krannebitter, one of the first examiners for the ACMG: "When will these new guides get experienced? When they are making decisions with people's lives in their hands?"

Krannebitter is an Austrian guide whose not so unusual story of moving to Canada to work for a season and getting stuck for decades began in 1973 when he became, at 20, the youngest Austrian to be certified by the UIAGM. A year later he decided to try ski guiding for Hans Gmoser in Canada for one year. Although no longer working for CMH, 33 years later he was still leading skiers in the Columbia Mountains and threatening to move back to Austria. In 2007, Krannebitter returned to his homeland. He was a notorious examiner for the ACMG for many years and earned the nickname Rudi Ankle-biter for his ruthless attention to detail and sky-high standards; but he is also held in the highest esteem. The legend is: "Where others climb, Rudi walks." While following Rudi at breakneck speed down a particularly icy run at the Panorama ski resort, I began to understand the mystique that surrounds the man. He skis without risk in his movement, brimming with that eerily quiet confidence in the face of danger that the likes of mountaineers, helicopter pilots and serial killers manage to attain. He is a strong proponent of the individual's judgment in the mountains and that the systems, however advanced, need to allow for individual freedom, intuition and last-minute changes in plans.

Without exception, as rookie climbers or skiers we make decisions that we look back on years later and wonder how we lived through our learning years. Every day in the mountains is an education, so the best training program in the world is not complete without full immersion in the world of mountain adventure without the parameters and oversight provided by a human instructor. The mountains are instructors, too – arguably the best instructors – and no amount of snow science and rope techniques can shortcut the education to be found while rambling in the mountains as a young adventurer with no guidance beyond the end of your nose.

Ski guides often begin as ski bums in places like Whistler or Banff. They learn to ski the ice, the crud, the corn and the powder; they get lost in the woods, set off avalanches, freeze their toes, break bones and skis, lose partners and have close calls of all flavours before they ever get paid to turn a ski. They feel the snowpack under their skis during big winters, lean winters and deadly winters and could discuss snow types with an Inuk. They ski for fun, on the race team, for escape, to avoid growing up, as an athletic passion and because it feels good. Then, at some point, they decide they want to do more than wash dishes or shovel snow to pay for their obsession.

Before even considering the life of a mountain guide, rock climbers typically go on vision-quest-style road trips to test their mettle against the most famous climbs around the world. In North America, there are big walls of tremendous difficulty in places like the Bugaboos in British Columbia, the Cirque of the Unclimbables in the Northwest Territories and Zion in Utah. But to complete their passage to the big time, they must visit Yosemite, California, where the 1000-metre wall of El Capitan has been the proving ground for big-wall climbing since it was first climbed in 1959.

Of the big three, alpine training is perhaps the most demanding, simply because it involves the route-finding, snow and avalanche elements of skiing as well as the rope work, vertical terrain and gymnastics of rock climbing. Canadian mountaineers are some of the best in the world thanks to their demanding home ranges. Many of the average alpine climbers in the adventure-sport meccas like Canmore or Golden could be sponsored alpine athletes in other countries. Canadians have no need to travel internationally to become world-class alpinists, but many do in order to experience the world's mountains.

CMH guides are easy to perceive as being nothing more than ski guides in their uniform yellow suits and full-time commitment to the ski program. But they all have lives outside of guiding and many climb and ski on their days off, though you'd never guess it while sharing an après ski pint. On December 8, 2006, Dan Griffith, a CMH guide, finished climbing the continents' Seven Summits in seven months. Bruce Howatt, manager of the Bobbie Burns, has made five ascents of El Capitan and, although he humbly dodges credit for it, was the first Canadian to climb 5.13 – a rock-climbing grade indicating difficulty similar to an Olympics-level gymnastics routine. Todd Guyn, assistant manager in Revelstoke, climbs 5.14. Dave Gauley, assistant manager at the Cariboos, made a living as a professional skier for years, skiing such terrain as the sustained 50-degree west face of Mt. Deborah in Alaska, a face better suited to climbing than skiing.

Traditionally, by the time aspiring guides enrol in guide training, they already are skiers, climbers or mountaineers. The training is then guiding-specific, an adjustment period for experienced climbers and skiers to learn to take care of less-experienced partners in the mountains. The way the ropes and group management are used to protect everyone on the team at all times, paying attention to timing and conditions with slower and weaker partners, and finding the path of least resistance – all are practised incessantly by aspirant guides. The more subtle soft skills are harder to practise. Taking mountain neophytes, even adventurous ones, into the wilderness and directing them through mountain hazards while they are a quantum leap outside their comfort zone requires a tactful approach to communication. This is often far more of a challenge for many guides than the technical aspects of difficult climbing and skiing.

In an interview Hans summed up what it takes to be a guide:

A guide needs a thorough knowledge of the mountains in the winter and summer, with an understanding of all the different conditions the mountains display and an ability to anticipate these conditions. Further, a guide should be able to move through the mountains with relative ease, grace and speed under all conditions. He needs a profound love for his mountains, much respect, humbleness and a strong desire to share his mountain experience with others.

As one newspaper journalist put it, back in 1979: "The guide becomes a combination of ski instructor, cheerleader, wet nurse and father confessor."

All told, the variety of skills required to be a full mountain guide is mind-numbing, and a university-based guide education will never replace the experience required to become a world-class guide. "I still learn things all the time," says Kobi Wyss, a soft-spoken expat Swiss who is likely among the top ten working CMH guides with the most vertical footage. Kobi skis and manages groups with an ease that defies logic. While skiing, his body scarcely moves. When everyone else is bouncing up and down and working hard in unruly snow, Kobi seems to just stand there on his skis, carving with

THE MOUNTAIN GUIDE'S DIVERSE
WORLDS: ROCK, ICE, ALPINE AND SKI.
THE EDUCATION NEVER STOPS.

the force of some inner meditation. While managing groups, his quiet demeanour is at least as effective at getting cooperation as the more verbose style of many, more extroverted guides.

These kinds of skills can't be taught in universities, so most full guides would encourage graduates of guiding programs to pursue a mentorship with the mountains and spend much time outside of guiding institutions and training programs to hone their abilities and judgment. These personal experiences then become the foundation for future decision-making and guiding philosophy. Rob Rohn, CMH's operations manager, views the guide certification process as only the beginning of the learning. He explains, "The guide qualification is really just the first step to becoming a guide. The day you think you've got it all figured out is the day you get a big lesson."

A note on the guides' office wall in the CMH Valemount lodge sums it up: "The least experienced press on while the more experienced turn back to join the most experienced who never left in the first place."

Training and experience are both important to the modern guide, but a guide with training but no experience is little more than a university graduate with a diploma and no résumé. Consider Hans Gmoser and his contemporaries. They had none of the snow science or advanced modern training that is available today, but they had experience. A typically matter-of-fact piece of Hans's 1960 report of the 150-mile

Icefields Traverse attempt between Banff and Jasper, five years before the beginning of CMH, reveals experiential guide education at its finest. Almost every sentence has a mountaineering lesson in it as Hans describes the trip:

We were up while the moon was still high, and with the first daylight we started to climb up the Mons Icefield. The going was very easy and we had plenty of time to view the spectacular icefalls coming down from Mt. Cambrai. At the end of the valley there was a small headwall where we took off our skis. I went ahead to clear the ice off some rocks in a little chimney. Once through the chimney, we kicked steps up a fairly steep slope and climbed over a small cornice on top of it. We were on the Mons Icefield! This manoeuvre actually took quite some time, as it was necessary to pull up everyone's skis and we also had to set up a fixed rope to climb up the chimney. Going over the cornice provided some excitement, as a portion of it broke off, carrying Kurt Lukas with it. He fell 60 feet with pack and skis, but by some miracle stopped himself on the steep slope. When asked what he thought as he was falling, he only replied that he was mad as he would have to climb back up again!

During the night the storm really set in and by the next morning so much snow had piled on our tents that we could hardly move inside them. We had to shovel our camp out, stretch the roof and readjust all the anchors. Visibility was absolutely nil and we could do nothing but stay in our sleeping bags and rest. That was fine for the first day as we were all tired, but when there was still no improvement on the second day, we began to get a bit restless. Since the next cache (of food) was only one mile from our present camp, Kurt and I decided to try to find it. We carefully set our compasses in the direction in which we assumed the cache would be and started out into the snow and wind. No sooner had we gone 50 paces then we couldn't see our tents; there were only our two black skis and the snow drifting across them at a terrific speed. Ice formed on our beards and the wind practically blew through us. After 15 minutes of this, I was worried that we wouldn't find our tents again so we turned around 180 degrees and after another 15 minutes our tents rose out of the fog.

And a few days later:

The upper icefalls are only passable on the left side and are very treacherous. Steep snow slopes lead up towards Mt. Farbus and were heavily laden with new snow. All of a sudden we heard the noise of an avalanche and saw it coming right at us. Luckily there had been several slides before and the terrain was so broken that it stopped when it hit the glacier. Cautiously, we threaded our way through a labyrinth of crevasses. The visibility was so poor, however, that it was impossible to find a straightforward route.

MULTI-DAY SKI TRAVERSES ARE PART OF A SKI GUIDE'S TRAINING REQUIREMENTS. HERE, THE FIRST TEAM TO ATTEMPT TO SKI FROM RADIUM TO ROGERS PASS FEELS THE EFFECTS.

We constantly had to detour and retrace our steps. On one such occasion the snow gave way under me and I felt myself falling for the longest time. When I finally landed on my head and back I was far down in a crevasse. Some light came through a small hole (he had fallen through) about 70 feet above me and, after discovering by some miracle I was all in one piece, I managed to climb up through it (after they threw a rope down the hole) and establish contact with my friends. On top, it was blizzarding and, I must admit, it was much more comfortable down in the crevasse.

By 1963, Hans had lived through a number of broken bones and successful expeditions on unclimbed faces on Denali, the highest peak in North America, and on Mt. Logan, the highest peak in Canada. For a decade of winters, he had been on skis more days than not and was pioneering rock climbs at the cutting edge of the world standards on cliffs like Yamnuska near Canmore. When the first discussions of an association of Canadian guides got to the point of choosing a first president, Hans was the natural choice. The Association of Canadian Mountain Guides (ACMG) was formed in 1963, and in 1972 it became the first non-European association recognized by the IFMGA. By this point, the CMH project was fully underway, and it took guiding into the limelight like it had never been before. Canada has since become the place to train as a ski guide, in part because of the sheer volume of exposure heli-skiing demands and in part because of the standards set by Hans Gmoser in the early years of the ACMG.

The introduction to the *Technical Handbook for Professional Mountain Guides* reads: "The concepts and skills described and illustrated here are based on the wisdom and efforts of many guides spanning over 200 years."

Neurosurgeon Betty MacRae's parallel between guiding and medicine holds true in the amassing of mountain knowledge, and it would be accurate to call guiding a "practice" like a martial art or medicine. The guides in training now piggyback off the discoveries and systems considered cutting-edge today and slowly usher in new techniques and philosophy. In acknowledgement of this fluidity of the profession, the *Handbook* has a disclaimer that reads:

> Actual guiding standards and technical performance can only be achieved in applied situations. If words like "should" and "must" appear, they are not intended to limit guides with hard and fast rules or regulations. They are meant to indicate common practices which may need to be modified or revised to meet the needs of a given scenario or situation. There are seldom "right" or "wrong" answers in guiding. Guides must be prepared to modify techniques, change approach, and make (to the best of their knowledge) judgments based on what is required and appropriate at a given time or place.

Even the most experienced guides often answer questions with "I don't know." Ken France, manager of CMH Kootenay, says: "People find it hard to believe we don't know what we're getting into every day. They often say 'What's it going to be like out there today?' and then respond with disbelief when I reply that I really will not know until we get out there."

When Hans Gmoser received his guide's licence in the 1950s, he was required only to complete a one-page questionnaire. Personnel changes in Parks Canada instituted the first Canadian guide training with a four-day test of ice- and rock-climbing skills followed by a written examination. But in 1958 a letter of recommendation by Hans Gmoser was enough to get the busy Parks office to issue a licence to several new guides in lieu of the assessment.

Hans felt that if all he had to do was write a letter it would be easy to recruit guides, but that this would not set a healthy precedent for the profession. After Hans voiced his concern to Walter Perren, the alpine specialist for Parks Canada, Perren suggested the guides themselves form an organization to take guide training and certification out of the hands of the government and into a group of guides who knew what was really going on out there. On May 23, 1963, with Hans and Leo as two of the eight founding members, the Association of Canadian Mountain Guides was formed.

Like starting into a medical profession or devotion to a martial art, the decision to become a guide is a committing one, and today the process is much more involved than merely obtaining a letter of recommendation. In mountain communities around the globe, it is easy to pick out the men and women who are training to be guides. Good enough is not enough for them; they are the ones spending extra time digging snow profiles, practising various rope techniques on all manner of terrain from the most precipitous to the most innocuous, and the look on their faces is one of concentration and learning while everyone else in the hills is seeking unadulterated recreation.

Guides are expected to fill their quiver with skills on their own, and guide training courses are a time to put them to use under the eye of a master, to hone the edges and learn from each other's missteps and moments of genius. Guide trainers have intimate understanding of the ruthless world where guides practise their craft, so courses are designed to challenge, frustrate, test, push, teach and make or break potential guides by taking them to their limit in terrain where they may or may not actually take paying customers.

Dave McNeil, a journalist for *Western Living* magazine, observed a 1983 guide training and described it as if the examiners were playing a child's game, "one that shows a picture of, say, some painters painting a house, and you have to pick out all the mistakes in the scene: the paint can is upside down, the painter is using his hand not the brush, and so on."

Instructors don't so much teach, in the classical sense of standing in front of the group and lecturing about how it's done, as go into mountain situations with the aspirant guides and then verbalize the lessons the mountains reveal and make sure there are no missed opportunities for learning. The courses cover a vast array of subjects, including backcountry ski techniques, wilderness ski instruction methods, mechanized guiding techniques, guides' information exchange, national and international avalanche standards and response, weather and snowpack observations, navigation, glacier travel and crevasse rescue, winter camping and cooking, rope handling and basic mountaineering.

Besides these guiding-specific courses, guides are also required to take advanced first aid and level one and level two avalanche courses. Anyone can take a level one course, but level two requires at least two years of experience as an assistant guide or fieldwork with another professional avalanche organization. Ski patrol, highway crews, avalanche forecasting and consulting services all look at snowpack in a similar way.

The full ski guide exam is a gruelling, eight-day, dawn to dusk ski mountaineering ordeal where participants take turns playing the guide role while skiing or climbing up and down an exhausting route chosen by the examiners. When the trainees are not leading, they follow quietly behind, avoiding any influence on the current leader's thinking. The examiner mostly follows quietly as well, taking notes and occasionally asking questions. Marc Piché, an examiner for the ACMG and an experienced heli-ski, ski touring, ice- and rock-climbing guide, is fascinated by the dynamic of training and says, "You can kind of tell how well you're doing by the kind of questions the examiner asks."

During the week-long ski guide exam, dawn to dusk ski tours give the examiners time to see everyone leading in a variety of terrain. At the end, even the fittest young athletes return bone-tired, wondering whether they pulled it off and are free to guide for the rest of their lives.

AN ASPIRING GUIDE GETS AN EARLY
START DURING THE ROCK GUIDE
EXAM ON RAPTOR, NEAR CANMORE.

If they pass muster on their first attempt at the exams – and about 40 per cent fail and must pay for a second attempt – certification includes ten courses plus three exams and costs about $20,000, not including first aid and avalanche education.

Even with the advances in the profession over the last 40 years, some guides wonder if new procedures limit their profession without making their jobs noticeably safer. More information can be good if it prevents an accident, but at the same time it can backfire if the individual guide's intuition is taken out of the picture by operating guidelines.

Bruce Howatt, the Bobbie Burns manager and a fan of individual decision-making, explains the potential danger of rigid systems. "If we make a run green during a hazardous period, we often end up skiing the edges in the search for fresh tracks where we may ski in more dangerous spots than we would on some red runs if we picked careful lines. Green doesn't mean a run is absolutely safe and red doesn't mean a run is absolutely dangerous!"

Therein lies the double-edged sword of industrial-strength guiding. With ever more systems in place, the guide's intuition and on-the-fly decision-making is squeezed thin. Rudi Krannebitter acknowledges that the systems make skiing safer for less experienced guides, but feels that experienced guides need to be able to make instantaneous decisions without working against a predetermined game plan. To his credit, he is one of the few guides with a comparably vast experience base who has never been caught in an avalanche. Certainly he's been fortunate, but to heli-ski guide for three decades without taking a ride in an avalanche is unusual in a profession where many guides have been caught in small slides – and some in big ones.

"In the beginning, it was all about terrain and snowpack. Now we just produce material in case of liability," laments Rudi. "The system inhibits new guides' learning." For over 40 years, CMH guides evaluated accidents and close calls industry-wide, and most of the technical directors for the ACMG worked for CMH at some point. The guides invented the systems to increase safety, and now they're legally obligated to work within them even when occasionally they are incongruous with the very reason they were originally designed – to help guides make good decisions.

Rudi's perspective is not lost on the senior guides at CMH. Tom Gruber, an assistant ski guide, took his full ski guide exam in the spring of 2006 after a winter of heli-ski guiding in the Cariboos. He didn't pass. During the guide training, he conferred with Colani Bezzola, one of the most respected guides in the profession, about the reason for his poor marks. Tom told Colani: "I think my individual decision-making was dulled from following the lead guide all winter long."

Colani leaned towards Tom and said frankly, "It's hard to learn to lead when you're in a program that leads for you."

Bruce Howatt shares the individualist perspective, but he also sees the potential in the combination of experience and modern training. "Guides used to have a lot of other guiding experiences outside heli-skiing with other ski guiding before getting involved. Now they come into a structured program without that experience," he says, but then adds, "You have to find experience yourself, but there are some excellent guides coming up, no doubt about it."

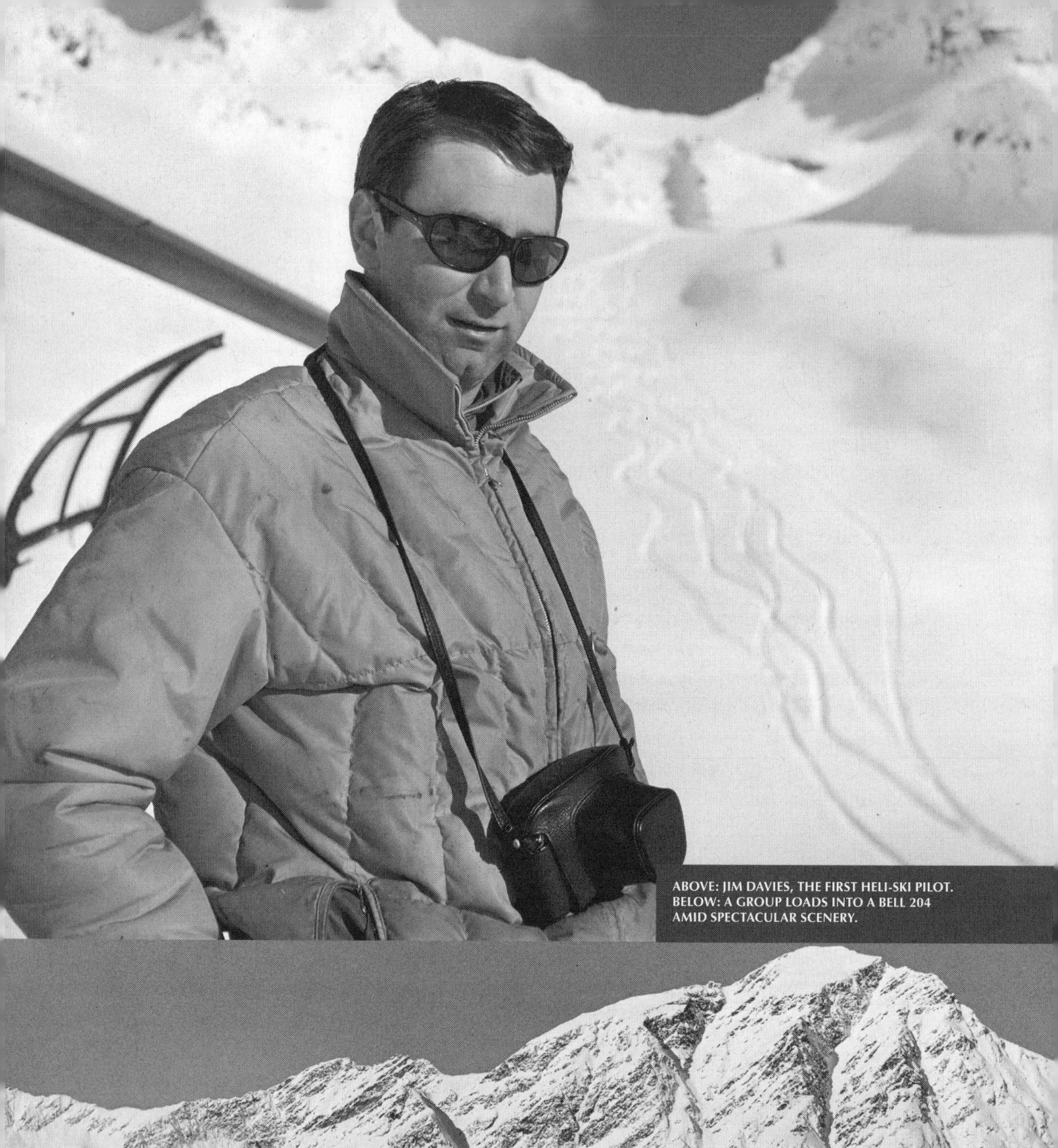

ABOVE: JIM DAVIES, THE FIRST HELI-SKI PILOT.
BELOW: A GROUP LOADS INTO A BELL 204 AMID SPECTACULAR SCENERY.

ABOVE: CHASING SHADOWS IN THE SIXTIES.
BELOW: EARLY CMH GUIDES.

ALOUETTE III FLYING PAST SPIRES IN
THE BUGABOOS IN THE LATE SIXTIES.
OPPOSITE: NEIL BROWN, SHARKA
SPINKOVA, HANS GMOSER AND
HEINZ KAHL ON BRUSSELS PEAK.

SKIERS ON WALLACE, A RUN NO LONGER
SKIED DUE TO GLACIAL RECESSION.
OPPOSITE: SUN, SNOW AND SKIER.

HANS GMOSER, ROCK CLIMBING
ON YAMNUSKA, 1965.
OPPOSITE ABOVE: LEARNING MOUNTAIN
LOGISTICS ON MT. LOGAN, 1964.
OPPOSITE BELOW: LEO GRILLMAIR SKI
TOURING ON GRIZZLY RIDGE
BETWEEN THE BOBBIE BURNS
AND THE BUGABOOS.

ABOVE: HELI AND SHADOWS.
BELOW: THE ORIGINAL BUGABOO LODGE.

ABOVE: HANS GMOSER CAMPED AT THE BASE
OF BUGABOO GLACIER DURING HIS FIRST
SKI EXPLORATION OF THE BUGABOOS.
BELOW: JIM McCONKEY, HANS GMOSER AND
MIKE WIEGELE EXPLORING THE BUGABOOS.

162

LLOYD GALLAGHER EXPLORING THE
STEEPER PARTS OF THE BUGABOOS.
OPPOSITE: THE FIRST GROUP OF
COMMERCIAL HELI-SKIERS IN
THE BUGABOOS: APRIL 1965.

A SNOWBOARDER PLAYING WITH THE
DEEP SNOW AND PILLOW DROPS
IN THE MONASHEES.

MONASHEES POWDER AND TERRAIN
CHANGED TREE SKIING.

AN OCEAN OF POWDER IN THE BOBBIE BURNS.
OPPOSITE: BIG TERRAIN AND STEEP SKIING IN THE BOBBIE BURNS.

SKI GUIDES ENJOYING
A DAY AT THE OFFICE.
OPPOSITE: ROGER LAURILLA
DANCING WITH SNOW GHOSTS
IN THE MONASHEES.

173

ABOVE: A TEXTBOOK EXAMPLE OF BREAKABLE CRUST. BELOW: SNOWBALL DANCING IN THE MONASHEES. OPPOSITE: STEEP-CAMP TERRAIN IN THE CARIBOOS.

ABOVE: FIT HIKERS
CRUISING IN THE ADAMANTS.
BELOW: REFLECTIONS IN THE UNICORN
MEADOWS OF THE ADAMANTS.
OPPOSITE: THE FIRST ZIPLINE ON THE
ADVENTURE TRAIL IN THE BOBBIE BURNS.

178

ABOVE: CROSSING THE SUSPENSION
BRIDGE OF THE MT. NIMBUS
VIA FERRATA IN THE BOBBIE BURNS.
BELOW: HIKING ABOVE THE CLOUDS
IN THE ADAMANTS.
OPPOSITE: A GLIMPSE INTO THE FUTURE
OF HELI-SPORT? REMOTE CLIMBING
IN THE ADAMANTS.

ABOVE: BUGABOOS STAFF HELP SHARPEN
A PILOT'S MULTI-TASKING SKILLS.
BELOW: STAFF AVALANCHE RESCUE PRACTICE
IS MADE AS REALISTIC AS POSSIBLE.

ABOVE: HELI-GLISSADING IN THE ADAMANTS. BELOW: WITH DEEP POWDER SKIING AN UNWRITTEN ELEMENT OF THE JOB DESCRIPTION, SMILES ARE PART OF THE UNIFORM.

HANS AND HIS ZITHER, BATTLE ABBEY 2006.
OPPOSITE: FRANZ FRANK'S STATUE
OVERLOOKS THE DINING ROOM
IN THE CARIBOO LODGE.

ABOVE: NOSTALGIA WEEK GUESTS 2005.
BELOW: SKIERS AND HELICOPTER
TRADE PLACES IN REVELSTOKE.

ABOVE: DRESS-UP NIGHT GETS
A BIT WILD SOMETIMES…
BELOW: AN EXCITED SNOWBOARDER
AT THE FRONT OF THE LIFT LINE.
OPPOSITE: MONASHEES SNOW GHOSTS
OVERLOOK THE PURCELLS.

THE CONTRAST OF WILDERNESS AND
HOSPITALITY WERE INSPIRED BY LIZZIE
VON RUMMEL AND ARE STILL PRACTISED
BY THE STAFF 50 YEARS LATER.
OPPOSITE ABOVE: LUNCH
IN THE BOBBIE BURNS.
OPPOSITE BELOW: THE BOOT DRYER –
NOT THE BEST-SMELLING ROOM
IN THE LODGE.

ABOVE: TRYING TO KEEP THE MICA
CREEK HOTEL ABOVE THE SNOW
IN THE MONASHEES.
BELOW: MARGARET AND HANS GMOSER
CELEBRATE 40 YEARS OF HELI-SKIING
IN THE BUGABOOS: 2005.
OPPOSITE: EVERYONE LEARNS TO
BUNDLE THEIR SKIS FOR THE SKI BASKET.
HERE, HANS HELPS A YOUNG
ROBSON GMOSER LEARN THE TRICKS.

ABOVE: A BELL 212 APPROACHES AN EXPOSED PICKUP IN THE BUGABOOS. BELOW: A BELL B-1 EQUIPPED WITH PONTOONS IN THE MID-SIXTIES.

ABOVE: A BELL 206, AKA LONG RANGER, IN THE BUGABOOS.
BELOW: A GROUP OF SKIERS WATCHES A BELL 212 LIFT OFF AMID A CLOUD OF SNOW IN THE BOBBIE BURNS.

MOUNTAINEER'S-EYE VIEW OF
A PICKUP IN THE ADAMANTS.
OPPOSITE ABOVE: A GROUP FLIES AWAY
FROM THE RAIN IN THE BUGABOOS.
OPPOSITE BELOW: ROKO KOELL TEACHING
GUIDES IN SKIING INSTRUCTION
AT SUNSHINE RESORT, ALBERTA.

195

ABOVE: A SUNRISE VIEW ACROSS THE CANADIAN ROCKIES FROM A SUMMIT IN THE BOBBIE BURNS.
BELOW: A GROUP LOADS INTO A BELL 204 BELOW SPECTACULAR SCENERY. AT THE END OF THE DAY, IT IS JUST A MATTER OF A FEW MINUTES' FLIGHT BACK TO THE LODGE.
OPPOSITE: THE ULTIMATE POWDER HARVESTING TOOL: A BELL 212 AND TRACKS IN THE BOBBIE BURNS.

199

As of the 2007/08 winter season, eight of the 100 ski guides working for CMH were women, but the number is slowly growing. Traditionally, the guiding profession was exclusively men, but in its modern form it is a profession ideally suited for equality between genders. While sitting in on dozens of guide meetings during the research for this book, often with one female guide in the room, I never observed anyone treating them any different because they were women. In an e-mail exchange with Jocelyn Lang, one of the first Canadian woman guides and the sole survivor of the ride in the Baystreet avalanche, I asked her about the female perspective on the tragedy. She replied, "I cope the same way as anyone in the same situation, so I'm not sure the female perspective is valid."

In conversations with men and women guides, the overriding sentiment was that women are no different than their male counterparts when it comes to doing their job as a guide. Climbing and skiing in general are great arenas for gender equality. Relative to many sports, the difference between the world standard for women and men is small, and in any group of climbers and skiers it is not uncommon for a woman to be the best on the team. In the mountains these days, men who are not comfortable with women skiing and climbing circles around them end up looking like the north end of a southbound caribou.

Diny Harrison was the first North American woman certified as an IFMGA full mountain guide and has received media attention for the achievement, but a handful of women were training at the same time and any issue of "first" is more of a technicality. In the late eighties, Yana Paplikova, Jocelyn Lang, Sharon Wood, Diny Harrison and Alison Andrews were the first women to break the mould of Canadian guiding as an all-male profession.

Alison Andrews works at CMH Revelstoke, trained under Rudi Krannebitter, has been ski guiding for 20 years and shares Jocelyn Lang's sentiment that the differences between men and women guiding are hardly worthy of discussion. She did note a difference in how some nationalities reacted: "North Americans are used to women being in these roles, but sometimes the Euros are surprised. Once, at the end of a week, a Euro group said, 'At the beginning we weren't sure about having a woman guide, but we just wanted to say it was great.' I always felt like it was not a liability to be a woman."

Kitt Redhead, a 28-year-old assistant ski guide, pursued both the institutional training and the mountain experience with aplomb and became something of a poster girl for the future ski guide. While training at the highest level during ACMG courses and exams, as well as CMH in-house training, she gained the most advanced ski guide education possible anywhere on the planet. On her own time, she chases visionary mountain experiences that are a page out of Hans's own book. After she finished her 2006/07 season in the Monashees, she departed on a traverse from Stewart, British Columbia, to Anchorage, Alaska, using a combination of ski mountaineering in the coastal ranges and cycling on the Alaska Highway. Afterwards, during the summer months, she pushed her rock-climbing standards in Squamish, Canada's granite testing ground near Vancouver.

If Kitt continues with the guiding path, by the time she's a senior guide she will have a quiver of experiences to rival today's old guard, an educational background of doctorate-level hours and intensity, and tools like Thierry Cardon's historical-information-sharing program to work with.

Heli-ski guiding started with a group of guys finding a way to take people skiing in an entirely new way. It fuelled a $100-million industry in British Columbia. But when it comes down to standing on top of a frosty peak and pointing the skis towards a distant valley bottom, it's the same as it ever was. Alison Andrews says, "If you talk about what has changed, you have to talk about what hasn't changed: being in the mountains with someone living a dream. The essence of why people guide hasn't changed."

Mike Welch, the manager of Galena, doesn't hide the thrill of ski guiding: "We get pretty excited about certain lines. Sometimes it all falls into place with the timing, the fuel, the other groups, and you know you're gonna get the line. You can see it coming from miles away and you're just like 'yeahhh.'"

"I don't know anyone else who hangs pictures of their office in their home," says Roger Atkins with glee.

In many CMH staff, the inner ski bum is thinly veiled under an aura of extreme professionalism. Dave Cochrane, the manager of the busy Bugaboo lodge, stopped on top of one run in ideal corn snow after having skied it once, turned to his group and said, "You all know where we're going now, so you don't have to keep up just because I'm going to ski this one really fast. I've got to ski this one for me." Dave pointed his skis down the hill, let gravity take over and was soon a small yellow dot snaking down the glacier. He waited on the glacier below, a big smile splitting his sunburned cheeks as he watched everyone make their way to the pickup.

Indeed, there are few guides who would get out of bed each morning to face the risk, the weather, the demands of people expecting their ultimate ski fantasy, and the time away from family if not for those timeless moments when the decisions have all been made and everything disappears except for an untouched blanket of snow rolling by, and the only thing that matters is putting the first track down the mountain.

8

A SLICE OF LIFE

All the days of storm and stress we bore together, with all the anxieties, hardships and risks, all the glorious long climbs and brilliant sunny days, all the hours of merry singing and savage cursing welded us into an ever closer band of friends.

And we shall remain brothers forever: brothers in life, brothers in work, brothers of the snow.

— Luis Trenker, Brothers of the Snow

One second we're turning through downy early season fluff spread over Galena's undulating terrain, lost in the reverie of the bouncy rhythm and the hissing of crystals pouring past our ears; the next second the spell is broken by a piercing scream: "Somebody help! We've had an avalanche!" Just below us, a man is buried up to his armpits in the snow. His delirious voice continues even after he sees us. "Somebody! Help us!"

His head lolls back, arms flailing at the snow around him, goggles half-torn from his head, eyes glazed with fear and desperation. The tail of a snowboard sticks out of the snow below him at an awkward angle, and past him the outline of an avalanche spreads onto a frozen lake below.

We gather at the top of the slide path, quickly forming a search team. One man grabs a radio and alerts the Galena lodge and the rest of the guides before turning to the group. His job as lodge baker has been transformed into rescue leader. "Everyone, turn your Barryvoxes to 'search' and let me check them!"

One skier, whose housekeeping job now includes conducting a hasty search for avalanche victims, continues down the slope to quickly cover the rest of the avalanche path. The bartender kicks off her skis to uncover the delirious man, who was working in the ski shop just hours earlier and is still yelling at the top of his lungs while the rescue team spreads out across the slope. Two other housekeepers have found a signal near a small tree and are digging like possessed badgers, one with a shovel and the other with her snowboard.

Within a minute, the maintenance man has located another signal and found the victim with a probe. Snow is flying from frenzied digging and the air is thick with the sound of heavy breathing from the effort punctuated by the life-saving chirps of the transceivers – the double beeps, as well as their purpose, eerily similar to the sound of a heart-rate monitor. Another minute passes and the rest of the staff is spread out on the lake near the end of the path in small groups digging or wallowing through the deep snow looking for the remaining signals. Everyone is working as hard as they ever have. One girl collapses from the effort. The girls near the tree are pulling a ski suit from the deep hole at their feet. The arm is bent in half and the head flops lifelessly.

Even though it is merely a one-piece ski suit stuffed with snow, a beacon zipped into a pocket, and buried by the guides for the purpose of training the staff to respond to an avalanche scenario, the intensity and urgency of the rescuers is entirely realistic. The guides stand at the perimeter of the slide path, watching the rescue for anything the staff could do to improve. They have done everything they could to simulate a difficult scenario. Some victims are placed close together, others against trees, some shallow, others deep, and they even buried a transceiver away from a suit, as if the transceiver had separated from the skier, so that after the staff uncovers the transceiver they must form a probe line to find the suit. This year, the snowpack is quite stable, so the slide path is an area stomped by feet and skis into a debris-like alluvium, but in other seasons the guides drop a bomb to release an actual avalanche and make the exercise even more realistic. After all the suits are recovered, everyone gets one more ski run – this time on Freefall, a run with so many cliff bands running its entire width that from below it looks like it would be impossible to ski.

While the season will open with banner conditions just days later and continue with record-breaking snowfall for the next couple of months, no group that year has more fun on Freefall than the appreciative staff. Kids in a candy store is an understatement – they're more like ravers on ecstasy. Hooting and hollering, giggling and squealing maniacally, they pour over the mandatory drops, some fearless and fast and others slower and nervous, but all with face-cramping grins plowing through the choker face shots. Back at the lodge everyone gathers to watch a video of the exercise, the nature of their winter job changed forever.

Working in a remote ski lodge is an employment experience unlike any other. Much has changed, but for everything that has gotten easier other things have become more complex. Skiing is where it began, and skiing is what it's all about, but turning a remote lodge into a comfortable resort for the world's most pampered skiers did not exactly come naturally to the ski bums who joined Hans Gmoser in order to live the skier's dream. There wasn't always a specific maintenance man with professional-grade skills. Putting skiers in charge of the chemical balance in the Jacuzzi resulted in a period where the staff's chest hair turned blue. There wasn't always fresh food flown into the lodges every week. When Lynne Grillmair was first hired as cook in the Bugaboos, following the interview in Hans's hospital room where he was so battered from a crevasse fall that he could hardly talk, all the food was brought in at the beginning of the season before the road drifted closed, and only a case of apples and oranges was brought in fresh with each group of skiers.

Lynne not only cooked but also managed the lodge and did the housekeeping. While there are more staff today to help with the load, there are still more jobs than people. Everyone has to wear multiple hats, and the area managers have one of the most unique skill sets in the modern world. During the day, they are lead ski guides dealing with snowpack evaluation, route-finding and helicopter logistics. One journalist wrote in *SKI* magazine, "The man who does the helicopter scheduling has to be an Einstein, getting all five groups to different areas – depending on their ski skills – and time it so it's waiting at the end of the run? Fantastique."

The moment the managers walk into the lodges and take off their ski boots, their role changes to hotel manager dealing with personnel issues, guest needs and whims, lodge maintenance and the details of a remote and self-sufficient building. Kris Newman, one-time manager of the Bugaboo lodge, was known to ski while wearing his work clothes under his ski suit so he could more quickly make the transition.

Today, fresh food is flown in weekly, but expectations and standards have changed, so the kitchen is still constantly scrambling to deal with operating in such a remote location. Chantal Gainer, a pastry chef, explains: "Since there is no supermarket, and supplies aren't replenished until the following Saturday, there can be some pretty stressful moments when you realize that you are short on things. The 'oh my god!' mantra is used often in times such as these: the case of meat in the freezer that you thought was beef tenderloin is actually breakfast sausage, or no milk or dairy came in on the order, or it is Monday and there is almost no fruit in the house. Being in this remote lodge setting requires you to think quickly on your feet and, mostly, be extremely adaptable."

Greg Gauld, the maintenance man at the Bobbie Burns lodge, describes his job as mechanic, carpenter, electrician, plumber and expert in water and waste treatment, occupational health and safety and environment issues management, shipping and receiving, landscaping, snow safety and avalanche blasting in the winter, and part-time hiking guide in the summer.

He didn't even include rescue team member on the list. Every other staff member tells a similar story. It is a job more like an expedition, where everyone must be ready to do whatever needs to be done. The staff is the fire department and rescue team, and most of the time there is no way to leave without a helicopter and help is a long way away. The isolation breeds a much higher level of responsibility than in similar jobs in civilization, more akin to working on a boat in the Arctic than at a ski resort.

Yet somehow everyone finds a bit of time for enough irresponsibility to balance out the stress and expectations of delivering the ultimate mountain holiday. In the seventies, the ski shop manager, Peter "Lusti" Lustenberger, got drunk one night and was talking with the lodge manager about how badly the Bugaboo lodge needed a new window. "I got a chainsaw and started faking like I was cutting a hole in the wall. The other guys were telling me to fire up the saw. I turned it on . . . "

Within minutes the new window was cut. At the year-end party that year, Hans presented Lusti with an award for cutting the new window. "Hans always recognized motivation," remembers Lusti, "even if sometimes it was misdirected."

All the skiers, hikers and climbers who visit the lodges are on vacation for a short time and likely one of the most cherished experiences of their lives. Anyone with a penchant for drink usually rolls up to the bar after a dreamy day in the mountains and

THE FIRST HELI-SKIERS BAR IN THE WORLD HOSTS APRÈS SKI, 1960s STYLE, IN THE ORIGINAL BUGABOO LODGE.

tips the first of many cocktails. Every winter evening during heli-ski season since 1965 has melded into one huge après ski party in the collective experience of the staff.

In the beginning, CMH had no liquor licence and guests brought their own booze into the lodge. Some groups found skiing made them so thirsty they needed an entire helicopter load to transport their week's liquor and beer. Since space was limited in the lodge, guests lined the baseboard with fine wines and top-shelf liquors. Hans enforced a ten o'clock curfew, but with the short winter days and the tendency of skiers to disregard rules, they found plenty of time to party.

In Europe, responsible drinking is considered reasonable even while skiing. To this day in the Alps, where schnapps and mountaineering are inseparable parts of the culture, there are slope-side bars in ski areas where you can sip a schnapps without even taking off your skis, and beer and wine are a perfectly accepted accompaniment to lunch.

In the early days of heli-skiing, guides sometimes carried a bottle of champagne all day and then popped the cork to celebrate at the very moment a guest reached so many million feet of heli-skiing. One skier built a custom ski pole fashioned into a flask, with a cap on top of the handle that could be unscrewed to fill the pole with his liquor of choice. Passing around his ski pole became a tradition, and a few skiers remember tipping the ski pole a few too many times, resulting in wobbly turns and close calls in the trees. During the early seventies, two bottles of wine for lunch was the allowance for each group. Eventually an American lawyer ended the fun, and maybe saved the business, by informing Hans that if there were an accident following a bit of lunchtime tippling, the courts could end the whole show. From then on, the booze stayed in the lodge, except for one occasion when an Austrian guide discovered the tasty apple cider in the kitchen and didn't realize it contained alcohol. For months, if the ski groups came into the lodge for lunch, he pounded a glass of cider – and then wondered why he felt so low energy while skiing all afternoon. Eventually he looked closely at the label and saw the alcohol content, and the reason for his afternoon doldrums became clear.

One of the first heli-skiers, Brooks Dodge, has a video, black and white and grainy, of skiers racing along a track around the Bugaboo sawmill camp. At the end of each lap, the racers ski up to the camera, grab a beer and sway back and forth on their skis as they drink, then take off again, heavily weighting their ski poles and charging towards a victory – or at least a hangover.

With the intimate atmosphere of the lodges and the festive state of most of the skiers, it is impossible for any of the staff with a penchant for drink not to get involved.

One day, guide Bob Geber was too hung over to ski. At the guide meeting, Hans said, "Where's Bob?"

"He doesn't feel well," said another guide, trying to cover for Bob.

"He was drinking last night!" said Hans. "If he is well enough to drink he is well enough to ski!"

Geber was rousted from bed and went to work. That was where the line was drawn – partying was fine so long as you could ski or work the next day. Worldwide, celebrating is a part of the culture of skiing, but at the isolated lodges the intimacy adds a new flavour. The atmosphere is so memorable that one Australian skier had an exact replica of the Galena bar built in his own home.

Luckily, the demands of skiing temper the drinking to some degree, and Hans had a surefire way to handle a group of heavy drinkers. When a group of them arrived and immediately got into the booze, Hans let them imbibe on the first night, and then skied them into the ground the next day. The second night, the booze bags were in bed by seven and took it a bit easier on the sauce for the rest of the week.

The après ski party has adjusted with the times to a more responsible level, but it still is the stuff of legend. Take the Gothics winter party, for example. The staff has been known to create a full dance club outside in the deep snow complete with a disco ball hanging from the trees, a full-service bar with benches carved out of the huge snowbanks and a dance floor packed by snowmobile. Chris Geber, jack of all trades CMH employee, Bob's

A NEW YEAR'S EVE PARTY CULMINATES WITH A BURNING MAN CELEBRATION OF THE CARIBOOS VARIETY.

nephew, and one of the instigators behind the Gothics hoedown, explains one of the unspoken rules of working for CMH: "We go out of our way to make things fun!"

Staff parties are legendary – and necessary. It offers a chance to have a small piece of life outside of work. One party was on the birthday of one of the pilots. For his cake, the staff put him blindfolded and nearly naked on a table and spread icing all over his body. The women proceeded to lick off the icing, but stepped back and the men surrounded the pilot before tearing off his blindfold so he would think they did the licking. The giggling and messy faces of the women in the room blew their cover. Someone said, "Isn't it great to have a workplace where you can put something sticky and sweet on a co-worker and lick it off – and not get fired for it!"

Pranks escalate. Once, a group raided the staff women's rooms and built a piñata stuffed with their underwear. The women discovered the theft, but couldn't figure out where their undergarments went until later when the piñata party climaxed with their underwear and lingerie flying through the air. To get even, the girls whipped up a heinous concoction of leftover food, blended it and spread it around the boys' bathrooms to look as if someone had gotten sick.

Rumour has it there is a small shack hidden in the woods near each of the lodges where staff can go to blow off steam after a hard day's work. In the shack there is supposedly a dance pole, disco lights, cases of beer stashed in the snowbank and skis mounted on the ceiling so if anyone is late to the party they are hung in their ski boots from the binding. With 30 staff in constant contact with each other, working hard in the confines of the lodge to meet the high and sometimes unrealistic expectations of heli-skiers and hikers, finding small pieces of personal space is essential.

In the winter, a bit of cross-country skiing is an ideal escape. In the summer, running or mountain biking serves the same purpose but also has the adrenaline element inspired by the possibility of running into toothy wildlife. Once, chef Chantal Gainer was riding her bike on the logging road near the Bobbie Burns and noticed a strong smell as she pedalled along. She didn't think much of it until she rounded a corner and saw a tiny grizzly cub standing in the road. While seeing the chubby little fur ball from so close was a rare opportunity, Gainer didn't take time to enjoy the little animal; the strong smell was surely momma bear, somewhere all too close. Without hesitation she wheeled the bike around and raced like Lance Armstrong all the way back to the lodge.

And there is the ultimate escape: the mountains. When a guest gets hurt skiing, the staff are genuinely sorry for the injured, but they can't help but look at the bright side when someone gets tired and comes in early – another seat open on the helicopter! The staff rotate through the ski opportunities, and when it's ski time, even the parties lose importance. Mike Welch, the Galena manager, enjoys watching the staff's enthusiasm for skiing. He says, "They get it figured out and when their (ski) day is up they'll not party the night before, wax their boards and leave their ski pants tucked into their boots like firemen."

This way, when they get the word that the helicopter is coming in for fuel and there is a staff seat, they can be ready before the machine even lands. René Clark, the Galena lodge manager, says, "As with any job, there is a lot of bullshit, but the thing that keeps me coming back is the friends, the silliness and of course the skiing."

One of CMH's longest-standing employees until she retired in 2007, Marion Kingsbury, has as much experience as anyone with the scene and says, "I don't know of anywhere else where people work so hard and are so lovely silly at the same time."

The party atmosphere is not pub-like, not student drink-until-you-get-falling-down-drunk style. It is more a celebration of everyone, staff and skiers, simultaneously having the time of their lives, more common pleasure than alcoholic madness, and often alcohol isn't involved at all.

The atmosphere inspired two staff women to volunteer to serve lunch to the skiers. They were flown out with lunch in the small 407 helicopter and stepped out wearing one-piece fluorescent skin-tight suits with feather boas. During lunch, they dusted the helicopter, striking alluring poses every chance they could, and skied the rest of the afternoon in costume.

A family-style dinner is the symbolic core of the Hans Gmoser way, learned from Lizzie Rummel at Mt. Assiniboine. Guests and staff eat together, and guides and housekeepers alike serve dinner to their respective tables. At the beginning of the week, it is done as formally as it can be in a remote mountain lodge, but after that, as people begin to get caught up in the irreverent nature of the ski holiday, and depending on the group, the atmosphere can become more like a family reunion than a catered vacation.

Even the most stoic employee eventually gets caught up in the atmosphere of close dinnertime interaction among people who are having the time of their lives together. One manager was going for the record of carrying the most desserts at one time by putting four plates on each arm, one on his head and one in his mouth. As he left the kitchen he stumbled, wiped out, and sent ceramic and cream in every direction.

Most weeks, a dress-up night is in order late in the week when everyone is familiar enough with each other to dress as silly as possible. Some skiers, like Shirley Bridges, make dress-up night a primary focus of the trip, with suitcases full of clothes. Everything from edgy and sexy to the utterly ridiculous is fair game. The lodges have closets full of costumes left by skiers and creative staff.

There is a strange relationship between skiing and nudity. Perhaps it is the contrast to the heavily clothed nature of the sport and the striking difference between cold snow and hot skin. The resort of Crested Butte in southern Colorado became famous for a naked ski day on the last day of the season, and in many areas, from the backcountry to the resorts, the pale flash of a skier's bum, free at last from a long winter in polypropylene, is not an uncommon sight. Skiing naked has hardly caught on in the cold of heli-ski season, but it is nevertheless inseparably part of the culture. While everyone is out skiing, female staff sometimes go out on the deck and flash pilots as they fly over the lodge on the way to refuel. Legend has it that dinner was served to one group by staff wearing nothing but paper bags over their heads. An area manager went naked to meet a helicopter full of returning guests, and while he knew everyone on the helicopter, he didn't know that Hans was also on board. When the manager opened the door to see his boss staring at his birthday suit, he probably wanted to disappear. In typical Gmoser leadership style, Hans didn't do a thing or even mention it afterwards, placing full trust in his team's judgment and letting the manager carry on with his antics.

Most of the time, things are not so wild. Heather Lyon, a ski shop guru, says one of her favourite thing about the lodges is "watching people sitting around entertaining each other telling stories or playing guitar."

Most of the time, the small skeleton crew is working like mad to keep the experience as nice as possible for everyone. House managers treat their lodges like their own home. The more legendary house managers, like Nicole Laliberté, who poured her heart and soul into the Cariboos, left a legacy of a polishing-wood-against-the-grain and shining-metal-in-the-toilets sort of perfection. Hans inspired managers by trusting them absolutely, and they reciprocated by leading their teams as if their lives depended on it. Just as nudity provides some balance to the heavy clothing of skiing, random silliness by night provides a balance to the high standards instituted by Hans and demanded by the calculated and serious world of heli-skiing.

Across the heli-ski industry there is a lot of talk about where the snow is deeper, the slopes steeper, the pace faster or the mountains bigger, but it would be hard to find a ski experience where skiers have a better time on and off the snow.

Heather Lyon explains the magic of working for CMH: "When I walk into a coffee shop, I feel like I have a little secret about how fun work can be. I'd rather be staff than one of the guests. The lodges are their own entity and when you're there it is your whole world. People say it is a great thing for the guests, but they forget how great it is for the staff. The guests miss half the fun!"

It's not just employment in the remote lodges that makes for an all-consuming lifestyle. Hans's leadership encouraged a die-hard work ethic while working with him in any role. Even the office staff ended up skiing and getting caught up in the buzz of heli-skiing, then returning to work with newfound motivation. "Hans always wanted us to experience what he was selling," says Marion Kingsbury.

Linda Haywood, Hans's secretary during the seventies and eighties, explains how the state of the business motivated everyone: "It was teetering on the brink all the way through and the things Hans would get done in a day – he could get more done in a day than anyone I ever knew. I would try to keep up and just wear myself ragged and not even come close."

The people who worked in the office with Hans remember his style with a mixture of awe and fear. "It's a miracle I ever started working there," says Haywood, shaking her head. "I still remember my first time walking into the CMH office. It was about the size of a small bedroom and when I walked in Hans was roaring at his secretary with the most amazing verbosity. It still makes my stomach seize up in knots just thinking about it! But he was the best boss I ever had. When times were tight he always took care of his people. He'd tell me when I was paying bills to 'pay the little guys first; the big guys can wait until later.'"

SHIRLEY BRIDGES IN ONE OF HER MANY ELABORATE COSTUMES DURING DRESS-UP NIGHT.

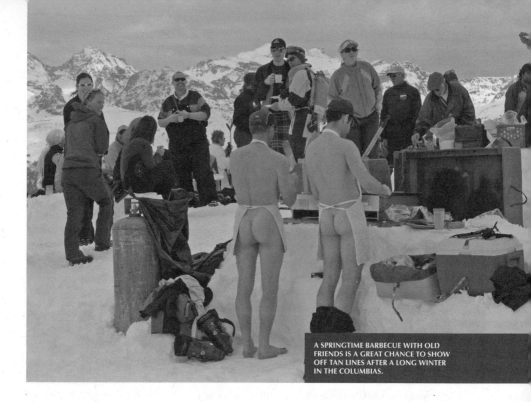

A SPRINGTIME BARBECUE WITH OLD FRIENDS IS A GREAT CHANCE TO SHOW OFF TAN LINES AFTER A LONG WINTER IN THE COLUMBIAS.

A mixture of leading by formidable example, and by ferocious expletive when dealing with issues, delegating with utter confidence in everyone, and caring for the team as family, made Hans a leader who inspired people to devote their lives to the project. Marion Kingsbury explains that "deep down inside you knew you were part of something really special."

Working for Hans Gmoser was a chance to live a mountain fantasy, but it came at a price. The first European guides were tradesmen, like Hans and Leo, and the business couldn't afford to hire anyone else, so when it came time to build lodges and make things happen besides the skiing, the guides did the work. Guiding legend Rudi Krannebitter remembers those guides with respect. "In the beginning, you were the company," he says. "Those guys worked all the time, putting in all kinds of time for free. If they'd been paid for everything they did, CMH wouldn't have worked."

Kiwi Gallagher remembers the guides helping with the construction of the Cariboo lodge. "It was miserable work," he says. "It was like being in prison camp, except there were more mosquitoes."

When the skiing began, the guides worked nine weeks straight, then later it was four weeks on and one off. They were paid $69 per day, even the week off, until the guides revolted against their wages because they were lower than European ski guide standards, and threatened to quit if they didn't get a raise. Hans's reaction was typically considerate: "If we raise you, we have to raise the girls." The guides got their raise and so did the lodge staff, but the paid week off disappeared.

The original guides and staff committed their entire lives to the project. Bob Geber's plan was to spend a year in Canada to learn English and have a bit of adventure rock climbing and skiing. After two years, he wrote a letter to his father explaining why he was staying longer: "My English is not so good."

Dad believed him, but after a third year and another letter with the same excuse, he wrote back, "Are you really so stupid to not learn English after three years?"

Canada was becoming a big part of Geber's life. After five years he went home briefly, but by then the wilds of western Canada had snuck under his skin. He'd found a mountain range and a country full of emptiness and wildness long gone from his homeland of Bavaria in southern Germany. He began taking people heli-skiing in the Bugaboos with Hans Gmoser and sealed his fate as a Canadian. What could be better than making the ultimate mountain vacation into your career?

In Geber's case, the "year to learn English" turned into the rest of his life. He is now 72 years old and is still leading skiers down the glades and glaciers of the Columbias. Not everyone can claim to have given their life to the world of heli-skiing, nor does everyone want to, but the business takes a piece of everyone who works to make it happen.

The snow, the mountains, the chemistry of personalities in the skiers and staff, the stresses of running a complex operation, the remoteness of the lodges and the potential seriousness of the endeavour conspire to keep the staff absorbed for weeks, months, years and eventually decades. To work at a remote lodge, be it for one season or 40, demands a hefty toll from the rest of the staff's world of family, friends and career ambitions.

Living and working in isolation, with a new group of excited skiers calling the lodge home each week, keeps the energy at a manic level. Pastry chef Chantal Gainer sees the effect, both good and bad, of working in the desert-island remoteness of the lodges:

> It is not unusual for people to forge lifelong friendships at the lodge. You get to know someone in hyperspeed fast-forward up there. Everyone eats, lives, plays and works together for weeks at a time, and you sure get to know a great deal about someone in that situation awfully quickly! Occasionally, you make such deep friendships with people that it can be frightening how much fun you can have together. The end of the season when everyone goes their own ways can be a tearful parting and a tumultuous separation!
>
> I won't lie, work is work in whatever job one does and eventually some of the glamour wears off. Aside from all of the perks, there are definitely some drawbacks to the job. Lodge life is not a life for everyone, and I can honestly say, after eight years of working for CMH, that if you are a person who does not have a generally happy, easygoing disposition, then this place is not for you. There is such closeness of quarters at the lodge that it is imperative that you are able to live and breathe the mantra "water off a duck's back," or your ship will sink – hard and fast. Slacking off will not make you any friends, and cutting corners will only make your day even longer tomorrow. One of the greatest challenges that exist in the

lodge is having to tough out an entire season with a co-worker you really don't jive with. In all of the CMH kitchens, the chefs work so closely to each other that I assure you, the long days can be hell when you don't get along with your co-worker, and unfortunately, it happens.

For everyone involved, the environment is ultimately stimulating, but at the end of the week, most guests go home, leaving the staff to do it all over again. Week after week, year after year this cycle continues. Within it, the dramas of a soap opera, the surprises of a reality TV show, the epics of an expedition, the education of a university, and the political issues of a parliament make for a world unto its own. Margaret Gmoser calls the show *As the Rotor Turns,* after the soap opera *As the World Turns,* and it is now running into its fifth decade. She explains the drama: "Some women guests would come and expect to 'have' a guide as part of their week. One woman must have 'had' three guides in one week!"

The promiscuity is no worse than at any resort or vacation destination where fit young people party with uninhibited holiday revellers, but temptations are distilled by isolation and small numbers of people, so affairs are transparent and secrets hard to keep. After a couple of glasses of wine, and with great mirth, Lynne Grillmair remembers episodes of *As the Rotor Turns.*

"The Euro guides were so aggressive. They felt like they could do whatever they wanted. It was kind of a shocker. Once you were attached to someone there was no trespassing, but if you weren't tied up it was all fair game. It was kind of a culture clash for a while."

It didn't help that Hans decided it would enhance the Alpine atmosphere of the lodge if the staff women wore dirndls in the push-up, cleavage-enhancing Bavarian tradition that squeezes even average bodies into curvy, buxom sex symbols. Margaret Gmoser recalls the dirndls as being "not only dirndls – mini-dirndls. We used to pour ourselves into them."

And if things did get a bit intimate, which they occasionally did regardless of attire, it always seemed like a good idea at the time. Lynne continues, "Things are so intense and you're your own little community, so of course there is energy between people. Then you get out into the real world and you're like 'oh my god, what have I done?'"

Abigail Elvy, Mark Kingsbury's daughter, recounted one of the most outrageous affairs. The Kingsburys were at home having dinner when the CMH phone rang. As president of the company, Mark had a CMH line directly into his house that could interrupt the family at any time for anything from accidents to personnel issues. Whenever the CMH phone rang, there would be a moment of tension as everyone in the house would fear there had been an accident. This time, though, it was a wife and husband with a baby, the wife staying at the lodge to take care of the baby while dad skied powder. She managed to get involved with one of the European guides, and the husband returned early from skiing to catch them in the act. A full-speed chase around the lodge ensued, with the guest stopping once at the bar to reassure the bartender, "Don't worry, I'm not going to kill him, just beat him up!"

The family was flown out early, too stressed to enjoy the rest of their vacation, and the guide returned to Europe with two black eyes. Mark returned to dinner and shared the madness with his family at the table. Abigail remembers him shaking his head and saying, "Jesus, what's next?!"

Even legitimate trysts were hard to keep private, especially in the early days of eight-person bunkrooms. Lynne describes their efforts at privacy: "We used to hang green towels on the doorknobs of our bunkrooms, and everyone knew that meant we were not to be disturbed. Then there were other places. The laundry chute, the laundry table and the old sawmill camp. Then later there was the heli-shack and the generator shack. The sauna was the best place, but you had to make reservations."

Valerie Legault, a 21-year-old housekeeper at the Gothics, explains, "When you're working so close, everyone has some story about affinity with people. We live at the rhythm of the season and the weather. The rest of the world disappears."

For the young, single and adventurous, working at a remote ski lodge is an ideal seasonal job. However, lodge staff average eight years with CMH and guides stay with the company for an average of over 12 years. This means most find it a profession rather than a one-season affair with the world of heli-skiing. To have a life outside of work while committing a decade or more to an all-consuming job is a difficult task and often relationships pay the price.

Guide Colani Bezzola describes the marital issues simply: "It's gotten better, but in the early days there was not one who was married who stayed married."

Today the work shifts are shorter to give people more time off, but the profession is still hard. One guide, only partly joking, said, "I'd be divorced too if I could find time to do the paperwork."

Maya Geber, former wife of guide Bob Geber, says of the remote world of the lodges, "That life is an artificial life." Bob shared a different perspective from a pub in Banff. Waving his hand at the street full of cars, shops and materialism, he says, "What's so real about this life anyway?" In the end, the difference was too much for their marriage, and like many other CMH relationships, they went their separate ways. Unlike many, they remain close friends and share a beautiful duplex overlooking Banff and the surrounding Rockies.

As a guest of CMH, it is easy to forget that the very people who make the magic of the lodge happen also have families and lives away from the world of powder, tundra and alpine isolation.

For the guides and staff to have a life outside of work, they essentially learn to live in two different worlds: the world of heli-skiing and the world of home. Some deal with the two by having very little life outside of work, others by having extremely full lives away from the lodges, complete with families and other career ambitions. Either way, most are constantly walking a tightrope between the two worlds. CMH Revelstoke, where the operation is based in town and anyone who lives in town can go home to their families at night, has a waiting list of guides wanting to work there.

While all the fun, skiing, hard work and camaraderie are happening in the back-country, families are growing up, wives and husbands are doing chores and life goes on. It is the secret cost of the remote heli-skiing project. The lodge staff is a relatively transient crew, coming and going with the seasons. A few stay on to eventually become managers or guides. While the reasons for leaving are many and varied, the most common is family. The lifers in the heli-ski world see the problems clearly. Marion Kingsbury speaks with the knowledge of a mother who raised three children while both parents worked for CMH: "All month I'd be working on certain things with the children and then Mark would come home and blow the whole thing out of the water. The whole system would be disrupted. I guess the kids took the brunt of it in the end."

Just about the time the family gets used to having two parents again, it's time for one to leave. Ular Wiatzka was five years old and tired of his dad, Bernie, a Galena guide, being away from home. One day as Bernie was packing his bags, Ular asked pleadingly, "Dad, why do you have to leave all the time?"

Before Bernie could respond, Ular's mother, Cindy, jumped in. She replied, "We need to be able to buy food." Ular had the perfect answer to keep dad home. He ran to the refrigerator and opened the door. Pointing to the stocked fridge, he said excitedly, "Look! There's lots of food!"

After working in the wilderness for weeks on end, the staff try to make up for lost time at home. Marion continues, "Mark would come home Saturday night after four weeks of guiding and on Sunday morning we'd be skiing with the kids at Norquay."

"Dad said to go get an education, get a job and then go into the mountains for fun," says Aita Bezzola, a 19-year-old working at the Bobbie Burns lodge during summers between semesters at McGill University. She cleans rooms, works in the kitchen and does whatever is needed to keep the lodge functioning. She plans to do one more year of school before taking a winter off to work at the lodge and taste a bit more of the legendary skiing. Aita is taking her first careful steps onto the CMH tightrope: more than one well-meaning student has worked in a remote lodge for a season and ended up there a decade later wondering what happened but knowing that whatever it was involved a whole lot of good skiing.

Aita, however, is also a second-generation CMH employee who knows all about the failed marriages, dropped careers and sordid affairs that go along with living and working in a remote ski area. Her father, Colani Bezzola, is the current mountain safety manager and a 33-year veteran guide for CMH. Colani was the manager of the Bobbie Burns lodge during Aita's first years of life, and she saw first-hand the world of heli-skiing. Before entering public school Aita's home was the Bobbie Burns lodge. Her playmates were adult skiers and hikers and her sisters Madlaina and Martina.

When Aita's older sister Martina reached school age and moved with her family to Parson, a small town at the beginning of the logging road leading to the Bobbie Burns, Colani saw a need to change his job to be able to spend time with his family. He approached Hans with his dilemma. At the same time, Hans felt the network of guides between the areas needed a common eye and perspective to make sure the snowpack evaluation was being done in a similar way. Colani moved into his current job, which allows him to work in the alpine wonderland he loves and also be with the family he loves even more.

Still, Colani is away from home most of the winter, travelling between lodges and keeping up with the various guiding teams. While many daughters with a father who was away so much would feel cheated of the father figure in their lives, Aita has a perspective only someone who knows other CMH families could have. She says, "Dad was only away in the winters; he was around all summer. That's pretty good for a CMH kid!"

Many of Aita's friends had parents who worked at the remote lodges. "A lot of us had the same behaviour patterns while growing up." When asked for examples she explains, somewhat cryptically, "Like dreams and sleep patterns and similar issues at the same time."

Aita noticed the same disruption of the family system as Marion did: "When he came home he had no idea what was going on. It made for rough going when he came home in the spring, because we had this dynamic going."

Even with the chaos it caused at home, most of the children of CMH are somewhat fascinated by it. Troy Kingsbury is a full-time CMH employee. His first time heli-skiing was when he was 18 months old, in a backpack on his father's back. "He would tilt the pack sideways so I could see forward." He remembers, then adds, "I don't think they'd let you do that now."

Today, Troy works various jobs for the lodges and is training to be a heli-ski pilot. He says proudly, "I was born because of it, into it, and haven't really left it." Then, taking a page from his father's book, he adds, "I love it. Mostly for the people."

Aita shares Troy's fondness for the business but also clearly sees the difficulty the profession causes families: "You hear the stories of the outrageous parties they used to have, and as an eight-year-old you really don't know what to think of it. Now I think we're all kind of intrigued by the CMH thing. I think the only ones who have sour views of it are the ones whose parents got divorced because of it."

It appears that there are far too many. Some have managed the balancing act successfully, but none without difficulty. Former shop manager Peter Lustenberger now runs the ski shop at Panorama. He explained his reason for seeking different work simply: "If I didn't leave CMH I would come home and my kids would say, 'Who is that?'"

Bobbie Burns manager Bruce Howatt describes the difficulty with brutal honesty: "It's not just while we're away. When we're home we're always useless recovering or useless getting ready to leave."

More often than not, family was the driving force that brought guides into roles in the administration of CMH. Marion Kingsbury explained Mark's reason for stepping into the office where he would eventually become president: "When our children were very small, he realized that the lifestyle of a mountain guide did not enable him to care for his family the way he wanted, and he made an agonizing decision to leave the guiding profession which he absolutely loved and threw himself into the unknown territory of an office environment. It was a decision he did not regret."

Even for management, the world of heli-skiing is demanding. Mark Kingsbury's youngest daughter, Lydia, explains her perspective on her father's business with respect, but her opinion of her parents' demanding business is not far below the surface: "I know it was something my parents had of lot of pride in, but even when he was home

ONE OF THE FIRST CHILDREN TO GROW UP AROUND HELI-SKIING: ROBSON GMOSER, SKI TOURING IN THE BUGABOOS.

his mind was on it all the time." Mark's death made making up for lost time impossible and solidified her view of work and family time: "I always wanted him around more, but I was more upset and mad after he died. Needless to say, I was happy to see my mom (Marion) retire last year." While Lydia's siblings are both involved with CMH, she prefers to keep her distance, teaching school in Calgary and mostly avoiding the heli-ski business. By the spring of 2008, she had given birth to Mark and Marion Kingsbury's first grandchild. True to the profound learning she received from her parents' lifestyle, she plans to split her maternity leave with her husband, Andrew. Time will tell how much time she and Andrew mange to devote to their family, but it seems family will be first priority. She concludes, "He (Mark) did a lot of things to make up for his time away, and I really appreciated it, but I think it's just hard being the child of a guide and mountain man."

9

BASE CAMP

It was quite obvious there were other places where one could heli-ski. In fact, virtually all the Columbia Mountains possessed the necessary attributes for good heli-skiing. The question was primarily one of access and accommodation.

— Hans Gmoser

Once the Bugaboos heli-ski model worked, the proliferation of heli-skiing was purely a factor of demand. The other valleys in the Columbia and Cariboo mountains were cloaked with deep snow and sculpted into ski terrain the likes of which people had not yet even dreamed of skiing. During the first forays with Jim Davies's Cessna onto the Canoe Glacier in the Cariboos, Hans Gmoser and Jim McKonkey were the first skiers to set eyes on much of the terrain. It was stunning. The Bugaboos have their crown-like spires and indisputably world-class skiing, but for pure skiing volume the rest of the Columbia and Cariboo mountains make even the mighty Bugaboos appear insignificant. The sub-ranges of the Monashees, Selkirks and Purcells lean against each other like fish on a string and together contain what is possibly the biggest stash of consistently excellent skiing on the planet. The area contains the only temperate rainforest on earth that receives most of its precipitation as snow, and the terrain is almost all steep enough to ski but not too precipitous to hold snow. One by one, between 1969 and 2003, CMH added 11 more areas to its mountain kingdom for a total tenure of over 15,000 square kilometres of ski terrain – that's over 200 times more area than Vail and Whistler/Blackcomb combined.

By 1970, the skier's lust for powder, helicopter capacity that made the business viable and timing with the provincial and cultural climate had combined into a perfect storm of incentive to expand heli-skiing into additional territory. Hans unveiled the potential of the new sport as a recreation industry in a ten-page letter written in 1971 to the BC provincial government. He explained heli-skiing simply as a new concept in ski area development, "To transport skiers by plane or helicopter is not new to this country nor other alpine areas of the world, but it has never been successful to the point where it can be looked upon as an entirely new industry. However, I believe this has been achieved with my approach to the operation in the Bugaboos."

At the time of the first expansion, into the Cariboos, CMH was anticipating growth of 25 per cent per year, and since the company had already built a full-scale model that was working spectacularly, the province had plenty of incentive to encourage growth in the industry and little reason to restrict it – so the guides essentially went heli-skiing wherever they wanted. While there were unlimited suggestions Hans could have made to the government, he outlined two simple requirements he felt were essential to the successful operation of the "helicopter ski resort": adequate space and exclusive rights.

In his letter, he warned the government of the impending explosion of interest in the sport, based on the CMH business trajectory, and concluded with a plea to establish standards by which CMH and other heli-ski outfits should be expected to operate. By writing the rules of the game in an effort to preserve the resource no matter how popular heli-skiing became, Hans ensured that the heli-ski experience would remain a wilderness one far beyond his lifetime, in more areas than just CMH's and beyond national boundaries. It took until 1983 – and pressure from CMH, Mike Wiegele and the other heli-ski operators of the seventies – for the government to take action and issue permits for mechanized ski tenures, but it was better late than never.

Hans did the math. More people wanted to go skiing with CMH than the Bugaboo lodge could handle. The year before Hans penned his sagacious letter,

THE 3-DIMENSIONAL MODEL UNDER GLASS IN THE CARIBOO LODGE SHOWS WHY HANS CHOSE THE LOCATION FOR HIS SECOND HELI-SKI AREA.

Mike Wiegele had begun heli-skiing at Valemount and fanned the fires of Hans's motivation still higher. Expanding the lodge and the operation in the Bugaboos would have been the most efficient strategy, but Hans, ever the skier at heart, thought about how increased numbers would change the very skiing he and almost everyone who tried it found so beguiling. Hans explained, "After a week without fresh snow in the Bugaboos, we were already finding it challenging and often had to poke around the edges to make fresh tracks and that's what people come for, the fresh tracks. If we brought more people we would lose the skiing that makes it worth the cost of the helicopter!"

In many ways, these guidelines are Hans's greatest contribution to the sport. If CMH had stayed in the ski touring business where it began, someone else would have gotten into the game with a helicopter. It doesn't take a genius to realize that an aircraft is a great way to get to the top of a ski run. If that someone had been equally entrepreneurial but less sensitive to the resource and the experience, the sport of heli-skiing could have ended up merely a very expensive way to go mogul skiing.

A visit to the backcountry lodges like the Bugaboo and Cariboo, or any of the other ten areas under CMH management as of 2008, is now a comfortable, catered experience, but when heli-skiing outgrew the Bugaboos, the business was not ready to pay for the building of another ski lodge. Besides, most skiers chasing Columbia powder at the time didn't care where they slept. Any building with enough beds to accommodate a group of heli-skiers was fair game, and many areas began with shoddy lodging until the popularity of the area was adequate to pay for a custom ski lodge.

Even before opening shop in the Bugaboos, Hans had been fascinated by the Cariboos' potential for skiing. Who among those who've ever strapped a board or two on their feet could miss it? After carving steep, round-bottomed valleys, the glaciers

left the drainages of the Rausch, the Canoe and the North Thompson rivers with architecture that has inspired more than one skier to say, "the Cariboos are proof that God is a skier."

Avalanches are the original ski run cutters, and when the slope's angle is consistent, the clearings left by avalanches tend to be parallel sided. When the angle increases, the avalanche paths narrow, and when the angle decreases, the paths tend to widen like water flowing in a river. The angle of the valley walls in the Cariboos is so consistent that mountains are striped with avalanche paths running parallel to each other like the teeth of a giant comb for as far as the eye can see – even from a helicopter. Each of the paths can be skied, and on many of them a runaway ski following the fall line unchecked will end up right at the pickup.

The terrain of the Cariboos is an amalgamation of all the different kinds of features that make up great skiing: the long, powder-cloaked old-growth forests, steep serpentine ridgelines, friendly glades, rock-edged couloirs, undulating glaciers, planar mountain faces and chaotic combinations of all of the above.

Without the advent of heli-skiing, the Cariboos would be unknown to this day. Even with 37 years worth of heli-skiers telling tales of Cariboos powder, and 28 years worth of heli-hikers returning home with photos of impossible fields of wildflowers below teetering glacial ice, the area is still described on the current website of nearby Wells Gray Provincial Park as "the wild untravelled country of the Cariboo mountains, with craggy peaks, icefields and hidden valleys."

Two years before the first skiers rode a helicopter in the Bugaboos, Hans flew with powder pioneer Jim McKonkey and pilot Jim Davies to the upper Canoe Glacier and began an exploration into aircraft-accessed skiing. During the trip, McKonkey built a kicker, or steep ski ramp, out of snow to jump over the plane as it sat on the glacier. Davies recalls turning the prop sideways to give McKonkey one less thing to hit if he cut it too close. After a few false starts, and one near miss where he slapped the wing with his skis, he stuck it. In a testament to genetics, Jim McKonkey's grandson is modern big-mountain ski visionary Shane McKonkey, the man called "the craziest man in skiing" by the film company Matchstick Productions for his invention of ski-basing, a gut-wrenching sequence that involves ripping a big-mountain line on skis and hucking off a huge cliff and a spectacular parachute-assisted descent.

So massive and obvious is the ski potential in the Cariboos that if there had been no sawmill camp in the Bugaboos to serve as an ideal base for launching the operation, heli-skiing in Canada would likely have started in the Cariboos. The mountainsides just beg to be skied. There are numerous safe and obvious drop-offs and pickups for the helicopter, and with the smaller craft of the day, the location of the present Cariboo lodge would have allowed more efficient access to varied ski terrain than the precipitous, albeit incomparably spectacular, Bugaboos. Thus, when the demand for heli-skiing exceeded the capacity of the Bugaboos, it was an easy decision where to ski next.

Hans was a leader in the mould of Ernest Shackleton and Meriwether Lewis: he led by putting absolute trust in his team. He was utterly confident in his ability to make the right decision, but to make the project move forward he surrounded himself with those he trusted most in the matter at hand and put enormous faith in their abilities and judgment. This rare quality of being a leader who built his decisions out of the input of his confidants created a team of unusual devotion. To make remote heli-ski bases work smoothly, Hans gave each team almost complete autonomy.

A German guide named Hermann Frank was put in charge of the Cariboos skiing, based out of the town of Valemount. For the winter of 1969 CMH still had the monopoly on heli-skiing, but in 1970 Mike Wiegele began offering heli-skiing out of Valemount as well. Hans planned to build a lodge in the Cariboos, but it took four years of bumping skis with his competition before the lodge was completed.

Skiing out of Valemount gave the team ample time to study the valleys of the Cariboos for the most suitable location to build a lodge. The Canoe River drainage was too swampy for logging trucks to navigate without significant road-building expense, and the timber within the valley was hardly worth the expense for logging companies to bother with. This gave the area obvious appeal for a lodge location. Even today, there are no logging scars visible from the Cariboo lodge.

However, the very same swamps and scruffy timber were also a hindrance to building a lodge. To accomplish the daunting task, Hans chose another close friend rather than an unknown builder. Lloyd "Kiwi" Gallagher had proved himself to be an unshakable spirit while handling the least desirable jobs and had invested his life savings in the project. He was the perfect choice. Just deciding where to place the lodge was a formidable decision. The ground cover was so thick that planning views, or even seeing more than a few feet into the dense bush, was impossible. Even after choosing the eventual lodge site, Hans, Kiwi and Philippe were unsure how it would turn out. "I clearly remember an epic day!" remembers Philippe. "Hans, Kiwi and I went thrashing through the bush in an attempt to find a better site – without results."

At this point, Kiwi dove into the Canoe Valley with his family and scarcely emerged until the lodge was finished. The building site became his home and obsession for two years as he managed the construction with the dream of making not only a beautiful heli-ski lodge, but also a place where he would feel at home. "Even today when I get a chance to go into the lodge," says Kiwi warmly, "I feel like I am going home."

The early guides were also skilled tradesmen and, with Kiwi at the helm, they poured heart and soul into the job of building the Cariboo lodge. For much of the timber used in the construction, they took trees from the building site and hauled them to a sawmill, where the logs were hewn into boards and beams. Then the wood was hauled back to the site and used in the construction. The beautiful woodwork in the lodge is made of trees harvested from the very land where the lodge now stands. The roads and building site were mud pits, the mosquitoes were thick and Kiwi remembers spending as much time pulling stuck trucks out of the mud as building. It was finished just before Christmas of 1974, complete with finishing touches like guide Franz Frank's wooden statue of his likeness with a rope over his shoulder and an ice axe in his hand carved into the spiral stairway of the dining room.

Ernst Buehler, the manager of CMH Cariboos for almost 30 years, is a product of Hans's leadership style. A mosquito-infested swamp next to the lodge was a huge problem for the summer season, so Ernst took it upon himself to turn it into a lake. After two years of wallowing in the mud, Ernst transformed the swamp into the clear, inviting pond it is today. Later, as corporate oversight crept into the daily operation of the various CMH areas, Ernst was turned down on a request for money to turn the old spa building into a staff house. Staying true to the needs of the lodge rather than the limitations of corporate decision-making, Ernst requested financing to buy a new truck for the lodge. The truck purchase was quickly approved – somehow an expensive truck seemed more important to the budget managers than staff lodging – and Ernst promptly took the money and built the staff house now known as the Chalet. "They weren't too happy about that," remembers Ernst, then added, "but Hans made us like owners and because of that we treated these places like our own." The Chalet still stands, a valuable resource for staff to have a place that feels like home, while the truck would have been scrapped long ago.

For skiing in the Columbias, location was to a large degree irrelevant in Hans's mind. He could run a heli-ski operation out of almost any valley and produce the requisite skier grins to fill a lodge and pay for a helicopter. So rather than look for the best terrain, Hans kept his ear to the ground for opportunities for lodging. Two hours north of Revelstoke, BC Hydro was in the last stages of building the Mica dam, which turned the northernmost point of the Columbia River, where it bends from flowing north to south, into the extensive Kinbasket Lake. The town of Mica Creek was a bustling village of 4,000 people. The gradual reduction of workers needed for the dam project left enough accommodation for skiers and Hans negotiated with BC Hydro to give skiers room and board for the winter of 1971 in the modular buildings used by the workers.

PHILIPPE DELESALLE'S ORIGINAL VISION OF THE CARIBOO LODGE. LITTLE HAS CHANGED.

COHOS DELESALLE & EVAMY
ARCHITECTS • ENGINEERS • INTERIOR DESIGNERS • CALGARY ALBERTA

The skiers ate with the workers in the mess hall, where, as Mark Taggart, one of the original Monashees heli-skiers, remembers, "The workers didn't really relate to the rich people from the USA who hired a helicopter to take them up the hill." The workers and skiers also shared the bunkhouse, which Taggart was sleeping in during what was almost heli-skiing's most lethal accident. At 2 a.m. Taggart was jolted awake by what he thought was a massive avalanche slamming into the bunkhouse, but as he came to his senses he realized the impact had been an explosion. The bunkhouse was heated with propane pumped through the space under the floor and a leak had ignited, lifting the entire structure from its foundation. Half dressed and wholly confused, everyone clambered out the windows and gathered in the parking lot. Taggart remembers people standing around, wrapped in blankets and staring in disbelief as the building "caught fire within ten minutes of the explosion and was totally engulfed."

Two bartenders were killed in the initial blast and one man was thrown from bed with such violence that he broke his nose on the ceiling of his room. CMH took the group to Revelstoke by bus, supplied everyone with clothing and called US immigration to inform them that 44 people would soon be crossing the border without passports.

After the explosion, BC Hydro built a cluster of houses and CMH leased them for the skiers. A number of Monashees skiers still talk fondly about the days of wading through waist-deep snow from their house to the dining room before a day of skiing. The houses served as lodging for CMH Monashees until 2002 when they completed their most upscale lodge, an edifice framed with colossal wooden beams and featuring walls of windows overlooking the northernmost shores of Lake Revelstoke and one of the most famous heli-ski runs in the world: rime-encrusted trees poking through deep snow for 1300 metres of otherworldly skiing ending at the water's edge and known as Elevator.

When Hans started skiing out of Mica Creek, little did he know that the area would become famous, even among the most experienced heli-skiers, for the combination of heavy snowfall and big-vertical, consistent-fall-line skiing in old growth forests.

Part of the reputation is due to the natural geography and climate of the area, but the Monashees got a reputation largely because of the ski vision of two of the area's first guides, Sepp Renner and Rudi Gertsch. Tree skiing has become the bread and butter of heli-skiing, far from where it began on the high summits and broad glaciers, but this transition was not because of a business decision. Renner and Gertsch started skiing the trees in the Monashees because it was possible in bad weather and accidentally found a whole new world of skiing. Not only was it more frequently stable enough to ski steeper terrain in the trees, but if they kept skiing the same slope during big storms and breaking up the slab development, they could continue skiing the popular slopes in safety even while the rest of the area was avalanching.

The first time Hans skied the trees with Renner in the Monashees, Renner remembers picking a steep line and when Hans arrived at the bottom he looked at Renner and said, "You're fuckin' nuts."

"Seppie was the one who showed us how to ski the trees," remembers Rudi Krannebitter. "We were all stuck on skiing the wide-open stuff and only skiing the trees to get to a (helicopter) landing. Seppie was a brilliant skier and he started leading groups through the trees from top to bottom in the Monashees. We saw this and it opened our eyes. He forever changed the way we look at ski terrain."

The drainage of Soards Creek became the tree skiers' holy land, a serpentine mountain valley studded with steep hillsides and covered with trees so ideally spaced for skiing that Monashees addicts get to the point where Soards is the only place on the planet where they are truly happy skiing. Twenty-year Monashees veteran Cliff Milleman said, "I tried heli-skiing other places, but I just found myself missing Soards."

Once dubbed the "Manashees," because of the testosterone-heavy nature of its skiers, many Monashees skiers are so committed to the place that they book the same week together for years. The fraternity of the Monashees is not entirely different from some groups in other heli-ski areas, but it is most prevalent in the Monashees. On the long bus ride, grey-haired men share earpieces from an iPod, one driving the tune selection and another guessing the song, giggling like a couple of high-school chums. The luxurious new lodge does much to dissipate the frat-house vibe, but it is there nevertheless. Hank Brandtjen has heli-skied for nine million vertical feet, all of it in the Monashees, and misses the old lodging where the construction-project atmosphere was better suited for pranks and manliness. Brandtjen once took all the avalanche beacons, turned them to "Search,' and hid them in everyone's rooms. It was the generation of beacons before the Barryvox, and they emitted an audible beep as soon as a signal was detected. Late that night, Brandtjen went out in the parking lot and turned his beacon to transmit, filling the lodge with beeping. After the lights in everyone's rooms came on, but before anyone had time to pinpoint the noise, he turned his beacon off. Then when the lights went off, he turned his beacon back on.

But although the new Monashees lodge has changed the comfort and aesthetic of the accommodation, the unbeatable skiing, the characters who are addicted to it, and the leg burn that comes from skiing your tenth thousand-metre tree run of the day are the same as when Sepp and Rudi first decided to point their skis into the forest.

There are some ski areas, whether heli-skiing or lift service, that are famous for their reputation, some that are famous for the lodging, some that are famous for the scenery, and there are some that are quite simply about the skiing. The Bobbie Burns is one of the latter. The area takes its name from a mining claim in the area named after the famous Scottish poet Robert Burns. Among students of poetry, Bobbie Burns is known for womanizing and writing poems of witchcraft and songs that have become traditional ballads. In skiing, the name is famous for massive daily vertical, non-stop runs, fit guides, a majority of non-English speaking skiers and an atmosphere soaked in hard-core ski elite. To minimize wait times in the big terrain of the Bobbie Burns tenure, the program runs with three groups rather than four and the skiers commonly descend 60,000 metres in a week – nearly double the guarantee of 100,000 feet.

The Bugaboos and the Adamants have an inseparable atmosphere of mountaineering thanks to the setting and history of those areas, but the Bobbie Burns has the strongest climbing culture of any of the lodges. The guides are often found training on the climbing wall and they are constantly looking for new climbs in the rugged peaks in the vicinity. The mountains are reminiscent of the great destination alpine climbing ranges in the world. Mt. Hatteras is shaped like a smaller Gasherbrum IV and the landmark Mt. Syphax looks like a diminutive K2 from some aspects, while Thumb Spire is reminiscent of the rugged peaks of Pakistan's famous Karakoram Range. Much of the skiing is in remote valleys with such precipitous drops into the Duncan River that even the logging industry has been unable to reach the timber. Skiing and hiking without views into cut blocks and logging roads enhance the big-mountain feel.

It is fitting, then, that the Bobbie Burns began as a ski experience more like an alpine climb from an exposed base camp than a catered heli-ski vacation. The Ruth Vernon Mine, with accompanying dorm buildings, powerhouse and cookhouse, existed near the head of Vermont Creek, a narrow drainage just downstream and on the same side of the valley as the current Bobbie Burns lodge. It was a natural choice after the success of the Bugaboos logging camp, and in 1977, when it was time to develop a new area to meet the booming demand for heli-skiing, the Ruth Vernon Mine was the easiest place to expand operations. There was one small issue: the camp was positioned beneath several huge avalanche slopes, and the skiing in the valley was exposed to large slides. During times of poor stability and bad weather, the skiing options were extremely dangerous and the threat of avalanches made life in the camp downright nerve-wracking.

So severe was the threat of slides in the camp that, according to legend, skiers wore their avalanche transceivers to bed. While one guest said he did sleep with a beacon in the Bobbie Burns camp, guide Colani Bezzola remembers it was never required – the camp was positioned on a small island of safety in the centre of the avalanche-prone valley. However, there were times he remembers firmly telling the skiers not to take one step away from the buildings, due to threat from avalanches, and one winter a huge slide pulverized the powerhouse. Massive avalanches frequently ran to within metres of the camp, and the path to the outhouse on occasion was covered with debris. With limited safe areas, the helicopter parked squarely in the centre of camp.

After big storms, the guides flew bombing runs in the cirque around camp. "I remember Frank Stark lighting the fuses with his cigar," says Colani.

When the bombs triggered the biggest slides, the ensuing powder clouds would engulf the camp, blocking out the sun and causing total darkness inside the buildings for a short time. Avalanche incidents have forever branded the early days of the Bobbie Burns with a notorious reputation.

Once, Colani was guiding and Conrad and Robson, the Gmoser sons, were along for the day. They were cruising through convoluted terrain when the slope on the opposite side of the valley released and slid far enough to bury Colani up to his knees. The Gmosers arrived in moments, but a few of the guests were nowhere to be seen! For a minute Colani and the Gmosers panicked and started back up the hill to begin a frantic search just as the others skied into view. Luckily, one had fallen and lost a ski before the slide, so they were busy digging for the lost ski in a safe place when the avalanche occurred.

Another time, Hans was skiing above guide Hans Peter "HP" Stettler's group when the slope fractured, releasing a huge slide. HP was directly downslope, but he had enough time and skill – and the slope was steep enough – to point his skis straight down the hill and tuck into the valley and far enough onto the flats to outrun the slide. The rest of his group was in the middle of the hill when it avalanched, but luckily part of the slab never picked up much speed, so some skiers were left perched on blocks while others fell between them. No one was hurt, but shortly afterwards HP changed careers and never went back to guiding.

Finally, the guides decided this base camp was a little too close to the action, so in December, before the ski season began, a group of modular trailers was brought in to the main valley to serve as base camp. For one season the trailers were home to the Bobbie Burns skiers, and the next year, 1981, CMH built the current lodge. In the early nineties, another danger threatened the lodge – economic recession. The Bobbie Burns was not selling well, so the manager, Bruce Howatt, encouraged CMH to drop the number of groups to three, and inadvertently created the fastest-paced ski program of any of the non-private CMH areas. Now the lodge is one of the first to fill and is a favourite among aggressive skiers. Marion Kingsbury summarizes the modern Bobbie Burns ski program: "It's not so much that you have to be good to ski here, but you need to be fit and fast. The Bobbie Burns is for people who want to ski!"

It's no coincidence that most of the CMH areas are found between the first two lodges, the Bugaboo and the Cariboo. Hans explained, "It was mostly flying between the Bugaboos and the Cariboos. It is a long flight, and most of it is over ski terrain. By the time we were thinking of expanding, we knew what was out there."

In the early seventies, access and accommodation trumped snowfall and terrain, and a man named Roger Madsen ran a business that took people skiing with a plane out of Radium, a small town just south of the Bugaboos. CMH had more skiers than space, so a brief collaboration ensued between CMH and Madsen, called Bugaboo-Radium Heli-skiing.

Madsen was a maverick during the most cowboy days of the profession. Long before heli-hiking, he had invented heli-golf. In the off-season he occasionally threw parties for his friends where the helicopter was the golf cart and patches of tundra scattered throughout the southern Purcells were the course. Madsen's heli-golf was never a business concept, but rather just a spectacular way to have a raging golf party in the mountains.

A series of plane and helicopter crashes rattled Madsen's nerves, and he offered to share management of the area with Hans and his established Canadian Mountain Holidays team, so Bob Geber took over management of Bugaboo-Radium Heli-skiing. While the ski terrain of the southern Purcells is huge, remote and varied – nearly ideal for heli-skiing – the area sits in the rain shadow of the Columbias and gets significantly less snow than the mountains just to the north and west. The winter of 1977/78 was especially dry and heli-skiing out of Radium was out of the question. The CMH brochure had advertised the Bugaboo-Radium option, skiers had already booked spaces and the only thing lacking was the one crucial ingredient: snow.

A young guide named Buck Corrigan was nervous about his job with no snow to sustain it, so he and Geber approached Hans for advice on what to do. Corrigan said, "Hans asked us, 'How long has it been since you've seen your parents at Christmas? Just go home and come back afterwards. There is always snow in Revelstoke. We can do something there.'"

Hans had explored the heli-ski potential of the Selkirks and Monashees on either side of town as early as 1970, so when he sent Geber and Corrigan over Rogers Pass to find a place with snow, Hans wasn't just shooting in the dark. Lodging was the first issue, and just by chance Geber walked into the Regent Inn and struck up conversation with the manager, a skier named Fred Beruschi. "We hit it off right away," remembers Geber. "Freddy was enthusiastic about the skiing in the area. I went and checked out some other places (hotels), but kept coming back to the Regent to eat."

When ski season arrived, CMH based out of the Regent Inn, and Geber and Corrigan led the skiers into the unknown nooks and crannies of the Selkirk and Monashee mountains on either side of Revelstoke. Remembers Geber, "It was a bit of a culture shock for Revelstoke to have a heli-ski company in town. On the local radio in the morning they would say, 'Good morning, heli-skiers!'"

In 2007 a ski resort opened just outside of town that will boast some of the most sustained fall-lines and the most vertical in North America – 1845 metres, or over 6,000 feet – once all the lifts are in place, and the town is buzzing with an infusion of money and energy. In the seventies, the place was little more than a rough logging and mining village on the Canadian Pacific Railway, so suddenly having the word's rich and famous walking the streets was earth-shaking. One group to arrive that winter included Princess Birgitta of Sweden with her entourage of personal ski instructors. In preparation for the visit from royalty, Hans told Geber, "If we can show her a good time, maybe the king will come." The week began with terrible weather, and after the second day of no skiing, the princess asked Geber, "What do you have in store for us tomorrow?"

To this impossible question Geber replied, "I don't know, but next door they have exotic dancing."

"I guess the boys would like that," said the princess.

The Peeler strip club is right next door to the Regent, and even today it is a legendary part of the Revelstoke ski experience. When Beruschi heard of Geber's plan he said, "You can't take the princess to a strip show!"

To which Geber said, "Aw, come on, some good Canadian lumberjack culture would be good."

"What would Hans think?"

"He wouldn't care, so long as she had a good time."

That night Geber went to the club with the princess, her two personal ski instructors, her brother-in-law and a German baroness. The next day Geber suggested the princess ski first down a run that had never been skied and named the run after her. Later, the King of Sweden did visit, so Geber's tour of Revelstoke nightlife and skiing must have received rave reviews from the princess. It is not known whether the king checked out The Peeler.

While Geber was the first manager of CMH Revelstoke, it was Corrigan who put it on the map. "Buck was the real pioneer around here," remembers Beruschi. "There is nobody who knows these mountains better than Buck."

Corrigan took over management of CMH Revelstoke and never looked back. The skiing is a little farther from town than the remote lodges based in the centre of skiing wonderlands, so it took a long time to explore the entirety of the area. Corrigan remembers, "The first ten years were the most fun. We were always finding new runs. It was a riot."

Although the world is only just beginning to figure it out, in many ways Revelstoke is the snow-sport epicentre of North America. Nearby Mt. Fidelity is home to the snowiest weather station in Canada: it receives the country's highest annual average accumulation, 1471 centimetres, and the peak gets 144 days of snowfall per year, more than anywhere else in the country. The coastal areas have more precipitation, but it often falls as rain or heavy snow and doesn't pile up with the feathery depth of Revelstoke powder.

Historically, every two decades another recreational user group discovers Revelstoke. Rogers Pass, an hour's drive into the Selkirks to the east, has been a mecca for backcountry skiers since the fifties. Then, in the seventies, heli-skiers discovered Revelstoke's snowy phenomenon, and snowmobilers, or "sledders" as the modern incarnation call themselves, discovered the area's vast and deep powder fields in the nineties. As of 2008, the word Revelstoke is circulating through lift lines and ski-area bars around the globe. The next decade will likely see the town become a household name among downhill skiers, and change the place forever.

An economic slump in the early eighties put CMH on the brink of bankruptcy, but by the end of the decade the future of heli-skiing had regained a rosy colour, and Hans's motivation to expand and accommodate more people continued with conviction. Walter Bruns, the director of operations, Mark Kingsbury and Hans Gmoser moved quickly to open new terrain to meet demand, and in just four years CMH started operations in three new areas. In 1987 available ski tenures were becoming few and far between. To avoid speculation and the possible leak of a new area, Hans secretly studied topo maps of the area between the Revelstoke tenure and the Monashee tenure, then drove around the logging roads to see as much as the view from the valley bottoms could reveal before chartering a plane for a day to see it all from the air. The research convinced him of the skiing potential in the region, and without telling anyone in his office, he applied for the heli-ski tenure to everything between the Revelstoke and Monashee terrains to the north and south, and everything between the great bend of the Columbia River where it turns from north to south. A modern mine near the confluence of the Goldstream River and the Columbia had adequate lodging, so CMH purchased a couple of ramshackle buildings from the mining operation.

The original Gothics lodge was the tackiest heli-ski base in history. Pink metal pillars and modular bedroom wings were connected by a hallway of plywood so long the staff would leave bicycles at either end to more quickly move through the claustrophobic tunnel. Today the pink pillars are long gone and the long plywood tunnel has been replaced with a glass hallway, a spa and an exercise and meeting room.

The Gothics are home to the longest named run in CMH tenure, Endless Journey, a 7,500-vertical-foot odyssey from the top of a peak at the head of Horne Creek. The biggest possible ski run in CMH is lost in history with the recession of glaciers, but according to legend, at one time 8,500-vertical-foot runs were skied in the Cariboos, and equally long runs are still possible. Today however, adventures down long descents are out of fashion, and fall lines are more important than exploration, so these long runs would be more of a ski tour than a fall-line ski run. The Gothics is also home to the most famous run in CMH tenure, Run of the Century. While skiing Century is a feather in the cap of any heli-skier, the guides will tell you there are better runs in the area, like the mind-blowing Downie Left, which has a lesser name but a better fall line for much longer. Indeed, the Gothics are all about skiing on stunning features. Many runs start on the very summit of a peak, and the mountain range itself is a testament to natural symmetry. From high viewpoints, perfect ridgelines recede into the distance, each the same angle and size, each with a perfectly pyramidal peak at the top.

The skiing in the Gothics is as diverse as it gets. Roger Atkins, creator of the Snow-base database used by CMH to track snowpack, animal habitat and other mountain issues, says, "The real judge of a heli-ski area is the skiing that's available in poor conditions." In this sense, the Gothics is one of the best. When only one elevation or aspect offers good or safe skiing, the options for high pickups are numerous and it is easy for guides to find fun skiing away from the big features that can send avalanches running up the opposite side of the valleys. And when conditions are stable, the options are limitless. The vast snow ocean of the Ruddock Creek drainage alone could keep an army of heli-skiers busy for days. Undulating alpine terrain drops into friendly glades and ends with the huge tree run of Cougar's Milk. Even today in guide meetings, discussions of new runs are frequent and nearly every year new runs are added to the run list.

The area not only is versatile for times of poor stability but also is uniquely suited for skiing with groups of mixed abilities. Mellow lines suitable for weaker skiers can be found right alongside steep runs that will steam the goggles of the most skilled. Big glacier runs with views of the impressive Gothics Range are easy enough for neophyte powder skiers, and nearby, the powder pocket of Marshmallow is considered a favourite run among CMH staff, who find the numerous terrain features a playground for snowboard aerials.

With the opening of the Adamants lodge in 1990, the area was split in two, with the Gothics severed by the tenure division from their namesake peaks and glaciers, which are now in the Adamants terrain, but Adamants and Gothics groups are known to poach each other's runs, since it is all part of CMH terrain.

Partly because of the mountains, and partly because of the energetic leadership of Claude Duchesne, the charismatic French-Canadian area manager, and Ian Campbell before him, the Gothics have developed a loyal following. Duchesne was working in the mine when he learned how much more fun the staff was having at the heli-ski lodge next door. He decided to get his guide's ticket and, as fate would have it, ended up managing the lodge years later. Guest Christian Gmoser (no relation to Hans) has made the trip from Finland to ski over a million feet in the Gothics. When the lodge was renovated in 2006, Christian travelled from Finland to pitch in with the remodel. By leaving the bar, dining room and kitchen wing separated from the sleeping quarters, skiers who want the après ski to last all night can carry on without disturbing those who want an early, quiet night in the northern Selkirks. "It's the best party lodge in CMH!" says Duchesne proudly.

Mark Taggart, a skier from Colorado who has sampled most of the Columbias' runs, remembers the Gothics as a combination of big snows and good parties. "When we arrived we'd reach down out of the window of the room to put our beers in the snow to keep them cool. By the end of the week it snowed so much we were reaching up out of the window to put our beers in the snow!"

THE MOST FAMOUS SKI RUN IN THE
COLUMBIAS: RUN OF THE CENTURY.

In the morning, with or without hangovers, it is time to go skiing. When conditions are good, the Gothics are still ripe for exploration. The big symmetrical peaks hide untouched valleys, and guides await the right group of strong skiers during a period of good stability with a big snowpack to discover terrain that has never been touched by a skier.

A ski guide sees tracks where no one has been, and even in the late eighties the CMH guides still had a vast horizon studded with unexplored ski terrain to choose from. By this point, the team had developed a deep understanding for what made for a smooth operation. Consistent snowpack, varied options for bad-weather flying and skiing, the thickness of the forest, the shape of the high peaks and the condition of the glaciers all made the difference between down days and powder days.

Skiers were crying for more heli-ski spaces, and there was unclaimed heli-ski terrain in the southern Selkirks, but the mountains there were unlike the other areas. The convoluted peaks that have become known as Galena are generally steep, rockier than the rest of the Columbias, heavily forested below treeline and exposed and steep above treeline. While the guides saw enough potential in the area to pay for the Crown-land tenure and build a lodge, the CMH management decided to build a less expensive lodge in case the area failed to attract skiers in the same numbers as the other areas.

"At the time, we thought we'd come across the perfect template for the future of heli-ski lodges," remembers the head of CMH marketing, Marty Von Neudegg. "Mark

(Kingsbury) and I thought we were so damn brilliant in the simplicity and economics of the design – and now we'd like to replace it."

Galena was the first remote lodge to be built since the Bobbie Burns, and was a significant departure from the design of the other three CMH lodges. The modular architecture is tastefully trimmed in logs and painted an earth brown, so the lodge avoids the trailer-park look, but the sleeping quarters are a string of ready-made dormitory modules attached to a simple three-storey living area and kitchen. Because the bedrooms were built at ground level, strong slats had to be retrofitted over windows to keep snow avalanches off the roof from smashing through the windows.

The Galena lodge is comfortable but utilitarian, and it feels more like a summer camp than a luxurious ski lodge, but there are no guest complaints and Hans needn't have doubted its popularity. Once skiers discovered the adventures waiting in Galena, the name became synonymous with technical skiing through old-growth forests in over-the-head powder. Now, a new lodge for Galena is on the drawing board. Some guests, however, have grown quite attached to the original building. A skier named Greenie, henchman of the hard-partying Australian group that invades Galena every year for the early season, has visited the other lodges but prefers Galena in part for the lodge's atmosphere. "I like this lodge best," he says with conviction. "I like the other lodges too, but they feel like resorts. This feels like a clubhouse – my ski clubhouse."

But even if CMH does build a new lodge at Galena, Greenie and his rowdy crew of surfers from Down Under will likely still make it home each December for one reason: they are utterly addicted to the skiing. If the Cariboos is proof that Mother Nature is a skier, Galena is proof that she is a skier with a twisted sense of humour. Most of the runs are Tolkien-meets-Dr.-Seuss epics through convoluted forests over plentiful pillow drops, and down ever-steepening faces. The trees, heavily laden with the tenacious snow of the southern Selkirks, take on personalities of all shapes and sizes.

Geology is at the heart of all ski terrain, but Galena's namesake and unique skiing is all about rock. Galena is a mineral, a crystal of lead sulfide, and the Galena ski tenure is along a heavily mined fault line between sedimentary and metamorphic zones that is generally younger than the rest of the Columbia Mountains. Geologists describe the area as "highly deformed," and skiers who've been there would agree. Miners took advantage of the exposed folds of stone to access gold and silver veins starting in the 1890s, and today their mineshafts are another hazard for skiers to avoid. The same forces of folding that reveal mineral-rich mines left mountainsides shaggy with millions of small cliffs yet to be smoothed by the powers of erosion. Add an annual snowfall of 18 metres and you get what Derek Marcinyshyn, a four-year Galena guide, calls "the best terrain park on the planet!"

John Byrnes, a die-hard Galena fan, describes a misadventure getting around a cliff on a run near Pair-a-Dice:

> But where in the hell am I supposed to go? Murray takes about 13 metres of
> air and lands it. After a totally immature celebration of the event, Fin manages
> to duplicate it. Shit. I'm stuck up here. Murray yells to go left. I thruch for

about ten minutes, but the smaller cliff he's aiming me at is ugly with rocks and trees and stumps sticking out, and is still eight or nine metres high. Finally Murray points out a small chute with trees growing in it. I commit to it, and start sidestepping down. I'm basically down-climbing this thing by lowering myself branch to branch like Tarzan. My skis are 190 cm, and the chute is a bit narrower than that and about 50 degrees. After stepping past a pongee-stump, I can finally jump in the air, pivot my skis downhill and take the final three-metre drop. I rated it 5.4 (a rock-climbing grade).

This is not the place to stand at the bottom of a run and admire your perfect tracks. Most of the time you look back and see three or four turns – or one. It's not only the trees; the undulating terrain prevents the picturesque but somehow homogeneous "heli-spooning" so common in other areas, where each skier lays their track right next to the track before them. To ski safely in Galena, skiers are expected to take on a bit more responsibility for their skiing than in areas where the guides can more often watch the skiers as they descend. Many runs descend truncated ribs, narrow ridges that split into two or more ridgelines with steep faces in between. Imagine following the edge of a massive pyramid that is cleaved off partway down the edge, leaving two edges. A skier who chooses a trajectory one degree different from the group on top can end up on the wrong edge, leading to an entirely different side of the mountain and ending at the bottom of the valley several kilometres away from the rest of the skiers. In microcosm the same holds true: skiing left of a tree island can be easy, while to the right is a morass of jagged boulders and big drops.

Galena terrain brings the best out of guides and guests. The guides typically explain the run from the top and point out the pickup and specific hazards before disappearing from sight in a ball of swirling snow crystals. It would be easy to mistake their hell-bent blast to the next strategic stopping spot as irresponsible, but in fact their reasoning is just the opposite.

Roger Atkins, a veteran Galena guide and a survivor of nearly every pitfall that can happen to a heli-skier, explained the reason for skiing with minimal delays: "If we stop frequently, people end up blowing past us in the trees, the group gets below me and the fall lines become harder to follow. If something goes wrong there's not much we can do in this deep snow except get a ride back to the top and descend again. If there is an issue, by waiting around in the trees we're just wasting time."

Guides in every area use the same strategy – and skiers encounter truncated ribs and deceptive terrain in heli-ski venues all around the world – but the volume of rugged terrain at Galena is unsurpassed. It is evident in the very bones and muscles of the Galena guides. During CMH guide training, an occupational therapist named Delia Roberts spends each evening giving therapy advice for specific ailments. On the night she announced, "Back issues will be the topic of the evening, so anyone with back issues raise their hands," all the Galena guides' hands shot up.

The spine pays the price for the mandatory drops that are the name of the game in Galena skiing. The terrain catches even the most veteran guides by surprise. Rock crevasses lurk in the forests and are traps of a sinister kind once they are buried in midwinter snows. Cliffs that seem benign from above turn out to be huge, and tempting rollovers reveal massive air.

"You ski over four of those things and it's a fun little rollover," says Galena guide Bernie Wiatzka with his eyes widening. "Then you ski over the fifth one – and it's a cliff!"

"It's the most challenging place to guide of all the CMH areas," another guide claims. Of course, the most difficult place to guide is the one with the worst conditions on any particular day, but even the easiest day at Galena holds a whole lot of question marks.

Just a year after the Galena opening, CMH divided their huge Gothics tenure roughly in half and built a lodge with a view to rival even the iconic Bugaboo lodge setting: the Adamants lodge, located near the head of the Goldstream River in the heart of some of the most rugged mountains in North America. When it opened in 1990 it was the most luxurious of the CMH lodges and set the standard for future development, but like the other CMH areas, the lodge is dramatically overshadowed by the surrounding mountains.

If a major highway crossed the Adamants, resorts would dot the area's phenomenal scenery, five-star hotels would be built on the most spectacular viewpoints, YouTube would have thousands of clips of the scenery, and the Adamants would join Yosemite, Chamonix and the Bugaboos as one of the most famous mountain areas in the world. Even when compared to the famous Bugaboos, the Adamants is the most precipitous area in the Columbias, but because the logging roads end shy of reasonable automobile access, much of the area remains exclusively the realm of heli-sport. Thousand-metre rock faces have yet to be climbed, massive cliffs have never been touched and skyscraper-sized spires are not even named.

The skiing and climbing in the area owes much of its exploration to the manager of the Adamants lodge, Erich Unterberger. The Austrian ski racer is famous for his enthusiasm for skiing and climbing and is another of the CMH guides whose athletic prowess is hidden beneath his professional persona. At 18 he became the youngest person at the time to climb the infamous north face of the Eiger in Switzerland. In the spring when the sun bakes the snow into velvety corn, he's been known to set gates on the glaciers for a few runs of heli-slalom. When the snow melts from the faces, he welcomes any and all climbers to the area and has been part of dozens of first ascents, ranging from easy ridges anyone could climb to the most difficult rock climbs in the area.

In the Adamants, it is the summer, when the snow melts off the vertical walls that form a surreal backdrop to the ski season, that demonstrates perfectly why the helicopter is the ideal tool for modern mountain exploration. The cliffs virtually enclose some valleys like the walls of a castle, and with the helicopter, hikers can explore the impenetrable gorges and climbers can scale the sheer walls and exposed ridges. The area is essentially a private Chamonix, a mountain-sport paradise for CMH guests and guides. On the eastern edge of the Adamants tenure, the Fairy Meadows hut serves as a base for skiers and climbers, but the sheer walls to the west keep even the most adventurous climbers and skiers out of the heart of the CMH Adamants terrain.

There is perhaps no other CMH area that is better suited to the vast potential of future heli-sport. Steep couloirs splitting faces of black stone have yet to be skied, and countless first ascents await adventurous climbers with enough cash to pay for the helicopter access. The Adamants guides are quietly waiting for the right guests to truly explore the area's climbing and skiing potential. In many ways, the summer is the future of the business. "The biggest potential for growth in our company is the summer season," explains Unterberger. "There are way more people who can do it."

While Unterberger loves the skiing and climbing as much as anyone, the motivation that keeps him in the Adamants has little to do with chasing his own adrenaline fix. He explains: "I'm intrigued by Hans's vision of the mountains and what brings people into the mountains and what the mountains can do for people. I draw inspiration from the how Hans saw the world."

Today, Unterberger sees the next generation of guides in the Adamants learning from the same things Hans used as teachers – the mountains themselves – and pushing the profession to continue to grow. "Hans had this way of putting you in your place, but not directly from him. He let the mountains show you. He never put himself above you, but he challenged you to do the most you could with what you had. I learned a lot from Hans, but now I have guides here that inspire me just as much. They come in with glowing eyes and see things Hans and I might not have seen."

In the mid-seventies, without any organized business effort, a group of skiers started leading heli-ski tours based out of the lakeside village of Nakusp, a sleepy town perched on the shore of the Columbia River where it is dammed into the 65-kilometre length of Upper Arrow Lake. For years, Kootenay, as the outfit was called, was arguably the most laid-back heli-ski operation in the country. Ken France, the current area manager, remembers the lawless days of Kootenay heli-skiing: "The guide pack (typically full of rescue gear) meant a six-pack of beer and a carton of smokes," he says with a smile weathered from thousands of days in the sun and millions of face shots.

The operation was run by a tight group of guides who learned their mountains as well as anyone has ever learned a mountain range. While the other heli-ski operations jockeyed for customers and reputation, Kootenay guides were content to just go skiing and the area maintained a low-key reputation and developed a loyal following of guests who loved the area, the steep Kootenay terrain and the après ski soaks in the area's famous hot springs.

Part of the guiding program in Nakusp is a close relationship with the nearby backcountry ski huts. One of the touring huts, Sol Mountain, is in the heart of the southern Monashees. Each morning, the Kootenay guides talk to one of the Sol Mountain guides, who is standing in the very snow the heli-skiers hope to ski. This way, the heli-ski guides learn exactly what flying and skiing conditions will be like in the committing Monashee terrain, and the touring guides learn what the heli-ski guides know from the vast network of information exchange and real-time weather information available online.

In the world of heli-sport, 1995 was the end of an era. Hans Gmoser completed a smooth retirement from the business by selling CMH to Alpine Helicopters. The entirety of the Columbia Mountains had become a jigsaw puzzle of heli- and cat-skiing tenures. The days of pulling out a map to circle a vast tract of ski terrain, then building a lodge and asking the government for permission later were long gone.

So a year later, when CMH president Mark Kingsbury had the chance to acquire the established local heli-ski business, Kootenay Heli-skiing, CMH purchased the business, with the Kuskanax Hotel for a base camp, and opened the 11th CMH area. Ken France describes the transition: "It was difficult at first because we were proud of what we had and didn't want anyone to tell us what to do, but it couldn't have been bought by better people. It (CMH) was an organization run by skiers."

With the Galena tenure right next door, Kingsbury knew Kootenay was a motherlode. Not only are there the nearly endless options of the southern Selkirks, but the tenure also includes the southern part of the Monashees on the other side of Upper Arrow Lake for those days when stability and weather are perfect and the big alpine terrain around Monashee Lake Provincial Park can be skied. Located between the Monashees and the Selkirks, Nakusp is a natural heli-ski base.

With ski terrain a commodity in western Canada, one flight over the Kootenay region will reveal why Kingsbury moved quickly to add Kootenay to the CMH web of ski paradise. "The difference between the steep skiing here and the steep skiing in Alaska," proclaimed one guest from Anchorage, "is that in Alaska you can see the steep runs because there are no trees. In the Kootenay we ski just as steep, but it doesn't look so steep because it is all in the forest."

According to Roko Koell, "The most stimulating skiing in CMH tenure is in Galena (just across Trout Lake from Kootenay), but the most bang for the buck, with straight fall lines and fast pickups, is Kootenay." The nature of Kootenay skiing is exemplified in the guy who had "Big Air" written on his skis instead of his name like everyone else to keep them straight in the transition in and out of the helicopter. After a few days, another skier asked him, "Why do you have 'Big Air' written on your skis? Do you like to jump?"

"Last year, I went off a 150-foot cliff," Big Air replied.

"Yeah, right."

"I spent days in the hospital and months in rehab."

"Oh," responded the skeptic, "and you still do this?"

"I love this shit. It's what I live for."

The Kootenay region is a maze of ridges with few taller peaks, reminiscent of Utah's Wasatch Range on steroids. Hundreds of pointed summits dot the horizon with steep faces on all sides. Daniel Zimmerman, an eight-year Kootenay guide from Switzerland, describes the Selkirks as "the kind of mountains shaped like children would draw."

The famous ski areas of Snowbird and Alta are almost indistinguishable from the surrounding backcountry, indicating minimal tree cutting was necessary to create a ski resort compared to the famous resorts in Colorado and other areas where many runs are virtually clear-cuts in thick forest. Likewise, the Kootenay region could be home to dozens of massive ski resorts, and not a single tree would have to be cut to make fantastic runs. CMH claims 230 runs, but the number is utterly irrelevant. The names are for reference rather than indicating any sort of boundary between the runs. There are hundreds that have never been skied, and it could just as accurately be said that the Kootenay region is one big ski run.

Zimmerman has observed that when guides from other areas work in the Kootenay, "they are always pointing at things and asking, 'What's that?' and I say, 'We never ski that.' And they are blown away that we don't ski such awesome-looking features. We just don't need to. There is so much terrain."

Some areas can become skied out during periods without fresh snow, but in Kootenay "skied out" is an unused phrase. Features like the huge Empress Bowl beg to be skied again and again. A frequent Kootenay guest remembers his group counting a thousand tracks down Empress Bowl by the end of a day. The southern Kootenay ski terrain takes time to learn. There are few big peaks to stand out as landmarks in the middle of the tenure, and every face of every ridge appears to be the best ski run around. A typical day includes so many different valleys that all but the most seasoned Kootenay skiers become lost within the maze of ridges and valleys.

After a dizzying day of skiing in Kootenay, the powderfest ends with a flight down Kuskanax Creek. Gazing out the window of the helicopter on the last flight is always meditative and gives time to reflect on the snow-soaked experience while appreciating the phenomenon of helicopter flight. Looking straight down into the powder-laden forest is an optical treat that verges on the hallucinatory. Trees appear to move from side to side as the machine flies overhead, their apparent motion caused by the subtle speed of the helicopter constantly changing the angle of view. While descending the Kuskanax, gazing into the depths of the forest below, you can see the hypnotic patterns suddenly interrupted by the sight of a large semicircular hot tub and upturned human faces peering out of the steaming water of the Kuskanax Hot Springs amidst the miles of frozen forest, and thus begins the most unique part of the Kootenay heli-ski experience. Before the lactic acid has even had a chance to settle into your thighs, you peel off wet ski gear and step into the therapeutic waters of the naturally heated spring. Because the springs are positioned several kilometres into the forested valley of Kuskanax Creek, it feels like part of the heli-ski day, not something that happens afterwards. For those who like soaking in hot water as part of their ski day, the complete Kootenay ski experience is utterly narcotic.

A short van ride back into town brings the skiers, drunk on deep powder and hot water, back to earth. Some of the Kootenay skiing is close enough to civilization that some of the terrain is visible on the high-resolution sectors of Google Earth maps. Zoom in above the Kuskanax Hot Springs and the undeniable symmetry of ski tracks can be seen slicing through a snow-covered meadow.

In the early eighties, the CMH marketing slogan was "The best, the most difficult, the most expensive skiing in the world." The campaign likely scared away at least as many skiers as it attracted, but one group, four skiers led by a French ski guide from Val d'Isère named Ary Dedet, came looking for the most difficult skiing in the world and found themselves unsatisfied with the pace of the skiing during their week in the Cariboos. Dedet was a private ski guide who had been leading groups in the

Alps, including heli-skiing, until heli-skiing was forbidden by the French government in 1981. In looking for a place with unlimited ski freedom, he found CMH and the Columbias and began organizing ski groups to visit the area.

While the Cariboos was expensive, his group was trained on the steep terrain of the Alps and instead of savouring the expected "most difficult skiing in the world," they spent a lot of time standing around waiting for the group ahead of them. Dedet explained, "The guide was upset with us because we kept passing him as he slowed down for the next group. We told him we just can't ski this slow."

The guide was Reinhardt Frankensteiner, and the conversation about staying within the confines of the skiing program continued all week. Near the end, Dedet told Reinhardt, "My group wants to stay an extra week, but not with a regular group."

According to Dedet, Reinhardt responded, "CMH doesn't do private groups." Dedet kept asking about the possibilities, so Reinhardt suggested Dedet contact CMH's main competition, Mike Wiegele in Blue River. After a single phone call, Mike was happy to arrange a private tour for the French skiers. Reinhardt called Hans to share the developments, and Hans told him, "CMH doesn't do private groups." Then, according to Dedet, Reinhardt said, "Wiegele said he'd do it."

When Hans heard he was about to lose the group to Wiegele, the issue quickly changed from a hassle to an opportunity lost to his most motivated competitor. Hans quickly called Dedet in the Cariboos. Dedet remembers Hans first asking, "You asked Wiegele?"

Dedet replied, "Yes."

"He said okay?"

"Yes."

"What do you want?"

"A private helicopter with Reinhardt guiding all week."

"What did Wiegele say it would cost?"

"It was something like $20,000," remembers Dedet, "and Hans said okay."

The next week Dedet got his wish and Reinhardt got the chance to go back to his roots of mountain guiding with a group of four skiers. With only a single group of skiers to consider, the program became much closer to ski mountaineering guiding judgment than the program Reinhardt was now accustomed to while leading 44 skiers around the Cariboos. Dedet remembers Reinhardt having as much fun as the skiers: "After he got comfortable with the group, we did a run where Reinhardt took out a rope and lowered us over a cornice at the top. He was so excited at one point he forgot his pack on top."

In classic Gmoser style, Hans passed the torch of leadership of the private programs quickly. To promote the new idea, he turned to Marty Von Neudegg, and as Marty remembers, "I think he already knew what to do, but he asked me what I thought we should do with smaller groups in Valemount."

Hans also went to the Cariboos with the guide he was grooming to be his successor as leader of CMH, Mark Kingsbury, to recruit a couple of guides as leaders of the private program. Danny Stoffel and Stefan Eder were in the Cariboos when Hans and Mark arrived. Stoffel remembers Hans coming up to the two guides and saying bluntly, "We want to talk to you two after dinner."

Stoffel and Eder looked at each other and immediately thought they were in trouble. Both had been involved in minor near misses over the previous few weeks, and Stoffel remembers, "It was a painful dinner – we were shitting ourselves."

After dinner, they met with Hans and Mark and were pleasantly surprised to find that, instead of a lashing, they were asked to lead a new private program based in Valemount. Stoffel remembers Hans concluding the conversation by saying, "It's up to you guys now. You can make it or break it."

The winter of 1987 was the maiden voyage for the first official private group, and they based out of the Alpine Inn in Valemount. Since then, the private areas of Valemount, McBride and Silvertip have developed comfortable lodging to go along with the steep price tags of nearly $150,000 for a week of skiing with ten skiers. The Alpine Inn was a far cry from the sort of lodging the wealthy skiers were accustomed to, though. Danny Stoffel laughs heartily in describing the lodging: "Each season we would convert one bedroom into a dining room, one bedroom into a living room, one bedroom into an office and one bedroom into a kitchen. A bathroom was converted into a walk-in cooler. We built a contraption over the toilet so you couldn't see it. At the end of each season we'd take it all apart and put it back together the next year."

Dedet found the skiing his clients wanted and started booking weeks right away, regardless of the lodging. The lodging was utterly irrelevant – it was all about the skiing. He remembers, "It was so funny to see these rich people spending so much money to spend their holidays in a third-rate motel. They would have never stayed in such a place except to go skiing!"

And according to Stoffel, the Alpine Inn was not only third rate, but beat up as well: "The deck on the hotel was slanted and after a few drinks it got even worse. There were cracks under the doors so big that after a windy night we'd have huge snowdrifts in our rooms."

They used a beat-up van to reach the helipad, and one day a wheel fell off, leaving the skiers stranded on the side of the road. Stoffel laughs remembering how the incident ended when "the cops drove us so we could go heli-skiing!"

Since then, the private tours have grown in popularity and are based from comfortable lodges exclusively used by skiers, and Valemount is booked years ahead with a waiting list for every week of the season.

With the freedom that goes with guiding a single group, Eder and Stoffel were able to range far from the base in Valemount. Eder explored the vast alpine peaks and remote valleys to the north and returned with reports of excellent ski terrain – enough to accommodate an entirely new operation. When the demand for the private experience exceeded Valemount's capacity, CMH president Mark Kingsbury asked guide Dave Cochrane to organize a single-group ski program out of McBride, a town with a population of 700 situated along the banks of the Fraser River near the northern limits of the Cariboo Mountains.

While the skiing is plentiful and the area is one of the biggest of the CMH heli-ski tenures, it took several years to arrange comfortable lodging. In 1992 Cochrane was managing a chaotic mix of sleeping in rooms at a roadside hotel, walking across the highway to eat, and even renting a lodge from a new heli-ski operation named Crescent Spur Heli-Skiing during the spring. Guide Kevin Christakos remembers one group of Austrian skiers that arrived in McBride expecting a remote mountain lodge, only to find the in-town lodging did not suit them at all. Before even tasting the skiing, they left, and Christakos remembers one of the skiers saying haughtily as he left, "We can be skiing the Arlberg by Tuesday."

With a suddenly vacant week, Christakos and fellow guide Greg Yavorski went out the next day to flag landings and pickups. Christakos recalls the two of them flying into the mountains on "a beautiful, cold, blue-sky morning." They flew over a shoulder of Roberts Peak where they had never skied before and saw a steep, wooded line where a fire had thinned the forest that promised good skiing. Christakos explains what they found: "It was steep tree skiing and the snow was just cold smoke. When we got to the bottom we figured we better name the run, so we called it Better than the Arlberg."

While Valemount is booked years ahead with a waiting list in case of cancellations, McBride, less than an hour's drive to the north, is booked only during the high season of February and March. An Italian skier named Andre, who has skied both areas, explained what he sees as the difference between the two: "The skiing is the same, the guides are great in both areas. The only difference is, there (Valemount) the lodge is in the woods and here (McBride) it is in town."

Due to the vastness of the area, McBride is suitable only for a single group of skiers. The flying time between the different areas would make it impossible for the larger-lodge, four-group program, as each group would spend more time waiting for the helicopter than skiing. For guiding and skiing, the area offers an experience unlike any of the other CMH areas. Christakos explains, "That's what makes it fun for guiding – it's such a huge, expansive area."

And for skiing, there is still opportunity for exploration. The bread and butter areas of McBride are the thousand-metre tree runs of the remote and pristine Betty Wendle Creek drainage and the alpine descents of Castle Creek that Christakos describes as a "land of rock walls, cornices and big terrain where you feel super small." But there are new areas to explore in the vast McBride tenure. During February of 2008, Christakos was excited by the already fat snowpack. With a gleam in his eye he said, "I expect to ski lines this year that have never been skied before."

The last area to be added to the CMH empire is also the most unusual. In the late nineties a private fishing lodge called Silvertip on the eastern edge of 100-kilometre-long Quesnel Lake caught Mark Kingsbury's eye – for good reason. Quesnel Lake is the deepest fjord lake in the world, and the double A-frame lodge is located at the end of the most remote arm of Quesnel, where it reaches deep into the Cariboo Mountains from the western side of the range. Guide Anjen Truffer describes the area: "For people who are looking for the true Canada – this is it." Even in the summer, a float plane or boat is necessary to reach the Silvertip lodge, located 72 kilometres along the lakeshore from the nearest road. As a ski destination, Silvertip is unrivalled for remoteness, but it is sandwiched between Wells Gray Provincial Park and Cariboo Mountains Provincial

Park, and thus a lot of the most appealing terrain in the area is off limits to heli-skiers. When Kingsbury purchased the lodge to use as a heli-ski base, his hope, according to other guides who followed the acquisition, was that some day the terrain would be opened to heli-skiing. According to Willy Trinker, the manager of CMH Silvertip, Mark's original idea was to begin offering remote fly-fishing as part of the CMH program. "When Mark died," explains Trinker, "the whole thing (flyfishing tours) kind of fell in the water." For now, the area is only practical for a single private group and they often ski in the western edge of the vast CMH McBride terrain.

As an experience, Trinker calls Silvertip, "the hidden little secret of CMH." It is the least popular of any of the dozen CMH heli-ski areas, but it offers something no other CMH area can. Trinker explains: "It is the most like the original CMH. It is so remote it's hard to imagine. One group even told me after they left that they had a great time but it was too remote for them."

Indeed, while all the lodges are in the wilderness, Silvertip has the aura of being entirely off the map. With a single group of skiers at any one time, in an area so remote that the nearest neighbor is the Cariboo lodge on the other side of the Columbias, Silvertip feels the most like the original heli-skiing days in the Bugaboos. "It's a grizzly-on-the-lawn kind of wilderness," says Trinker. "Once a lady went for a walk along the lake, and when she came back she told the staff, 'I didn't know you had a dog up here. It has the most beautiful yellow eyes.'

"'That's no dog,' someone replied. 'You saw a timber wolf.'"

Today the private lodges attract groups who want the exclusivity of having a lodge and staff to themselves, but in the beginning, and for many groups today, the sole reason for the private lodge is the most basic of all. As Ary Dedet explained, "It is all about the skiing."

When Hans, Leo and company built each of the lodges and developed the skiing, they made them parts of a single business, but then they hired committed individuals and gave them the freedom to run each area as their own. Today, each area is run by a radically different team, has a different skiing personality and geography, and an entirely different flavour. Roko Koell, who works in almost every area each winter and moves around weekly, says: "It's like being in a different country every week."

The collective entity that is Canadian Mountain Holidays is as multi-faceted as a bad snowpack. Hans's leadership style, built upon by Mark Kingsbury's touch while the industry changed, influenced this diversity by giving the area managers and staff both huge responsibility and huge freedom to treat the areas as their own. The managers ran their area with the conviction of an owner, not just an employee, from decorating the lodges to developing a skiing style, from the selections at the bar to the food in the dining room, from the fashion style of the staff to the daily schedule. By doing so, CMH became a business that offered not just one experience, but a dozen experiences to be had in different cultures of leadership and atmosphere as well as different topography.

As real estate, the CMH lodges are relatively worthless compared to their value as jumping-off points for recreation access, and as such, they will most likely remain bastions of hedonism for tight-knit groups of skiers, hikers and climbers who want to spend their careers or holidays in mountain isolation.

10
POWER TO SPARE

The helicopter, it turned out, opened a whole new, exhilarating world of possibilities that in fact promised to be ecologically feasible as well. The helicopter permitted the age-old emptiness of the wilderness to stay intact, free from the commercial hardware and gingerbread that a network of lifts would have imposed upon it.

— Hans Gmoser, from Lynne Grillmair's Bugaboos cookbook,
Gourmet in Paradise

FIRST ROW LEFT: JIM DAVIES BEHIND THE STICK OF AN OVERLOADED BELL 47 DURING THE FIRST YEARS OF HELI-SKIING.

FIRST ROW RIGHT: NANCY HOLLAND AND JIM McCONKEY EXPLORING THE HELICOPTER SKIING POTENTIAL OF THE CARIBOOS IN 1963 WITH THE BELL 47 G3-B1. THE LANDING SPOT IS MARKED WITH TREE BRANCHES.

SECOND ROW LEFT: THE SIX-PASSENGER ALOUETTE III IN 1969 TRANSPORTED ENOUGH SKIERS TO MAKE THE BUSINESS WORK, BUT THE MACHINE WAS PLAGUED WITH MECHANICAL PROBLEMS.

SECOND ROW RIGHT: THE FOUR-PASSENGER ALOUETTE II USED IN 1966.

THIRD ROW: HOLDING NINE SKIERS AND WITH BETTER PERFORMANCE THAN THE ALOUETTE III, THE BELL 204 WAS RETAINED FOR HELI-SKIING, AT PILOT JIM DAVIES'S INSISTENCE.

FOURTH ROW LEFT: A 212 WITH A BROKEN MAIN ROTOR AFTER AN ACCIDENT IN THE CARIBOOS.

FOURTH ROW RIGHT: SINCE THE EARLY SEVENTIES, THE 12-PASSENGER BELL 212 HAS BEEN THE BEST COMBINATION OF RELIABILITY, POWER AND PAYLOAD FOR CMH HELI-SKIING.

In 1886, Jules Verne, the legendary adventure writer who also introduced readers to the concept of the submarine, wrote about air travel using ships powered by rotary wings in his novel *The Clipper of the Clouds (Robur the Conqueror)*. Six years earlier, a French visionary named Alphonse Pénaud had committed suicide after a decade of frustration and ridicule while attempting to achieve vertical flight. During his short but brilliant career, he built a toy-sized wooden helicopter with two counter-rotating propellers and sold one to a bishop named Milton Wright. Wright gave the toy to his boys, Orville and Wilbur, who went on to make history with the first airplane flight in 1903.

The very idea for a helicopter was based on a centuries-old Chinese children's toy called a "bamboo butterfly": essentially a propeller on a stick that can be spun between the hands to give the little toy an impressive lift to soar through the air – entirely out of control. The potential of vertical flight was obvious, but in practice it was a desperate thing to achieve. Almost a century ago, in 1912, a Danish engineer named Jacob Ellehammer built the first rotary-winged flying machine that actually left the ground, a contraption he called a "screw plane."

Various inventors worked on the concept. One prototype required 16 blades, and another used a hydrogen-filled balloon to stabilize and assist the rotors with lift. A number of machines were built that flew – straight up and straight down – but forward motion and control were out of the question until 1922 when an American, Henry Berliner, built a machine that could rise to 20 feet off the ground – and move forward. He is known for saying "the way to fly is straight up," but he never developed a practical version. In conclusion to his efforts, he wrote, "The machine is not yet perfected to the extent of landing from any height with the degree of safety that is required."

It was a Russian, Igor Sikorsky, who finally built a helicopter with the same single main rotor design most helicopters use today. He was a veritable Mozart of flight, having invented a small rubber-band-powered helicopter at age 12.

Hats off to these bold inventors who committed their lives to realizing the complicated physics of the helicopter. They were visionaries who knew it was possible to fly straight up and were willing to risk life and limb to prove it could be done – and they probably never could have imagined that one day the machine of their dreams would lift skiers, hikers and climbers into the world's most rugged wilderness and land on a table-sized summit above the clouds where the passengers would disembark to chase the Holy Grail of winter fun. Since 1965, helicopters have transported CMH skiers to some 18.7 billion vertical feet of bliss in an average of 300,000 runs per year. That's a total of five and a half million kilometres. Joined end to end, the ski tracks would make almost 150 laps around the Earth or stretch from the Earth to the moon and back more than half a dozen times.

One of the many coincidences leading to the success of heli-skiing was the friendship that developed between Hans Gmoser and a young native of Banff named Jim Davies. Davies and Hans were introduced through Lizzie Rummel while Davies was studying art in Calgary. Although talented, Davies left art school after two years to get his pilot's licence. "I needed more action," he explains.

Davies was not only a quick study as a pilot, rapidly gaining experience in planes and helicopters, but he was also a skier. In 1956 Davies was 17 years old and the best junior skier in Canada, taking gold in every race he entered that year except one where he took silver. Hans had found a fellow skier with a valuable skill in his ability to offer air support for his wilderness endeavours.

Davies dropped supplies for Hans's icefields traverse expedition and delivered food to Lizzie's lodge at Mt. Assiniboine. When the discussion of using a helicopter for skiing arose, there was one element of the project Hans didn't need to waste any energy debating: Jim Davies would be the pilot. Davies can't exactly remember whether the first discussion about heli-skiing happened at the skiers watering hole called the Cascade Bar or on the chairlift at Lake Louise, but he remembers Hans talking to him about the Bugaboos and asking, "Do you think you can land in there and move skiers for me?"

To which Jim replied, "I'm sure I can."

The first helicopter used for heli-skiing was the piston-driven, turbo-charged Bell 47G3B-1. It was underpowered for mountain flying, hard to start, and could only carry two skiers at a time. The second year, an Alouette II was used for a short time because it held two more passengers, but the bigger and more efficient Alouette III was well tested in the Swiss and French Alps and was an obvious next choice. Holding six passengers, the Alouette III allowed a full group of skiers to make it to the top in just two laps.

It didn't take long for a guest to casually throw his skis over his shoulder and inadvertently stuff them right into the rotor assembly of an Alouette III. After that incident, placards appeared in the bathroom stalls at the Bugaboo lodge explaining helicopter safety and the pilots and guides collaborated to teach skiers how to behave around the machine.

Then, the first time Davies brought a tired skier back to the lodge at mid-day, a pair of skis blew out of the basket from the force of the helicopter's airspeed. The skis slammed into the main rotor, which chopped them in half as they in turn carved a dinner-plate-sized chunk out of the rotor blade. Davies was left to pilot a flyable though obviously damaged and wobbling machine with compromised aerodynamics, but he managed to maintain control long enough to land safely back at the lodge. Not only did no one get hurt, but the accident was a blessing in disguise. With skiing to be done and the helicopter damaged, Jim Davies found the company he worked for, Bullock Aviation, had an available Bell 204 he could use while waiting for new rotors for the Alouette III. He found the performance of the machine so superior to the Alouette III for heli-ski flying that even when the Alouette III was repaired, he told his company how well the new helicopter worked and requested, "You have to leave that here."

As coincidence would have it, CMH built a wing onto the Bugaboo lodge in 1969 to accommodate more skiers and the Bell 204 was introduced the same year, enabling nine skiers at a time to catch a lift to the top. Then, in 1970, just in time for the CMH Cariboos operation to get up to speed, Bell introduced the 212 model, and the modern CMH heli-ski system was born. With twin jet engines, the 212 is commonly called the safest helicopter ever made. When asked what was the single biggest factor in CMH's success, Hans replied, "It was the helicopter capacity. Once we had the 212 we had a business that could really work."

At the time, with most helicopters sitting unused in hangars during the snowy months, the helicopter industry was desperate for winter contracts. As a result, Hans and company got a low off-season price on the helicopter and pilots. As heli-skiing grew, the helicopter industry found the ideal off-season customer.

CMH experimented with the 214, essentially a 212 with a single huge engine, but it had greater fuel consumption and flew so fast that the second group arrived at the landing before the first group even had time to put their skis on. For a time, the 214 was used in the Monashees to lift skiers out of the narrow valleys to the top of the steep tree runs, but eventually the 212 won out with adequate power and superior safety thanks to the dual engines. If one engine fails, a computer automatically adjusts the transmission, and the other engine then drives the rotors alone.

Regardless of the helicopter type, any heli-ski pilot will tell you the skiing world is the most demanding flying there is. Some jobs require more precision, like placing a long rescue line in the hand of a rescuer, and others are more dangerous, like some military missions, but none have the combined issues of deceptive visibility and human factors found in heli-skiing.

When Art Patterson decided the combination of helicopters and skiing was a "chancy and expensive" undertaking, he was dead right. Add the high speeds of downhill skiing to the terrain of mountaineering, and the exposure to different scenarios is increased immensely. Throw a helicopter into the mix, and a can of worms is an understatement. Making it all work together – the mountaineering elements of route-finding, weather prediction and glacier travel; the skiing elements of skill, snow-condition timing and group management at high speeds; and the helicopter elements of machine limitations, mountain flying and orchestrating the flow of skiers in a huge area – was not exactly a natural thing to do. What Patterson could never have guessed was that equal parts tenacity, dumb luck, technology and fast learning would make the concept work.

Pretty much everyone involved agrees that the best days of heli-skiing are the ones when the whole ungainly operation works together: skiers pay attention and are in tune with their guide's leadership; guides and pilot put together a series of runs that minimize waiting time and maximize skiing fun; and mountain conditions cooperate with adequate visibility and good snow. There are a phenomenal number of great days, but a few bad ones have supplied a world of learning that has given everyone involved the knowledge that makes heli-skiing a much safer experience than it used to be.

The stories of learning are endless, and the ski basket is one of the main protagonists. From the original automobile ski rack used in the first days on Old Goat Glacier, the guides and Jim Davies simplified the system and strapped the skis onto the skids with elastic bungee cords. As helicopters got bigger, more skis needed to be carried, so a metal basket was welded together to hold them. After the first close call with skis flying into the main rotor, the guides realized the potential disaster of skis colliding with the rotors in mid-flight, but their solution, the two bungee straps to hold the skis in, created other hazards. It was Leo who involuntarily demonstrated the danger of the straps one day when he gave the pilot thumbs up indicating all clear to take off. Leo was wearing a pair of stylish Bogner ski pants with a stirrup under the foot to hold the pants down over the ski boots. As the machine lifted off, the hook on the bungee strap slipped through the stirrup and almost instantly Leo was flipped upside down, dangling off the helicopter suspended on the bungee strap hooked on his Bogner britches. The pilot had no idea of the disaster unfolding and within seconds the machine would have been hundreds of metres off the ground as it pulled away from the summit. Luckily, the Bogner pants were designed for industrial fashion instead of industrial strength, so the stirrup gave way once Leo's full weight was on it, dropping Leo on his head from just above the ground. Again, no one was injured, but the basket was proving to be a challenge to perfect.

During the seventies, shorter skis became popular, especially for skiing off-piste, and the combination of the less than perfect basket system and changes in ski technology conspired to create a deadly mix. A couple of staff had spent the morning skiing and were flying back to the lodge during a fuel flight so they could complete their afternoon's work. They were skiing on shorter skis, so the position of the bungees just barely held the skis in place. During the rapid descent, the skis worked loose from the straps and flew into the tail rotor. This time, the passengers were not so lucky – without a functioning tail rotor, the machine spun out of control, killing the two staff, while the pilot escaped with his life. After the tragedy, a metal lid was built to hold everything in the basket under any circumstances.

The helicopter is one of the only vehicles that can have a horrendous crash while standing still, and most of the near misses with the helicopter have occurred when the machine was moving slowly, near a landing. As a result, most of the helicopter crashes in heli-skiing have been hard on the machine but left the people involved unscathed. Bob Geber was involved in a few helicopter incidents in the early days before tighter safety standards and pilot experience made mountain flying a safer game.

Geber's first crash was while working for Roger Madsen's guide service out of Radium. A minor crash had put their ski plane out of commission, so they found a helicopter and a pilot to take skiers out the very next day. Geber remembers, "The pilot had a southern accent and no mountain flying experience. As we were landing, I looked down to enter flight time in my book – when I looked up all I could see was snow."

The pilot reacted at the last second and pulled up just before hitting the slope, so the helicopter crashed with much of the force on its skids instead if its nose. As the machine rolled backwards, a skid stuck in the snow crust, preventing a probably fatal tumble. When things stopped moving, Geber had one thought: "Shit! I'm still alive!"

During the crash, he slammed his head into something in the fuselage, and blood from the wound pooled in his eyes. His second thought was: "Shit! I'm blind!"

He could smell fuel, so he kicked open the door and started running away. After a few steps he had a third thought: "Shit, I'm the guide!"

Wiping the blood out of his eyes was a relief, as he realized he still could see. He turned around and helped everyone else out of the helicopter. No one was hurt, and there was wine in the lunch, so they grabbed the lunch and moved away from the helicopter to wait for a rescue. There was no long-range radio in those days, so Geber hoped it wouldn't take long for Madsen to realize the helicopter hadn't returned and send out a second ship.

They drank the wine and ate the lunch, and still no rescue was forthcoming. The short winter day was half over, so Geber decided they'd better try to get out under their own power before darkness fell. While the helicopter was bent, with pieces scattered everywhere, the basket had miraculously protected the skis during the crash. Everyone grabbed their skis and did what they knew how to do – ski. The only problem was the pilot. He had no skis and wouldn't have known what to do with them if he did.

The snow was too soft and deep to walk without floundering, so Geber had the idea to make a sled using the disk-like cowling that fits around the base of the helicopter's rotor assembly at the very top of the fuselage. There was enough room for the pilot to sit in it, like a child on a saucer, and the disk slid easily on the downhill. The group left the wreck and headed down the mountain, 11 skiers easily cruising along, and the pilot sledding behind on a piece of his mangled helicopter. When the terrain was less steep, the skiers attached a rope to the makeshift sled and pulled the pilot along, but when they hit a flat section, with deep, soft snow, it became impossible to pull. The pilot tried to walk, but ended up wallowing.

To make forward progress, Geber and one of the stronger skiers each gave up one ski so the pilot, with zero ski experience, could use two. Gently rolling terrain was perfect for the new system and they made good time, and the pilot even started enjoying the idea of skiing with the exhilaration of sliding easily down a few small hills. Soon they crested a bigger hill, and Geber was ready to change back to the sledding system, but the pilot asked, "Hey Bob, do you think I could ski by myself down this one?"

Geber thought there wasn't much of a hill, so he let the pilot go ahead. Geber remembers, shaking his head, "He went about 50 feet, fell over, and started squealing like a pig. We couldn't figure out what he could have done to himself in such a short distance and insignificant fall, but I skied up to him and he was holding his leg. Immediately I could see he had somehow gotten a compound fracture. The bone was obvious sticking out against his pants."

By now the day was well on the way to a guide's worst nightmare, in fact nightmare on top of nightmare. With a crashed helicopter and a pilot with a broken leg, Geber was in no mood to listen to the pilot's screaming. "I shoved 200 mg of Demerol up his ass, and pretty soon he was grinning stupidly, happy as a baby."

By this point, Madsen had recruited a rescue helicopter and soon found the crash site and followed the ski tracks to the beleaguered team. Madsen was happy to see the entire team, but they were gathered around someone who appeared to be hurt, so he got out of the helicopter and started running uphill – directly into the path of the rotor. To end the day, Geber ran at Madsen and dove at his legs with a football tackle, effectively knocking him over before he decapitated himself on the blade.

Geber told Hans about the incident afterwards, and according to Geber Hans's response was, "What do you think?"

"I thought I was dead." Geber replied.

"The best thing for you to do is go right back guiding."

Two days later, Geber was guiding in the Monashees. "Hans knew, if you're going to keep doing it, it is better to get right back to it as soon as possible before you have too much time to think about it."

Years later, in the Bugaboos, Geber found himself watching his helicopter nosedive into a forest, from the front-row seat. He had just finished skiing the run called 69 on one of the first trips of the day. "It was a year plagued by unusual winds," he remembers. "Just as the helicopter lifted off, a gust hit the machine directly from behind. We lost all of our lift and were sent right into the thick forest in front of us."

The pilot, Joe Sawkins, in a testament to the mental abilities of the best helicopter pilots, kept his wits until the last possible second and likely saved everyone on board. "He pulled an amazing move," remembers Geber. "He was dodging big trees while the rotor was slicing through other trees a foot thick and I could see pieces of the rotor flying through the air."

Then, just before the machine lost all controllability and hit the ground, the pilot pointed the nose straight up so the force of the crash would be absorbed by the tail boom as it collapsed. Bob says with reverence, "I think it worked."

Taking Hans's advice to get right back on the horse, Geber went out two hours later and took the group for a couple of runs. "It was good to do a bit of skiing – and then we went to the bar and got pissed to the gills."

Mark Kingsbury, the man whose glass was always half full rather than half empty, told Geber, who now had two significant helicopter crashes on his résumé, "Half the guides don't want to fly with you because you crash. Me, I want to fly with you because you always survive them."

The worst CMH helicopter crash, the only one with guest fatalities, was an event with a twist of fortune of the most dramatic kind. As the machine came in for a landing, the ski basket caught on a rock, spinning the helicopter out of control. When the helicopter slammed into the slope, its momentum carried it over the edge of a steep face and the violence released a large avalanche. The avalanche, with the helicopter riding in it, went to the bottom of the mountain. Sadly, the pilot, guide and four guests were killed, but incredibly, the other seven on the helicopter survived. A review of the incident revealed that the helicopter fell over several cliffs in its plummet, and speculation is that if the mass of the avalanche had not cushioned the tumble, everyone in the machine would most likely have died before it stopped rolling at the bottom of the mountain.

While there have been few fatal helicopter crashes in heli-skiing, there have been a number of close calls resulting in expensive damage and even more where quick thinking saved the day. Once, in the early days of Revelstoke skiing, it was storming too hard to land on the drop-off points on the west side of the range, so Hans decided to fly to the east side, where typically the storms are less severe. Rogers Pass gave them a road to follow in the limited visibility, so they loaded up and headed east in hopes of finding a window over the pass and into better conditions. As they approached Rogers Pass, a horrifying sight materialized out of the thick fog and heavy snow: the mortar-launching avalanche control stations on the pass were busily lobbing explosives into the fog at the known slide paths that threaten the road, and when the avalanche crew came into view they were pointing a mortar right at the helicopter.

Legend has it that Hans yelled, "They're shooting at us!"

Overloading a Sikorski helicopter once nearly led to a crash. The tail boom was accessible from the front and there was no ski basket, so the group loaded the skis from the inside and piled in. As soon as the helicopter took off, it was unbalanced because of the weight and started trending downwards on its side. Thinking quickly, the pilot yelled at everyone to jettison the skis. With the kind of urgency only the threat of death can inspire, everyone grabbed skis and threw them out the door. With the tail boom empty, the aircraft regained balance and the pilot regained control in the nick of time.

The potential disasters of the combination of helicopters and the mountain environment are almost unlimited. As the decades of heli-skiing passed, more disasters occurred – or came dangerously close to happening. A BASE jumper once said, in describing risk and experience in his sport of jumping from anything high enough to give a parachute time to open, that BASE jumpers have two jars, an experience jar and a luck jar. When they begin, their luck jar is full and their experience jar is empty. Every time they jump, they take one coin out of the luck jar and put it in the experience jar, and after enough jumps, their luck jar is empty and their experience jar is the only thing that keeps them alive. Granted, BASE jumping is an unusually dangerous sport, but the metaphor of risk fits the world of heli-skiing perfectly – and after decades of gaining experience, the luck jar was running out.

There was also the element of human interaction with the machine, like the skier who walked too close to the pitot tube, the hollow protrusion that sticks out of the nose of the helicopter and measures air speed. The skier stumbled and jammed the hollow point into his face. The pilot remembers, "I had to scrape a bit of flesh out of the end of the pitot tube." There was also more than one occasion when skiers slung their skis over their shoulders and right into the spinning rotor, causing incredible damage.

Then there was a problem with the machines themselves. They were simply pushed to their limits by the rigours of heli-skiing. Although they worked, the trustworthy 212s were often at the limit of their power. By the mid-eighties, a series of crashes had pushed the industry to the breaking point. Insurance companies were getting fed up with helicopters getting wrecked while heli-skiing, and even though the skiers usually walked away, the underwriters were threatening to withdraw coverage altogether.

Heli-ski pilot Bryan MacPherson credits Dave White, the VP of Alpine Helicopters during the late eighties, with saving heli-skiing by changing the way helicopter business was done from one end to the other. As Bryan recounted, "Dave said 'We can't keep crashing helicopters!' and was willing to shut down the whole operation in the name of safety."

Dave Gubbels, the chief operations officer for Alpine, explained how they dealt with the issues. "We made real changes," he said. One problem was that pilots were sometimes pushed by the guides and skiers to fly in dubious conditions. "So we gave the pilots more authority." Between 1986 and 1996, the entire helicopter element of the equation was redesigned. "The majority of accidents were weight- and power-related," Gubbels continued, "so we made modifications to the machines to raise their performance. Bell had already modified a 212 for government work in the Middle East, so we gave the government a blank cheque, essentially, to get FAA certification for the HP kit."

HP stands for horsepower, and the tricked-out 212s used at the CMH areas are essentially on steroids to make them safer in the high-demand world of heli-skiing. The kit includes a beefier transmission, a bigger tail rotor and a reinforced fuselage, and gives each 212 an extra 60 horses to pull it out of a jam. The $200,000 upgrade gave pilots more to work with, but rather than use the additional horsepower for everyday flying, they operate off the weight and power charts of the weaker machine and save the extra horsepower for emergencies. Like putting a truck into four-wheel drive to get unstuck rather than locking the hubs and going farther before getting stuck, Gubbels explains the way the kit is used: "The HP kit is purely an extra margin for safety. Our intent was to have that extra horsepower as a reserve."

MacPherson is proud to be a pilot of such machines. He says, "Alpine probably has the best fleet of 212s in the world."

When a pilot uses the extra juice, the passengers on board would never know it, but back at the shop everyone knows and the pilot will be buying a few bottles of wine for repentance. The term "overtorque" is used to describe tapping into the extra power to avoid a crash. Every pilot's goal is to make it through their entire career without an overtorque, but most will one day need it. Overtorquing requires expensive maintenance on the machine, and, more important, it means the helicopter was just a little too close to a crash.

Another change made by Alpine Helicopters to make heli-ski flying safer was the way time is billed. Traditionally, helicopter contractors charge for every minute the machine is running. In the mountains, this meant guides were always rushing around, loading skis hastily and rushing the skiers in hopes of saving on helicopter costs. Hans was always pressuring guides to minimize helicopter expenses. Once, during a time of financial duress, Hans was using a printout from the helicopter timer to keep track of each guide's time while the helicopter was on the ground. One guide decided to spin the numbers, and all day long he had his group bind the skis into a bundle with a cord so he could throw them all into the ski basket with one heave. While it was terrible for his back, at the end of the day Hans was flabbergasted that the guide spent so little time with the machine on the ground.

Pat Aldous, who until 2007 was president of Alpine Helicopters, CMH's sole helicopter provider since the mid-eighties, explained that another change was to pay heli-ski pilots in such a way that there was no perception that more flying meant more pay. MacPherson shared the current philosophy at Alpine Helicopters from the pilot's perspective: "I get paid really well to say no."

"There have been times we just left the machine for the night and called snowmobiles to come and get us," said Bryan. "The hard days are when the skiing is really, really good and I have to say no."

For the winter season, Alpine Helicopters removed the standard timers from the machines and installed timers on the collectives, the control at the pilot's left side that initiates lift, so today there is no charge until the machine leaves the ground. Heli-ski pilots are paid a fixed number of hours per day, regardless of how long they're actually in fight, so flying time has no bearing on their paycheque. Now, rushing is a mistake rather than a standard operating procedure, pilots can veto the day's plan with no questions asked if they are uncomfortable, and the number of helicopter incidents has decreased dramatically – but it's still a job the pilots take extremely seriously. Alpine gives safety bonuses to everyone on the staff, not just the pilots, because as Aldous says "We have to make enough money to keep the operation safe."

Individual teams and individuals are docked for safety-related mistakes, and the rest share the safety-bonus pool.

"Now," says Gubbels, "it is no problem to get insurance for heli-skiing." Aldous observes that it wasn't just Alpine that changed; at the same time, "the whole industry matured."

Even with the safety-conscious modern helicopter business, there are other factors that affect insurance costs. Lynda Murdock, Pat Aldous's successor as president of Alpine Helicopters, explains that after the World Trade Center disaster on September 11, 2001, aviation insurance costs spiked 85 per cent. Since then, the cost of coverage has decreased to a more reasonable level, but during that time, a number of people bailed out of the business, insurance companies folded and the whole industry readjusted. Now, helicopter expenses eat up about a third of the total revenue generated by CMH.

The helicopters themselves are expensive – a 212 costs about $3-million – but skilled pilots are Alpine's biggest asset. Alpine has contracts in heli-seismic remote drilling, forestry and firefighting support, air ambulance and rescue operations, sight-seeing tours and power and pipeline maintenance, so there is plenty of opportunity for experienced pilots, but heli-ski flying draws the best pilots in the business, ones who enjoy being part of a complex team. Most heli-ski pilots have at least ten years of flying experience before they take their first group of skiers, hikers or climbers into the Columbias in an Alpine helicopter.

To train for accurate flying in the early days, a pilot was put in a small Bell 47 and asked to hover in front of a stand of poplar trees. Gothics pilot Rocky Cooper remembers, "We would inch forward until the tip of the rotor was just tickling the leaves." Then he quickly adds, "That's not approved anymore – it was the old cowboy way."

However they learn, a mountain pilot needs leaf-tickling control of his machine. MacPherson explains the world of mountain flying as few pilots can. "You have to get to this point where the machine is just an extension of your mind. I can't even explain the movements I do to get the machine to do the right thing. I can anticipate the machine's movement before it moves, but I can't explain it." Like an athlete talking about his body as it performs, there is too much going on at the same time to explain, and control becomes an intuitive reaction rather than a mechanical series of steps. Surfers can't explain their every movement while interacting with a wave – they just do what feels right, and after years of experience, it is right.

Outside of the mechanics of helicopter flight, the mountains throw a lot of factors into the equation. Consider the helicopter that fell through a thick snow crust, trapping one skid under the tenacious layer. If the pilot had simply pulled power for liftoff as usual, the machine would have flipped and a horrendous crash would have followed. Instead, the pilot felt as if someone had tied his feet together, and as he slowly lifted off he realized something was not right. Everyone got out of the helicopter, and with no weight the pilot was able to wiggle out from under the trap. Even on pavement, a helicopter can freeze to the ground, creating the same dangerous liftoff condition. Many pilots "wiggle their feet" before lifting off so they know there is no resistance anywhere.

Mountain flying is challenging for many reasons, and the framework of heli-skiing complicates everything. On some days, pilots do a hundred pickups and landings in tricky conditions. Just the visual element of heli-ski flying is enough to boggle the mind. Pilot Roger Hoogendoorn says, "The hardest part of flying in the mountains is visibility. Our minds are easily deceived looking at snow." Horizon lines appear to be close but on closer inspection can be hundreds of metres or more away because of closer horizons blending with those in the distance. Flat light makes all detail disappear, and while it is unnerving for skiers, it is downright diabolical for pilots – and the resulting face plant in case of misjudgment is far worse for the pilot than the skier. The angle of a slope can appear almost flat from the air but actually be quite steep. Even speed of travel is illusory. While surrounded by whiteness, it is easy to be moving fast while all visual indications suggest you are standing still. The depth of the snow on a landing can trick the pilot into thinking he is almost on the ground when in reality a stable surface is still a metre or more lower. Temperature differences change the way the helicopter reacts to the air. The brilliance of the sun can blind a pilot at the wrong moment. Then, of course there is the mountains' tendency to change everything from one moment to the next.

Mountain guides are masters of dealing with the visual perception issues in the mountains, but even their craft falls short of the complications of flight. Even experienced guides defer to pilots regarding the visual tricks the mountains can play. Once, Hans was circling a landing with the original heli-ski pilot, Jim Davies, at the helm. Jim was having trouble seeing the landing in the whiteout, so Hans offered to jump out to give him reference, thinking they were just a few feet of the ground. Questioning Hans's perspective of distance, Jim said, "Throw your pack out first." Hans did, and the pack fell a long time before hitting the snow.

Years later, guide Christian Meyerhoffer was in a helicopter dealing with the same issue and the pilot gave him the same suggestion. Christian was young, and bold, and instead of taking the pilot's advice he jumped, hitting the ground from treetop height. Luckily, the snow was deep and he was uninjured.

In the guide meetings, the pilots are generally treated with a sort of reverence by the guides, not as superiors, but as equals with a different skill set where the guides cannot tread. Rocky Cooper, one of the most respected pilots at Alpine, understands the guide and pilot dynamic: "When the guides are uncomfortable, what are we doing there? When the pilot is uncomfortable, we really shouldn't be there!"

Making a day of heli-skiing run smoothly is a combination of a lot of diverse elements operating in sync, but the pilot is in a unique position in the whole process: he is utterly alone as the professional in charge of his specialty. The guides have a team, and they dovetail each other's expertise to keep the team strong even if one guide is

having an off day. Even the skiers can help the guides by being responsible for following the guide and being respectful of the dangers. But when it's time to get to the top of the mountain, the pilot shoulders the entire burden of safety.

Guides and pilots are cut from the same cloth, and their cooperation in the mountains is the kind that only soldiers and lovers achieve. A seasoned guiding team's keystone is the pilot, and a heli-ski pilot's biggest asset is an experienced guiding team. Guide Pete Harvey explains a lesser known role of the pilot: "The guide in the front seat vents to the pilot – it's like he's a priest or something. We all take turns at confession." With the guests deafened by the noise of the machine, it is a chance for the guides to speak their minds.

After enough times at confession, the sinners start to feel like priests themselves. Bob Geber explains, "Sometimes I almost feel like I could fly the helicopter."

When guide JF Lacombe is directing Gothics pilot Rocky Cooper in for a landing, Lacombe simply holds his hand up and Cooper sets the handle of the ski basket precisely in Lacombe's hand. All the guides speak with awe of their pilots' abilities. After a day of thick clouds and delicate flying in Kootenay when the pilot flew backwards down a ridge to avoid a whiteout, one guide said to the pilot, "Even after watching you fly for all these years, you amaze me again and again how awkwardly you can fly that thing."

Listening to pilots talk about their craft is like listening to a jazz musician talk about music. They talk about "finding the wind" by the feel of the machine. "The wind can be just as helpful as not helpful," explains Bryan. Pilots pass over a landing just to raise a snow cloud so they can see how the snow blows after the force of the rotors passes. Little snow features on the ground can reveal the direction of the wind and the softness of the snow. The feel of the tail boom is a big indicator of wind direction. Bryan continues, "There is just this happy helicopter feel when the landing is just right.

The 212 has this way of telling you when things are good. It's just all smooth, and then when things are off she kind of vibrates and tells you to watch out."

The wind is a living thing for a helicopter pilot. Explains Bryan, "Think about the air like a river: the air above an obstacle is clear, and below it is messy. To see the wind you have to picture the river. In mountain flying, you don't have to fly into the wind, but you have to know what the fuck it's going to do to you."

These eddies, rapids, pools of calm, and waves are all part of the equation the pilots are always trying to visualize and feel. On one side of a mountain, the wind can be strong but smooth; then, after it flows over the peak, it becomes turbulent.

When landing, the helicopter creates its own wind, called the rotor wash, and when the wind touches the ground it stirs up the snow into what pilots call a "snowball." When there is light snow on a hard surface like a rain crust, the snowballs take on colossal proportions from the ricochet effect of the rotor wash on the hard surface. In these conditions, the snowballs can rise 30 metres into the air, engulf the helicopter and blind the pilot at the most crucial landing moment, even on the clearest bluebird day. To combat the snowballs, the approach speed for the landing must be high enough to stay ahead of the blowing snow. Too fast and the momentum will carry the machine past the landing or cause it to hit the ground with too much force. Too slow and the snowball will overtake the helicopter and the pilot will have to pull up and wait for the snow to settle before trying again.

Matt Conant works at Galena and is a second-generation pilot and a master of low-visibility flying with specialized low-visibility training. He explains that heli-ski flying is a "challenging combination of instrument and visual."

Conant loves the whole package of flying for mountain sport: "It's more than just flying. For me, heli-ski flying is being part of the whole program, knowing where the four groups are and becoming familiar with the runs."

After a day of flying in heavy snow and challenging conditions, Conant commented, "Oddly enough, I enjoy days like today at least as much as the sunny days."

Pilots talk about the pleasure of performance as much as the skiers, and getting in tune with the mountains is a big part of it. Bryan explains, "There's this time when it all clicks with the groups, the flying, and it all becomes crystal clear. I can see how the fog is forming, the weather is changing, before it even happens."

The hardest part of mountain flying, according to most pilots and guides, is flagging the landings before the season begins. Some guides say it is the most dangerous part of their job. Landing on a white spot on a white mountain with a white snowball following the machine every time it gets close to the ground is no easy task. Sometimes they throw machine nuts threaded with orange flagging out the door to serve as a visual indicator, but in deep snow the nuts will simply disappear.

While every part of helicopter operation has gotten safer, there was something special about the devil-may-care early days of cheap fuel, no concern for carbon emissions, and letting a bunch of skiers loose in the mountains with such an incredible machine. There was the day when the ice machine broke in the Bugaboo lodge, so the pilot fired up the helicopter and flew up to the Bugaboo Glacier to get ice for the cocktails.

One spring a group of women were sunbathing topless near the old Bugaboos staff house, and the pilot saw them, so on his return flight with a group of skiers, he flew low and dusted the sunbathers with snow driven from the rotor wash. The women scattered, and the skiers lucky enough to be on the right side of the aircraft got a good view.

Another time, it was Leo's turn to clean the snow from the roof of the lodge, but he was tired of shovelling, so he had a bright idea to get the snow off the lodge without lifting a finger: he asked the pilot to hover over the lodge so the rotor wash would clear the snow. It worked perfectly and cleaned every flake from the roof. When Leo went back inside, smug with his innovation, he met an incredibly angry mob. The downdraft had also blown down the chimney, blasting ash and soot as if a bomb had gone off in the fireplace to plaster the inside of the lodge with a coating of black, tenacious dust.

While the days of fun and games with the helicopter are essentially over, the fundamental access it provides is the same as ever. An editor of *Powder* magazine, Don Patton, wrote:

> To me, the essential beauty of helicopter skiing lies in its simplicity. Not that helicopters, heli-ski vacations or the logistics of a winter campaign in the wilderness are simple, but that helicopters can transport you to simplicity. When you step out of that bird on top of a mountain, all of skiing's extraneous factors are eliminated, and skiing becomes what it was always meant to be: a simple relationship between the skier and the mountain.

And what will the future of helicopter technology hold? Unmanned rescue helicopters are in the prototype phase. Unmanned military drones are already in the air over the Middle East gathering intelligence and even firing weapons, but the heli-ski pilot's job is secure. An automated heli-ski machine is as unlikely as a robotic mountain guide – the human element is irreplaceable.

11

EYES IN THE FOREST

By 1973, when Mica Dam is completed, the Valley of the Big Bend from 60 miles north of Golden to 80 miles north of Revelstoke, as well as the apex of the Big Bend for 70 miles up the Canoe River will be flooded, creating a lake with an area of at least 500 square miles, and no provision is being made to thoroughly log and clean this area! The result is that you will have a huge body of water studded with dead trees, rendering the lake impossible for fishing, boating or any other water sport; and at the same time you are denied access to the whole of the northern Selkirks. It has been said that the cost of clearing this area is prohibitive; how can one talk about the cost when those who come behind us will curse us forever?

— Hans Gmoser, luncheon address to the Rotary Club of Calgary

It's 5:30 a.m. at Calgary International Airport and there's not a sleepy eye in sight. The energy on the bus is palpable, almost painful. French, Italian and German fill the air and "helicopter" is the only word I can understand – and it's spoken often.

We're bound for the Bobbie Burns, an area known for fast-paced, aggressive skiing, and even though I've been skiing since before I can remember, I'm intimidated. The young French all look like Olympians. The Austrians have custom racing jackets with a helicopter emblazoned on the back. The Swiss have the quiet confidence of serial killers. The Italians jab each other in the ribs and make gestures of wind milling their arms like a jumper off a cliff while talking loudly. Two Japanese near the back of the bus look like Zen warriors and speak almost in whispers. I try not to think about the flaccid ski touring boots I will be wearing all week and turn to the window to stare at the Rockies growing larger in the distance.

Sunrise greets us near Banff, low clouds parting as the sun hits the high peaks above the dark and jagged treeline. Elk and deer graze alongside the highway and cameras click and videos whir inside the bus. Heads snap back and forth like spectators at a tennis match while people try to absorb the 360-degree mountain beauty revealing itself around us – and we're still on the most boring part of the trip.

The bus leaves us at a landing pad, where we will trade places with the departing group. Few words are spoken between the groups. It's as if knowing how good it was last week could make our week less enjoyable if we get poor snow conditions. Or maybe it's like sober people walking into a bar while drunk people are walking out – they're just not on the same wavelength. The people leaving look tired and happy. Our group fidgets, edgy and impatient. Soon, the deep rumble of the 212 is heard, and eventually even the Italians dive behind the bus to hide from the flying debris stirred up by the powerful rotors as the machine lands and we climb aboard.

In minutes, we're hundreds of metres off the ground, powering towards a glistening white world where we will spend a week chasing the elusive elixir of the ultimate mountain experience. And so it has been for tens of thousands of people all over the globe, for whom the sound of a Bell 212 will always evoke a feeling of standing on the edge of a great adventure in the natural world.

Hans Gmoser was always reluctant to offer trips shorter than a week. He knew it takes time for the webs of life to fall away. It takes time for a group to get to know one another. It takes time to get into the rhythm of the mountains.

In the late fifties and early sixties, Hans was putting the entirety of his prodigious energy into sharing the mountains. If he wasn't skiing or climbing with a camera, he was showing and narrating promotional films on tours in Canada and the United States. Tom Briggs, a writer for Ski Canada, was at one of Hans's lectures in Toronto in 1962, three years before the first heli-skiing in Canada. According to Briggs, Hans stepped up on stage and told the crowd they were about to see the greatest powder snow in the world, all filmed in the eastern part of British Columbia. He then proceeded to challenge anyone in the auditorium to find better skiing anywhere.

Briggs describes the audience as "skeptical, unprepared to admit that the greatest of anything could be found in Canada." At the end of the show, Briggs wrote that Hans had "in effect, tapped them on the shoulder as they gazed across the Atlantic to the mountains of France and Switzerland, only to show them the magnificence of their own backyard."

While the snow and geography of the Columbias are the main reason why people recreate there, it was Hans's promotional films that first opened the eyes of the world to the wonders of the region. While guiding ski tours in Little Yoho, Hans would sometimes ski all day, leave his guests at the hut and ski out to his little Volkswagen, drive to Banff to give a presentation, then drive and ski back to the hut to be ready to guide the next day.

He eventually extended his tours into Europe. At one show in Basel, Switzerland, there was a student in the audience named Michael Pfeiffer. Pfeiffer had no money at

HANS GMOSER AND CAMERA ON
YAMNUSKA, 1965, PROMOTIONAL
PHOTO SHOOT.

the time but explained, "The way he presented it, the passion he had behind it and the pictures affected me greatly. I made heli-skiing my life dream."

For decades he couldn't afford it, but he never forgot Hans's presentation. Eventually, Pfeiffer found a means to go and has now heli-skied millions of vertical feet. Hundreds of people tell a similar story, and untold others decided to chase a life of mountain adventure after watching one of Hans's films.

Steve Komito was a young American with no interest in mountain sport until he happened to attend one of Hans's presentations. He said, "Hans's way of talking about the mountains affected me so greatly that I dropped everything I was doing, started climbing and skiing and made a life in the mountains."

Komito has never been heli-skiing and has little interest in it, but he has authored numerous first ascents in the Colorado Rockies and is a legendary cobbler of mountain footwear based out of a small workshop called Komito Boots just outside Rocky Mountain National Park in northern Colorado. He spent his every free minute for the last four decades skiing, climbing and chasing that freedom and passion he heard in Hans's stories and speaking style.

Joe and Anne Jones met Hans after one of his promotions while he was cleaning the auditorium, picking up the programs people had left so he could reuse them on his next show. Anne remembers, "We ended up going skiing with him for many years because we talked about skiing as we walked around with him picking up his programs. He was so frugal and so genuine."

The era of Hans's promotional film tours coincided with mountain sport leaving the realm of fringe exploration to separate into the sub-sports of rock climbing, alpinism and ski mountaineering. Yosemite's famous wall of granite, El Capitan, saw its first ascent in 1958. Whistler Mountain opened in 1966 with the biggest vertical drop of any ski area in North America. A climber named Yvon Chouinard began selling clothing with outdoor fashion and function in 1972 under the brand called Patagonia. By the late seventies, the world was enamoured of outdoor adventure, and heli-skiing was being promoted without Hans lifting a finger. An international Seagram's ad campaign featured snowboard pioneer Ted Shred waist deep in feathery powder (on skis) and sporting seventies ski fashion, including a pointy red hat and matching tight wool sweater without a flake of snow stuck to it. The ad read: "There's skiing. And then there's the Bugaboos. There's whisky. And then there's v.o."

Journalists took Hans's torch and ran with it in all directions. Some were ambulance chasers, arriving to cover avalanche and helicopter incidents, getting in the way of rescue efforts and leaving with quotes out of context and over-dramatized, over-simplified versions of a complex and tragic story. But most were professionals writing euphoric first-hand accounts of their experiences heli-skiing. The editorial power advertising the sport was more than Hans ever could have done alone, even though some journalists were about as comfortable as ducks without feathers in the world of big-mountain powder skiing and covered the subject with more fear than fact-checking.

Descriptions of avalanche transceivers are among the most often butchered by journalists, which is a little scary because they are put through the same transceiver drills as the rest of the skiers. One reporter wrote, "On certain days and in certain areas, you carry a small vertical-like package that is a blipper, sending out electronic signals – just in case of trouble." Another described the transceiver as a device that is used "in case someone gets lost."

Based on the CMH archives, between 1973 and 1979 the CMH story was told in nearly 400 magazine features and over 300 newspaper articles. The articles helped British Columbia to eventually rank alongside the world's most famous ski regions – and eventually to surpass them. Rainer Degimann-Schwartz wrote an article in 1974 for the *Christian Science Monitor* in which he describes an encounter with a baggage handler at the Munich airport. According to Degimann-Schwartz, when the man took his skis he said, "What a jerk, going to North America for skiing."

Degimann-Schwartz continues, "I really couldn't take offence at his opinion. Indeed, thousands of American skiers travel to Europe every year and bring news of super-modern ski resorts, sensational slopes and fantastic powder snow."

Six years later, Amanda Touche wrote an article for *Calgary* magazine profiling a Canadian named Gerry Doyle who was skiing at Kitzbühl, Austria, one of the centres of world skiing. On a ski lift Doyle met a man who asked him where he was from. When the Austrian heard Doyle was from Canada, he exclaimed, "Why would you come here from Canada?"

Doyle explained that he came for the skiing, to which the Austrian shook his head and leaned across the chairlift to reply, "But in Canada, my friend, you can heli-ski with Hans Gmoser."

The tide had turned. Hans had become a recreation icon, his story gracing the pages of magazines ranging from *Western Living* to *Esquire*. The influx of journalists was great for business, but now the guides had journalists to take care of besides their regular guests. Thierry Cardon pulls no punches in describing some of the media hounds who came looking for the story. "They come with all the clichés and then write all the same things."

Rudi Krannebitter added, "Some journalists showed up with price tags on all their equipment and had never skied before."

Many journalists and photographers were accustomed to getting a story by being pushy, but when journalists became demanding with Jim Davies, the pilot, he landed the helicopter about 50 metres from where they waited and made them walk through the waist deep snow to board.

The heli-ski culture Hans and Leo had created was not used to being studied by the outside world. Such was the isolation of the project that Margaret Bezzola, while helping her husband Colani manage the Bobbie Burns lodge, was perplexed by how many people came from a place called "Ellay." She knew they were Americans by their accents, and even studied a map of the United States closely, but never could find this city of Ellay where so many heli-skiers lived. It was quite some time before she learned that the mystery city was none other than the initials for Los Angeles.

The floodgates had opened. Every ski-film producer wanted a piece of heli-skiing. John Jay, Dick Barrymore, Warren Miller, Norm Clayton and Willy Bogner all visited

CMH in the seventies to make ski films and fanned the flames of its popularity with shocking visuals of skiers courting unending fields of powder. There was one common thread between all the venues where heli-skiing was portrayed to the world: everyone made it out to be as elite as possible.

"The biggest mistake we made, almost from day one," said Hans, "was thinking it was only for good skiers. It almost cost us the whole thing."

As heli-skiing caught the attention of the world, it was painted as the most radical thing a person could do. The hard-core ski elite spread the word about it, but even in the beginning, neophyte skiers found themselves heli-skiing. Ann Dodge, who was on the first heli-ski trip in the Bugaboos, recalls, "I was terrified! I didn't even know how to ski this stuff!"

The guides didn't help matters by skiing hard and fast, competing with each other, belittling guests who couldn't keep up, and generally coming to deserve their Swiss Mafia reputation. One group would ski as fast as possible in order to pass the group ahead of them in the helicopter cycle, and then yodel, heckle and razz the slower group as they passed. It was all in good fun, but only if you liked your powder snow flavoured with testosterone.

Journalists didn't help the sport's image, either, writing articles about the experience that made it sound like more of a Chamonix-esque death sport than a gentleman's holiday. At about the same time, a Swiss journalist wrote a self-test for skiers to see if they were ready for heli-skiing – most failed the test.

Still, until the early eighties, heli-skiing had the reputation of offering impossibly difficult skiing for only the world's best skiers. It didn't help the rap that the first line of the 1978 brochure read: "You have to be a strong advanced skier and in your own style be able to handle any kind of snow. You should be in very good condition to enjoy heli-skiing. The snow is very good 70 per cent per cent of the time. The rest of the time you'll find snow from very good to the worst that you can imagine. The skiing can be very difficult at times."

Journalists who visited CMH during the seventies took the elite theme and further raised the bar of perception for what it took to ski there. One writer, Alec Blasco-Ibáñez, had been a paratrooper for the French Foreign Legion, and with a background as a war correspondent, he made heli-skiing with CMH sound like a battlefield more than a fluffy playground. In his article for *SKI* magazine titled "The Bugaboos: Macho Skiing," he said that "in Gmoser's world there are no ski instructors or namby-coddlers."

Recounting his first day of heli-skiing, he wrote:

> I stop. I'm out of breath. I'm lost. All is quiet. There is no sign, sound or sight of my group. That is, the ten skiers in my class in the Cariboo Mountains. And it's been a long time since I last saw our peerless and absolutely fearless leader taking off over the steep side of a high, deserted peak where the whirlybird dropped us off, zooming down through the falling white like a maddened horsefly skimming wildly through the foam on the top of a pail of fresh warm milk.

While the colourful simile and adrenaline-pumping prose is surely a temptation to the elite skiers whose spouses don't mind their partners catching lifts on a giant steel insect with a thousand horsepower in its thorax, it surely scared away a number of people who were perfectly capable of enjoying the skiing and who would have been reassured to know the "maddened horsefly" was actually the safest helicopter ever built, and the "skimming wildly" was more like flying with the conservative precision of an eagle.

The very name, heli-skiing, didn't help the reputation, either. Even today many people think heli-skiing involves some simultaneous combination of helicopters and skiing. After a heli-ski trip, countless skiers are asked by well-meaning friends, "Is that where you jump out of helicopters with your skis on?"

The reality – calculated use of the helicopter as a ski lift that actually waits for you to get on and off, making it easier than a chair lift or gondola for accessing slopes ranging from the steep and deep to the widest beginner runs on the planet – was hidden behind a smokescreen of testosterone and the sport's reputation. Some areas, due to terrain and the pace of the ski program, are much more suitable than others for different

FORMER "SWISS MAFIA" MEMBERS
KOBI WYSS, RUDI GERTSCH AND
PETER SCHLUNEGGER IN THE BUGABOOS.

skier abilities, but at first it was all perceived, as well as advertised, as a rush for rich daredevils who could ski like Austrian racers.

By the late seventies, Hans realized that the number of elite skiers who could afford heli-skiing was limited – and he had already skied with most of them. "We were narrowing down a narrow slice of the market," he explained. "If we kept it up, pretty soon we'd have just one skier that fit our criteria."

Ski ability is a hard thing to judge, and off-piste and deep-powder skiing take a bit of getting used to even for the most crack athletes. As per Hans's style, it was the guests who motivated the change in the system. Every year more skiers came to CMH, and every year more intermediate skiers felt they were up to the task. Guides became ski instructors with no training in teaching at all and started teaching powder-skiing technique so people who were in a bit over their heads would have more fun.

Not every journalist made heli-skiing sound like a sport for expert skiers only, and by the late seventies a new trend began to emerge. Wendell Benedetti, a writer for *The Skier* magazine, visited the Cariboos in 1977 and described – a bit more accurately – the learning curve of trying to ski powder:

> With miles of open slopes beckoning, my first day was a complete disaster! It was a bright, sunny day – the only one that week – and I neglected to bring my camera! But what's worse is I stumbled, fell, landed on my side and generally tumbled all the way to the bottom of the slope, narrowly missing a disgruntled wolverine in the process!

Was I embarrassed! My touted powder technique that I had mentally reviewed all summer turned out to be a complete flop! I was sitting too far back and as a result had no control whatsoever. In other words, on my first run I literally shot down the hill like a careening bullet, nearly wiping out several of my fellow skiers.

However, I was not alone, in that nearly half the group needed help. So on the second day we were given a full morning of specialized instruction. Getting forward proved to be the first task to conquer, followed by linking figure eights with our instructor, and ending with practice on perfecting our somewhat shaky rhythm. We all progressed satisfactorily and by noon were getting ready to tackle more exciting things.

. . . Six days in the Cariboos passed quickly, so quickly that just when my powder technique was beginning to take shape, it was time to pack and get ready to head down the mountain.

While Hans and the majority of journalists were busy making heli-skiing sound as elite as possible, in the field a different kind of heli-skier was emerging. Over the years, a number of skiers, often staff or skiers' spouses, joined a heli-ski trip as beginners, or even had never skied before. With a bit of group juggling and special attention from a guide, the neophytes actually learned how to ski without ever using a traditional ski lift.

This new heli-skier was exemplified by a woman named Carolyn Damon, who visited CMH year after year with her husband, Ned, and learned to ski from day one in the big-mountain powder of the heli-ski elite. Damon proved it was possible to heli-ski at lower levels of ski competence than was previously understood. Suddenly, snobbish marketing campaigns that scared the glitzy, status-defining Bogner ski suits off of potential customers didn't seem like such a bright idea after all, and CMH began a new era of sharing the ski ultimate with more people than ever before. Damon's first ski run ever was Vowell Glacier in the Bugaboos, and she went on to hold the current women's record for the most vertical feet.

Roy Ostberg was about to quit forever after a hard day of crawling out of his own divots and chasing his group around the Bobbie Burns, when he felt a hand on his shoulder. He looked up to see Hans's piercing eyes looking into his. Hans simply said, "Roy, I'd like to ski with you this afternoon."

After a bit of personal attention from the old master himself, Ostberg improved dramatically. Now he's heli-skied ten million vertical feet and lost 45 pounds and ten inches off his waist. Ostberg is jubilant about his heli-skiing-induced life change. He says, "For my 110th birthday I want these words written on my birthday cake: 'It's all Hans's fault!'"

In the early eighties, Hans pushed hard to change the fierce reputation of heli-skiing. The handbook read: "We will ask what pace you wish to ski and then divide everyone into groups accordingly. This allows for smoother operation during the day's skiing for all concerned. If you come with a friend of differing skiing ability and wish to ski together, this is possible as long as you realize we will only ski at the pace of the slowest member of the group."

The promotional tag line changed from "The best, the most difficult, the most expensive skiing in the world" to "The best, most exciting skiing in the world."

Hans explained the change: "We needed to do whatever it took on our part to make sure people have a good time at all levels of skier. Sometimes it would take all morning to do one run with one skier (with an extra guide). They couldn't even slide slip in the morning, but by lunch it was a big success. By the end of the week, they were actually skiing. Pretty soon we were turning people away because we had no space."

In the mid-eighties, the popularity of heli-skiing was booming. Hans recalled, "By 1989, we had sometimes a three-year waiting list. We opened Gothics, Galena and the Adamants and we were selling spaces in Galena before the lodge was even built!"

While newspapers, magazines and films opened people's eyes to the ultimate ski experience, there were a handful of individuals who went heli-skiing and were so inspired by its appeal that they decided to make a business out of selling tours for CMH. The potential of commissioning international agents began to be realized in 1976 when a group of 44 Germans descended on the Cariboos, sparked by the entrepreneurial efforts of a man named Pepi Erben. Erben owned a travel agency called Aeroski that specialized in packaged ski tours to the best areas in the Alps. To try out this heli-skiing concept, Aeroski booked the largest group of Europeans ever to go heli-skiing together in the Columbias. Pepi and his son Viet accompanied the group. As Viet explained, "We didn't want to sell things we didn't know about ourselves."

According to Pepi, they found the Cariboos to "exceed our expectations by quite a bit," and the group introduced the Canadian ski guides to the "Arlberg Design" of spooning one track against the other for a visually pleasing and yet experientially homogeneous pattern in the snow. Discussions with Hans followed, and on a handshake Aeroski became the German agent for CMH heli-skiing. Other countries followed a similar model, with passionate individuals visiting CMH and starting a conversation with either Hans or Mark Kingsbury about bringing groups to go skiing and hiking.

A number of agents have now passed the job along to their children. Thanks to their sustained efforts, says Swiss agent Martin Gallati, "CMH and Western Canada are known as *the* place for heli-skiing."

Freddy Weiss was the first agent for Hans, convincing Austrians to give heli-skiing a try. Like many agents, Freddy's first experience was as a guest. But it wasn't the skiing that first hooked him on the experience; it was the camaraderie of the lodge. "My first time heli-skiing I came in, sat down at dinner and said, 'Hello, my name is Freddy.' Five minutes later we were all friends!"

Weiss started in the role of agent, as he says, "as a friend, for fun, and for no money. We wanted to come skiing! We [had] just quit racing and we wanted a new challenge."

In the face of modern business, the role of the CMH agents is utterly unique. They work together, trading spaces and doing promotions together, established agents helping newcomers work more efficiently. There is real competition because there are a limited number of seats, and yet everyone works with the philosophy that what is good for one is good for all. A dozen agencies sell CMH from ten different countries: Japan, Austria, Australia, Germany, Italy, France, England, Sweden, Spain and Switzerland.

Traditionally, there have been no official contracts. The agents' annual meeting, held at one of the lodges, is as much of a family reunion as a business meeting, and yet the agents account for nearly half of CMH business. Pranks are rampant, the party never ends and even those who are retired come back for the meetings.

Some of the agents represent the core of the ski culture of their countries. The grandfather of Miguel Arias, the Spanish agent for CMH, brought skiing to Spain by taking people skiing in the mountains above Madrid by using a donkey for transportation. Two generations later, his grandson is selling skiing that uses a helicopter.

The relationship with the agents is a direct result of Hans's and Mark's way of doing business through interpersonal trust and commitment, more like a climbing or skiing partner than a cold, hard business deal. Because Hans and Mark had welcomed them to be part of the CMH project, the agents returned to their home countries and sold heli-skiing as if they owned the company. With both area managers and international agents feeling this sense of ownership, everyone collaborated in an unprecedented recipe for success unheard of in the traditional world of capitalism.

The kinder, gentler face of heli-skiing leading to increasing guest numbers was what inspired the new area development of the late eighties, and to this day the powder instruction program of CMH is developing under the leadership of Roko Koell, who assists guides in providing instruction for skiers of all levels. And although the Swiss Mafia would never have believed it, family weeks, where groups of 12- to 17-year-olds go heli-skiing with their families and other teenagers, are the fastest-growing programs in heli-skiing.

Hans concludes the discussion on skiing ability: "In a business like heli-skiing, I'm sure there are a lot of people who could do it, could afford to do it, but who are afraid of it."

To communicate the new face of heli-skiing, Hans hired ski film legend Dick Barrymore to produce a promotional video. Barrymore built a storyline around a husband and wife going heli-skiing for the first time. Barrymore's nasal sporting-event voice narrated the film, and it was educational as well as inspiring. The voice-over went to great lengths to communicate to lesser skiers that heli-skiing would be possible for them: "Heli-skiing, sometimes labelled a daredevil, macho sport, can be enjoyed by anyone willing to give it a try."

The film explained some of the systems used to minimize risk, including the run list and snowpack assessment. "Gone are the days when skiers just jumped in the helicopter and went skiing."

The couple posed a few falls as if they were learning and then proceeded to ski perfectly, with the voice-over saying, "Carol caught up with Stanley and they skied happily ever after."

The production was partly sponsored by the Colorado beer company Coors, and it included skiers happily sipping cold beers in the bright sun during lunch. Almost as if everyone was a bit bolder after a few beers, Barrymore proceeded to fill the rest of the film with aggressive skiers ripping over wind rolls to catch massive air of nearly Nordic jumping magnitude, straight-lining down lines of house-sized pillowdrops and generally goofing around with superb skills on skinny skis. Everyone wore wool sweaters, the height of ski fashion, even in the blower powder sequences. There was not a single lodge sequence. The product being sold was the skiing, period.

Four years later, Hans produced his next promotional film. This one added a bit more reality with a section on skiing in less than perfect snow, introduced real tree skiing and included a soundtrack similar to wild west Hollywood productions. It included a section featuring Ted Shred, the surfer who brought the first snowboard heli-skiing. Again the film included outrageous jumping sequences with whole groups hucking in tandem. At the time, Hans was hooked on windsurfing, and taking a page from Warren Miller, the film included wind surfing sequences that couldn't have had less to do with the skiing they were trying to sell – but were fun to watch.

Other modern film producers wanted the powder of the Columbias in front of their cameras, and numerous CMH guides worked as models in various ski films. In talking to them, I discovered that the most common sentiment about these film projects was risk. Thierry Cardon has no hesitation when he says, "The most dangerous thing we do is these film shoots."

The goal changes from skiing something safe to skiing something that looks good on film, and hazard mitigation takes a backseat to aesthetics. Film groups are always pushing the limits, and avalanches and crashes were more frequent in film projects than in the daily routine.

Roko has a scar on his arm from a big crash that happened while filming with John Eaves, one of Canada's premier snow athletes and cameramen. "You have these guys, you have the film crew and you just go a little too far."

Roko stuck his ski pole into his arm and the force of the impact was so great that only the ski basket kept the pole from going all the way through his arm. Roko looks out from under his bushy hair and says sheepishly, "The next day someone had to feed me."

Pat Morrow, one of the world's most accomplished mountain photographers with both still and film cameras, has shot 25 different weeks in CMH terrain. He says, "Working with heli-skiing it's mind-boggling how many possibilities your lens is exposed to in a single day, but I always felt the vulnerability of the skiers."

In the end, for all the risk, creativity and effort, it wasn't the films that made more people fall in love with powder skiing than ever before. It was an innovation in the mid-eighties that changed the game forever and completed the transformation from heli-skiing as a daredevil's adrenaline fix to a sport for the old, the young and everyone in between: the fat ski.

Roko says the biggest thing the fat ski changed was the people who came skiing. "It makes it so [that] much-less-skilled skiers can experience nirvana." It also made it so that older knees could keep on skiing. Hans estimated that "the fat ski added 10 years to everyone's ski life," then added, "but I never learned to ski on them." You'd never guess it by watching him rip on fat skis in the last few years of his life, effortlessly floating through thick crud as if he was on a groomer at Lake Louise.

At the same time as the fat-ski revolution, other mountain sports felt a surge in popularity. Almost overnight, trails formed from foot traffic to remote destinations, and the extremes of the Earth from Antarctica to Mt. Everest became tick marks on the life

checklists of motivated sightseers. In 1968 Hans gave a pleading luncheon address to the Knights of the Round and prophesied the future need for regulation of wilderness areas even as his business depended upon freedom to operate in them.

He told the Knights:

> If we try to look 50 years down the line, providing we haven't blown ourselves up, the changes which will occur are in all probability beyond our imagination. One thing, however, is clear: we are in for some major social upheavals. There will be a much better system of distributing the wealth we are able to generate already today; people will spend less time providing for themselves and much more time to educate and amuse themselves. Because of an ever-increasing population, we will have to curtail our individual freedom, and there must be a much better control and preservation of our environment. How all this will manifest itself in practice I can only guess.

In the sixties, it was common practice among wilderness users to dispose of garbage by simply digging a hole in the ground and burying it. Gasoline consumption wasn't even a consideration, and the idea of "leave no trace," a wilderness ethic encouraged in most modern countries today, was the last thing on outdoorsmen's minds back then. Hans, however, was intuitively concerned about man's impact on the world. Mike Wiegele remembers Hans making people carry their trash out of the wilderness before anyone else even thought about it. Hans was willing to try heli-skiing in the first place because it was a ski lift that didn't leave a mark on his beloved wilderness.

During July of 2007 a group of heli-hikers were enjoying the peace of Rocky Point Basin on the edge of a provincial park, a magnificent valley closed to all wheeled access to protect the fragile tundra and alpine ecosystems. Suddenly the sound of motors broke the reverie and a few minutes later a group of dirt bikes roared into the basin. The heli-hikers snapped photos of the bikers as they high-pointed on steep slopes where tenacious plants struggled to make the most of the short alpine summer, and tore though lush tundra, their knobby tires munching forget-me-nots and moss campion. They left tracks just as skiers or snowshoers do, but rather than in the shifting snows that erase a track in a matter of hours or days, the bikers left theirs deep in the very flesh of the alpine ecosystem. Then they rode away, perhaps having no idea what they had just done, but Marc Piché, who was managing the Bugaboo lodge at the time, described the dirt bikers' visit as having done "irreparable damage" to the basin. Heli-hikers were the only ones to witness the impact.

The wilderness today bustling with people: heli-skiers, heli-hikers, dirt bikers, sledders, skiers, climbers, hikers, fishers, hunters and even car campers often feel like the only people out there. The truth is, there are lots of other eyes in the forest and our actions affect other users of the resource. Groups from sledder organizations to heli-ski companies are educating their people in taking care of the wilderness where they play.

At CMH, guides and staff try to instill a respect for the natural world in every person who visits a lodge, and there is ample opportunity for guests to be touched by nature. The lodges are in the heart of the wilderness, and animals behave accordingly.

Once, a window was left open in the lower level of the Bobbie Burns lodge, and sometime during the night a bear climbed into the room. The staff member who was sleeping in the bed awoke to find he was sharing the room with a confused bruin. The man struggled to get out the door and the bear struggled to get out the window – both equally scared. That morning, when he told the rest of the staff of his wildlife encounter, lodge manager Vicki Hemmingson didn't believe it – until she went to the room and saw the scratch marks where the bear had struggled to get out of the room.

Another time, Viet Erben was visiting Valemount and with three other guys decided to make a surprise visit to the Cariboos. With Hannes Webenhoffer driving one snow-mobile and the other two on another, they headed up the road. A heavy snow year had narrowed the road with high drifts, making it a natural passage for wildlife. They came around a bend to find their way blocked by a massive bull moose. Viet remembers, "He turned to us as if to say 'you don't belong here,' so we decided to wait a while to give him time to move away."

They shut down the machines and waited, then drove around the next curve only to find the moose standing just 30 metres away. Viet turned to Hannes and asked, "What do we do if he charges?"

"Jump in the forest," Hannes replied.

The moose lowered his head and charged. The manly-heli-skiers-turned-terrified-victims scattered in all directions. Viet dove off the snowbank and filled his face with snow, effectively blinding him from more defensive manoeuvring. Hannes fell down a tree wall and the others hid behind trees. The moose proceeded to smash the fronts of the snowmobiles with his hammer-like forefeet before ambling on his way.

There were other times when the antics of the animals seemed more comical than terrifying. Thia Klebaur was guiding a run in the Monashees during a big storm cycle when he came across a moose. He directed his team around the animal and skied down

MOTORCYCLES IN THE TUNDRA OF
ROCKY POINT IN THE BUGABOOS.
ONLY HELI-HIKERS WERE THERE
TO WITNESS THE DAMAGE.

a different way to let the local continue on undisturbed. As they cut back across the valley bottom to reach the planned pickup, suddenly the moose came cart-wheeling out of the forest after losing its footing in the deep snow. To see a moose tumbling out of control like a wayward skier in bottomless powder is something few humans have ever seen and a glimpse into the difficulty of living in such a snowy world.

For much of the wilderness where CMH operates, the guides, pilots and guests are the only human monitors of the areas. The recession of the glaciers, the changing of wildlife habits and populations and the health of the forest are all part of the daily routine of the guides.

The mountain caribou are a prime example of an element of nature that needs to be monitored. These unique animals live in the very terrain where heli-skiers and heli-hikers play. Mountain caribou are about the size of deer, but they have hooves closer to the size of those of elk and moose. These natural snowshoes allow them to live in the snow-laden high country of the Columbias while most of their ungulate cousins are forced to lower altitudes. Unfortunately, their numbers are declining at an alarming rate. Over the last decade, the population has dropped by 50 per cent. Numerous factors are contributing to the animals' reduced numbers. The loss of old-growth trees coated with the lichens the caribou feed on in the winter, hydro-electric projects that limit their movement, and other human-caused developments seem to be a significant issue for the animals. During the nineties, a study revealed that the most common cause of caribou death was accidents, particularly avalanches. Limited terrain forces the herds into the higher and more exposed valleys where avalanches are more frequent.

The pressure is on the heli- and cat-skiing industries, as well as snowmobilers, to avoid stressing the caribou's already delicate existence. The effect these sports have on the animals is not clearly known. Heli-ski guides have observed that caribou tend to live near logging operations, most likely because the freshly felled trees reveal the lichens that sustain the animals during the snowy months, and the trucks and machinery break up the snow, making it easier for the caribou to move around.

Of all the winter users in the backcountry, snowmobiles are perhaps the most startling to caribou because the driver cannot see them as he approaches, and by the time the animals come into view, they are already running. Helicopters too can disturb the animals, but it is much easier for the pilot to see them from a distance and avoid startling them. For guides, respecting local wildlife is a goal on par with keeping skiers out of avalanches. They track the herds and monitor their populations with the Snowbase database to observe their behaviour as well as stay out of their way. A single wayward caribou will change the day's plan for an entire lodge full of skiers or hikers. Helicopters fly longer routes to avoid herds, and prime skiing areas are left alone for weeks to allow a herd to maintain its natural patterns without interference.

Most of the guides express similar sentiments about their impact on the wilderness: they don't want to damage the land, and if there are strong data that suggest their activities are causing the decline of a local species, they will change how they do business to protect the animals. So far, the rate of decline of the herds is the same both inside and outside heli-ski tenures, but the guides know the survival of the animals and the survival of their business are closely intertwined. If the naturalists decide the recreational use of the wilderness is killing the caribou, the heli-ski industry is doomed.

Hans would happily have given up his life's work if it meant the wilderness would be preserved, but since he was allowed to run a business in his cherished wilds, he endeavoured to instill a respect for nature in everyone he skied or climbed with. His business brought more people into the wilds than any mountaineer or skier had ever done. In some ways, it must have been hard for Hans to watch his enterprise shuttling truckloads of people onto the tundra and to see skiers whose only interest was in cataloging vertical feet. On the other hand, he built a system by which everyone who came to CMH became in some small way a watchdog of the changes in the natural world. His guides and guests are not only tourists, they are the monitors of a region where much damage could be done without anyone ever knowing.

The guides have become so attuned to the habits of the caribou that their understanding of what is happening with the animals living in their area may be greater than that of the professionals assigned to protect the herds.

One guide remembers an incident when the authorities arrived to monitor the heli-skiers around the herds: "We were running out of good skiing because the stability was poor and we really wanted to ski the run where a herd of caribou were hanging out, but they just wouldn't leave. They were there for weeks and normally they stay in one area for a few days and then move on." The skiers continued to avoid the slope until a couple of biologists flew into the area and landed on top of the run where the caribou were living to see if the heli-ski operation was butting in on the animal's habitat. According to the guide, the biologists watched the heli-skiers all day and then skied right down the middle of the very glade the heli-ski groups had been avoiding for weeks on account of the caribou.

This kind of thing can be frustrating for guides, with the land managers viewing their business as a potential problem for the local wildlife, while the guides feel like the true stewards of the mountains and the only ones who are there all the time to see real changes. Luckily, the ultimate goal of the land managers and the guiding industry is the same: to preserve the wilderness as much as they can.

How much man is affecting change in the wilderness is hard to measure, but change is happening fast. Glacial retreat is one of the most striking changes. The skier's perspective of glacial change is more sensitive than any other non-scientific measurement – not that it takes a precision instrument to measure such significant changes. Guides point out places where the retreat of the glaciers is most rapid. It's hard to miss a vertical cliff rising 20 metres above the glacier when just 15 years ago it was a broad dome that could be skied right from the top with no rock visible anywhere. Other runs will never be skied again, and some, like the legendary Vowell run through the centre of the Bugaboo Spires, are much shorter now because of dangerous icefalls forming where once a smooth glacier allowed unlimited fun. Vowell is in danger of breaking up and becoming unskiable sometime in the next few years if the current warming trend continues.

One thing we know for sure is that energy consumption is the major issue of our time and will remain so into the future. A full group of 44 skiers running a 212 main helicopter and a 206 support machine will burn about 57 litres of jet fuel per person per day, or 2500 litres per day in total. The average SUV driver will burn about the same amount of gasoline in six months, but the similarity stops there – heli-ski operations are acutely aware of the fuel consumption of their machines. The seemingly impossible task of finding alternative fuels for aircraft is underway. The US Air Force is collaborating with four prestigious research universities in the US – Princeton, Case Western Reserve, Pennsylvania State and the University of Illinois, Chicago – to better understand the characteristics of jet fuel so alternatives with similar combustion qualities can be developed. NetJets, a private jet charter and aircraft management company, is concurrently working with Princeton to develop new jet fuels with near-zero net greenhouse gas emissions.

Unfortunately, it will be a long time before helicopters are powered by anything except petroleum products, and until that time it is up to individual heli-skiers, heli-hikers, heli-mountaineers and heli-sport operations to find ways to offset their energy-intensive recreation. CMH recognizes the impact of their operations, and thus it has developed the Second Nature program, an employee-driven initiative that has been responsible for everything from decreased packaging in the food and beverage department to installing fuel sensors on remote fuel caches to enable immediate response in case of a leak. Second Nature is involved with other programs, including Friends of Bugaboo Park, a group committed to preserving the qualities of the popular area. Other elements of the program include reducing generator use at the lodges through monitoring energy consumption, and orchestrating the cleanup of abandoned mine sites.

With nature driving every element of the remote lodge operations, and in honour of their founder's legacy of stewardship, CMH has taken a leading role as one of North America's most environmentally active wilderness tourism companies. It began with having a couple of pigs at the Bugaboo lodge to take care of food waste and has evolved into an award-winning program. Lodge staff are proud of their efforts to have the least impact possible. Carlee Hughes, a bartender, observed, "The local communities here don't even recycle, but here we are recycling at the lodge. I'm really proud to be part of a company that puts their money where their mouth is."

It doesn't stop at recycling. From installing micro hydro generators in nearby streams, to pumping wastewater through a sand filter before letting it run into the ground, to installing $60,000 composting systems, the operation of the company has carried on Hans's legacy

with aplomb. In 2007, the United Nations World Tourism Organization awarded CMH the inaugural e-Tourism Climate Change Award for the educational elements of the CMH website. In 2005, the Council of Tourism Associations of British Columbia presented CMH with their Environmentally Responsible Tourism award. In 2004, the Tourism Industry Association of Canada chose CMH as the winner of their Parks Canada Sustainable Tourism Award.

While the ownership of the company has changed several times, the individual lodges are still largely free to develop systems and utilize technology to minimize their impact on the wilderness that is so essential to their very existence. Time will tell whether the current leadership will pass on the legacy of stewardship for the world, and for each other, to the next generation of skiers, hikers and climbers to be lucky enough to spend a part of their lives playing in the Columbia Mountains.

By the end of my week at the Bobbie Burns, our group was sitting around a campfire outside the lodge and the lines between our countries dissipated like our ski tracks under the next storm. We'd skied a smorgasbord of mountain features together in variable but wonderful snow, speaking the same language of unbridled enthusiasm for a wilderness feast of the senses. Beer was stashed in the surrounding snowbanks, each nationality took turns singing songs, and stars reflected off the nearby pond. As the night grew colder, everyone drew closer to the fire, and Hans's vision of showing the world the magic of Western Canada while instilling in them respect for the wilderness and for each other, was alive and well in the expressions revealed by the dancing flames reflecting off the faces of new friends around the fire.

TAKING CARE OF THE ENVIRONMENT
MEANS EVERYTHING FROM TEACHING
GUESTS TO PICK UP THE SMALLEST PIECES
OF TRASH TO USING MICRO HYDRO POWER
AT SOME OF THE LODGES.
OPPOSITE: THIS CAIRN WAS BUILT IN 1990,
MARKING THE TOE OF THE VOWELL GLACIER
AT THAT TIME. SINCE THEN, THE ICE HAS
RECEDED AS SHOWN IN THIS PHOTO
TAKEN DURING THE SUMMER OF 2007.

12

A SKI TOUR WITH HANS

Many people wouldn't think in terms of skiing unless they had a lift to carry them to the top of the slope. To be bound to one slope, even to one mountain, by a lift may be convenient but it robs us of the greatest pleasure that skiing can give, that is, to travel through the wide, wintry country, to follow the lure of the peaks which tempt on the horizon and to get away from all the noises of our technological age and into some clean, mysterious surroundings.

—Hans Gmoser

HANS TAKES A BACK SEAT WHILE
MARGARET GMOSER PLAYS THE SAW
AND FRANZ ROECK, TONI NOICHL
AND BERNHARD PLATNER ACCOMPANY
ON ZITHER AND GUITAR.

The industry born in the deep white powder below the black-and-white-streaked granite of the Bugaboo Spires owes much of its health and success to the depth of the friendship between Hans Gmoser and Leo Grillmair. They formed a team based on complete trust, on shared hardships and a clear understanding of their roles in chasing their mountain dreams. Hans was a leader with rarely matched ability to rally his team towards any goal. Leo was a steadfast second in command. Their friendship never wavered and their mutual history in war-torn Austria had much to do with their commitment. After the horrors of war, the rest of their lives were easy by comparison. Hans spent most of his youth with his stomach crying from hunger. After a particularly brutal bombing, Leo walked home from work, stepping across bodies, mostly children and elders, in the streets of Linz. Even the hardest days of cutting wood, hauling water and shovelling snow in the Bugaboos were dreamy compared to their childhood years. The tragedies of avalanches, helicopter crashes and business struggles were not enough to fracture their friendship or deter their focus on providing the ultimate mountain experience.

After the business grew beyond Hans's wildest expectations, and the world credited him with the invention of an industry, he took every opportunity to tell people how many individuals had contributed to the project. He strongly felt that, as visionary physicist Sir Isaac Newton once wrote, "If I have seen farther, it is by standing on the shoulders of giants."

Rudi Gertsch put it simply: "He just wanted to make it a business so we could all do what we liked to do."

Hans felt the other people involved in the project never received enough credit for their part in its success. To honour them, he threw a heli-ski party in the Bugaboos during April of 2005 in appreciation for everyone who helped make it happen. Guides, staff, investors and guests were all invited. The entire Bugaboo lodge was reserved for two weeks to fit everyone. The first week was mostly old guests, and the second was reserved for the old guides and staff.

It wasn't the first such gathering. Almost every year, the characters most involved in the building of CMH would get together for what they called Nostalgia Week. It was typically scheduled during April, when the days were longer, the weather milder and the snow reliable. It was a time for old friends to get together and relive a most precious piece of their individual and shared histories. But the 2005 weeks were different. With conviction, Hans declared it the last Nostalgia Week. He stood up in front of the room full of his closest friends and said: "I get a lot of credit, but in actuality, in truth, I've just been a very lucky person who met loyal, excellent people who made all of this happen.

"This is the last week, because I'm getting too old to ski. It is bittersweet, but there's too much pain." His voice cracked and his eyes sparkled with a hint of tears, but he recovered with humour as he added, "Maybe they won't let me stop. They'll keep dragging me out like the Pope."

Hans didn't want to be wheeled anywhere like the Pope, and fitting to his accidentally prophetic manner of running his life, he threw his final party less than 15 months before his death.

It had been a decade since Hans sold CMH to Alpine Helicopters, years he spent cycling the most scenic roads in North America, Europe and Japan, skiing and hiking with his family and making up for lost time devoted to the business.

Near the end of his time as a businessman, changes in the industry, shareholder and skier expectations, and avalanche tragedies took the project far from the days of the sawmill camp. Hans's success was beyond anything he could have dreamed for a mountain guide, but it came at a price. His devotion to the business cost him valuable time with his family and he saw a future of the business without him, and in that future was a guide named Mark Kingsbury.

Kingsbury, a New Hampshire native, started working for Hans in the 1970s, eventually becoming a ski guide. Like many guides, Mark wanted to work closer to home and asked Hans if he would sponsor Kingsbury returning to the US to go to business school. Hans replied, "I'm not going to pay for you to leave, but if you stay I'll teach you everything I know." This was just what Kingsbury needed. For the next decade, he worked at Hans's side and treated CMH as his own. Mark had an uncanny way of interacting with people, and true to Hans's knack for delegating responsibility to the ideal person, when it came time to pass on the operation of CMH, Hans couldn't have picked a better person than Mark Kingsbury.

Fred Beruschi, owner of the Regent Inn, where CMH Revelstoke bases its operation, watched Hans pass the management of the operation to Mark. He explained, "Hans knew what he wanted, but he needed a guy like Mark to make it happen. Mark had a way with people – not that Hans didn't, but he could be a bit rough."

Age has a way of smoothing the sharpest edges in people, and Hans was no exception. Cook Hannelore Achenbach remembers an incident one evening when Hans's fuse was still quite short. He was lending a hand in the kitchen, cooking steaks for a group of skiers, when somebody got impatient and yelled into the kitchen, "Where's my steak!"

Hannelore watched in disbelief as Hans stepped into the room, yelled "Here's your steak!" and proceeded to throw a steak across the room.

Mark stepped into a decision-making role at a time when the needs of the industry were becoming less suitable to Hans's style of management and communication. The world of doing business in the wilderness had changed from the freedoms and follies of the sawmill camp to a system of tenures, regulations, and legal and governmental oversight. Hans said once, during a meeting with land managers, "If I had to do it all over again, with all these rules, I wouldn't have bothered."

Viet Erben, the German agent for CMH, remembers Hans saying, "Mark is much better than me at this stuff. I lose my temper too easily." Hans knew it was time for a change. Viet continued, "Hans had a clear picture in his mind that he would transfer the business to Mark."

According to those close to Hans and Mark during Hans's last years as owner of CMH, Mark was just what the company and the industry needed. Marty Von Neudegg of the CMH marketing team commented that Mark "brought a lot of humanity into the company. Hans was more severe. Mark would never lose his cool in public, while Hans was famous for losing his temper."

Kingsbury was a master of dealing with bureaucracy and had confidence in the potential of British Columbia long before today's rush for real estate, recreation and investment in the region. Beruschi said, "Mark was a visionary, not just in heli-skiing, but in tourism."

In 1991 Mark took over leadership of CMH and presided during a time of increased regulation and competition. He saw the industry grow for a decade until a fateful day in 2001 on the Trans-Canada highway. He was returning home from visiting his son, Troy, and Brady Beruschi, Fred's son, in Revelstoke. Mark had taken the two young men fly-fishing to celebrate Brady's recovery from a broken back suffered in a snowboarding accident. After catching a few fish, Troy had business to attend to, but Mark had breakfast with Brady before heading home. Mark was travelling on a recent gift from his wife, Marion, a Harley-Davidson Softail motorcycle, and he was surely looking forward to the ride home. Brady remembers Mark saying, "The black ribbon is calling. I gotta go." On the way home, Mark decided to stop to visit Rudi Gertsch's Purcell Helicopter Skiing office just outside Golden and was waiting for traffic to pass in the other lane before turning left when a truck driver didn't see him or the brand new Softail he was riding.

When a mountaineer dies in the mountains, family and friends find solace in saying "at least he died doing what he loved." But if the death occurs on the highway or from other factors, it is somehow harder for the brotherhood of the mountains to accept. Most of Mark's family stayed involved in the business his passion helped build. Marion continued to work in reservations until retiring in 2007 and was considered the soul of CMH by many agents, guests, guides and staff. Daughter Abigail now sells CMH heli-skiing in Australia, and Troy is right at the heart of CMH in any job he can get his hands on. Lydia, the youngest of the Kingsbury children, lives in Calgary, farthest from the family business and prefers a life away from the mountains. Troy explains her distance as being at least in part because of missing her father: "I think she feels a little ripped off, timewise, on how much she got."

Abigail likes her job as an international agent for CMH but explains that her attachment to her father's business is not without reservations: "I like it from a distance. As my mom says, it haunts me when I come home, and I think that's a little bit true."

In describing her father, excitement shows through Abigail's usually stoic countenance: "Everyone loved him. He had a great relationship with everyone; even kids who were normally quiet liked talking to him." Then the striking blue eyes she inherited from her father grow distant and she says, "It would have been nice to have had more time to learn how he was always so nice to everyone – and patient. He was a good dad – a good everything."

Fitting to the tradition of the workers running the company, with Mark's passing, another guide, Walter Bruns, stepped in as president of CMH. Bruns had initially been hired by CMH to drive a truck. With a masters degree in physics he was slightly overqualified for the job, but Hans always respected someone who would do any work that needed to be done, and Bruns stepped into any position where he was needed, from cleaning up after the construction of a new lodge, to managing the intricate operations of the entire company. It was a natural progression for Bruns to lead as president.

While working on an article for *Powder* magazine throughout the 2005 Nostalgia Weeks, I watched Hans dodge compliments effortlessly, and give everyone except himself credit for the invention of heli-skiing, and I wondered what part of it, if any, he felt was entirely his contribution. He gave Ethan Compton private tours in the smaller 206 helicopter, skiing all of his favourite runs with the man who first had enough faith in him to sell him skis on credit so he could begin his career. He spoke in front of the group every night, taking the time to recognize everyone, even those who couldn't be there, beginning with Compton and down the list to Mark Kingsbury, who took the reins at a time when Hans needed to move away from the business. For two weeks Hans used the Bugaboo lodge for the last time as a place to pay respect to everyone who contributed a piece of their lives to the project, and he honoured each one with a story and a toast.

On the last day, it was snowing too hard to fly, so the old skiers hung out in the exercise room to watch Brooks Dodge's film footage from the early days, some wearing beacons with the transmit indicator light flashing through their clothing as they watched films of themselves skiing in the sixties. Wrinkled grins and sparkling eyes reflected in the light of the flickering black-and-white films, and they debated whether they could still make turns on 220 cm skis. Hans presented his version of the history of CMH, continuously recognizing everyone involved.

A year later, I fell in behind Hans on the skin trail in one of the places most dear to him – the ski touring terrain of Battle Abbey. After becoming fascinated with his passion for the mountains during the Nostalgia Weeks, I wanted to spend a little time with Hans away from the rotors, comforts and pace of heli-skiing. I wanted to have a chance to talk to him in his ideal mountain element – on a ski tour. When his son Robson invited me to join his family at Battle Abbey in return for some promotional photography, I said yes immediately.

While heli-skiers may disagree vehemently, most people who have tried everything the ski world has to offer find touring to be unquestionably the best. Compared to the heart and soul experience of ski touring, lift service skiing by any means could be compared to paying for sex: the motion is the same, but the foreplay and everything else is missing. Hans knew this from day one, and while he built a business out of getting people effortlessly to the top of a mountain, he enjoyed ski touring far more than even the most epic day of heli-skiing.

Battle Abbey is one of a growing number of huts and lodges used by ski touring groups who use a helicopter to access the hut and then spend a week ski touring in the area. It is also one of the most remote, a 20-minute helicopter ride over the full width of the Purcells, over the Duncan River Valley and well into the Selkirks. Before aerial photography, the maps left a blank spot, with the words "Battle Range" written across the unsurveyed region. The hut is perched at treeline on a mountainside in a valley impenetrable by snowmobile, in the centre of the Columbias where even the wide-ranging heli-ski operations don't often fly.

The rustic hut uses solar and wind power for electricity and sleeps 14 guests, and while it has a view as scenic as any structure on earth, and easy ski access to some of the least-known terrain in the Columbias, it is a different world from today's heli-lodge comforts of spas, hot tubs, massage therapists and master chefs.

Hannelore Achenbach, who cooked for CMH groups for 39 years, suspects part of Hans's reason for building Battle Abbey in 1978 was "he wanted a place where he could do skiing like the old times." Hans built the hut with Bill Putnam, an American climber who, according to Achenbach, "wanted a piece of Canada for his own." CMH ran ski tours out of Battle Abbey until 2005. Explains Achenbach, "It was never a moneymaker for CMH; it was for Hans's sake, a tradition."

When CMH cut ski touring from the program, Putnam gave his share to Roger Laurilla, long-time manager of CMH Monashees, and Hans gave his share to his son Robson. Robson and Roger now share management of the hut, booking themselves and other guides into the area throughout the ski touring season.

On the skin trail out of Battle Abbey, I jockeyed to get in position behind Hans to catch him alone where I could ask him about his contribution without him considering anyone else. It didn't happen for a few days, but a lot of time on the ski trail behind the rest of his family told me much of the toll the CMH project had taken on their family. Either Robson or Conrad could have taken the reins of CMH if they had wanted to, but by the time they were old enough to think about it, they simply knew too much. They knew it

HANS GMOSER SKINNING AT BATTLE
ABBEY, FOLLOWED BY HIS WIFE,
MARGARET, AND HIS SONS,
ROBSON AND CONRAD.

drove their mother, Margaret, to take the kids and live alone for over a year in Calgary because Hans had no time for them. Separately I asked both Conrad and Robson if they ever wanted to take over CMH from their father. Both answered with a resounding no.

"We asked them at one point if they were interested," remembered Margaret, "but they didn't want anything to do with owning the business." The Gmoser sons had seen the difficult side of the heli-ski business from the beginning and wanted nothing to do with it. Not that it had been a bad childhood. Robson and Conrad remember skiing behind their father and other guides when the snow was so deep they had to stay in the track to stay above the snow. They grew up with a group of hedonistic skiers as friends. One skier remembers a sign posted on the basement wall in the Bugaboo lodge that read, "Do Not Feed Candy to Conrad."

Conrad chased his own passions entirely, studied architecture and is now is a brewer of some of the best beer in Canada with Vancouver's Steamworks Brewpub. Robson was enamoured of skiing and mountain adventures, and after taking ski-guide training he found himself back in the Bugaboos for a couple of months each year working as a guide. The rest of the time he spends guiding ski-touring, backpacking and river-paddling trips.

The week at Battle Abbey started with a massive low-pressure system clearing from the area, leaving us with a metre of new snow. We wallowed around, choking on bottomless powder in the trees while the alpine terrain stabilized. I eventually found myself skiing behind Hans, as he broke trail through the deep snow. He appeared to be working hard, so I offered to break trail for a change. He insisted he was fine. Since he was breathing like a sprinter, I kept quiet instead of asking him to talk. I didn't know it at the time, but a pulmonary issue had left him with only about 20 per cent of his lung capacity, and spinal problems from injuries forced him to wear a full torso brace while skiing. Considering his history of accidents, it was impressive to watch him ski at all. He pushed through the thigh-deep snow, finding the most efficient line up the hill.

I wondered if I'd be ski touring when I was 73 years old, and was fascinated watching his movements, his frame bent and uneven from bone-shattering injuries. His backpack, an old CMH guide pack embroidered with his first name, and the rest of his clothing and ski gear, while functional, was at least ten years old. One shoulder hung several centimetres lower than the other, and as he pushed through the snow his head hung below his shoulders like an old plow horse. At one point, he cut across a steep rollover and the snow depth rose to where he was cutting a track deeper than his waist. Again I offered to take over the lead, but he declined, slowed down and methodically broke through the drift. Pain was obvious in his movements, but for him to stop would have hurt in other ways. Once on top of the rollover, he said nothing, but took one big step to the side, the age-old ski touring signal that says "it's time for someone else to break trail now." I was next in line, and it's not good ski touring etiquette to shirk your turn to break, so rather than stop with Hans to ask my question, I plowed into the deep snow.

The next day, the storm cleared. Soon Robson was taking us down the steepest ski runs in the area, dragging us to the summits of the biggest peaks, and each day ended with a sunny afternoon on the deck of the Battle Abbey hut toasting with one of Conrad's hearty ales. Evenings of silly games and storytelling gave me a chance to get to know Hans a little better, and eventually I got my chance to ski with him alone. He was lagging behind the rest of the group on the morning climb, so I stepped aside to take a few photos and to join him without appearing to wait. It was one of those days where the Columbias are the most beautiful place on earth. The sun shone brightly against a blue sky, yet thick clouds roiled between the peaks, isolating them from one another and hiding trees and ridges in between. Without the living things our minds use to give us a sense of scale, the mountains appeared unfathomably huge.

He stood on the ski track catching his breath as I skied up to him. While we both were motionless I popped the question: "Of all the things that everyone contributed to heli-skiing, what do you think you contributed?"

He caught his breath with the remaining 20 per cent of his lung capacity, chuckled, said nothing for a minute, and then replied, "The business of it. Getting enough people here so it could happen."

Those dozen words said it all. Hans made guiding a profession in North America and through helicopter access he unintentionally crafted an industry.

His business strategy was, in many ways, the opposite of the bottom-line, profit-driven models. Rather than focus on profit, he was willing to risk financial ruin to give his guests what they wanted and keep his staff inspired. Rather than insulate his leaders from risk, he put them right in the heart of the action, where their very lives were threatened if they made a mistake. Rather than delegate the dirty work to others so he could focus on the higher-level managerial work, Hans often donned his coveralls and jumped into the muck to do the job nobody wanted to do at a lodge, leaving the high-level work to his managers. And rather than draw the line of commitment to his staff at the office door, he took care of them on and off the clock.

The value Hans put on the people around him is exemplified best by the story of an accident far from Canada, in the Cordillera Blanca of Peru. A group of climbers, including a young CMH guide and talented climber named Rob Rohn, were acclimatizing on a peak called Quitaraju before trying the difficult high-altitude peaks in the area. Rob recounts the moment when things went wrong: "We were crossing what looked like a fairly benign slope when ice blocks the size of small cars fell from above. One of the blocks hit me, breaking my back and leg." Climbers helped evacuate Rob to a lower altitude where a helicopter pilot would be comfortable landing, but the Peruvian government refused to send a helicopter unless someone paid for the flight. They wanted $17,000 before the helicopter would leave the ground. The Canadian Embassy contacted Rob's parents and Rob's father called CMH. Marty Von Neudegg was in the office at the time and remembers sitting in a room with Mark and Hans when the call came in. "There was really no discussion," remembers Marty. "Hans and Mark just said to send the money right away." The helicopter rescue was initiated as soon as the money was wired to Peru.

CMH recovered the money through Rob's insurance, but at the time the decision was made to pay for the rescue, recouping the money was not even mentioned. Today, Rob works as the head of operations from the CMH office in Banff and is quick to point out that "the commitment the company had towards me strengthened my commitment to the company."

Hans led with this unprecedented commitment to his team, at the risk of losing his business and his family, and by putting complete responsibility in the hands of his managers and guides. When Mark Kingsbury came along with talents for management and natural compassion that exceeded Hans's own, Hans saw a path to retirement that would leave his people in good hands.

The managers responded with such conviction to both Mark and Hans that even today they base many operations decisions on their interpretation of Gmoser and Kingsbury ideals and then lead the staff accordingly. At pre-season setup in the Gothics, manager Claude Duchesne told the staff, "Hans believed strongly that what our guests want is to be disconnected from the world, so please don't leave newspapers lying around the commons area."

Mark's way of making people feel comfortable was a refreshing change from Hans's thundering temper. Hans was feared for his prodigious attention to detail and, when something went awry, his milk-curdling invective. He had an uncanny knack for the meaning of language, and he used it to the limits of both profanity and tact. So feared were his outbursts of dissatisfaction and insistence on high standards that even a vague rumour of a visit by the chief sent tremors through the staff. Once, a large wheel of cheese intended for the Adamants arrived at the Cariboos. They threw the cheese on a later flight between the lodges. As the pilot approached the Adamants he radioed ahead, "I'm on my way and I have the big cheese on board."

The Adamants staff flew into a frenzy of organization and maintenance to make sure everything was up to Hans's standard and avoid the dreaded Gmoser tongue-lashing.

Time passed and Hans never appeared. Eventually, someone went outside to see where Hans might be, only to find the block of cheese sitting alone on the helipad.

Hans's communication was legendary for its wrath, but also for its accuracy. Most guide services call their customers clients, but for the world of heli-skiing from a remote lodge with only snow machine or helicopter access, there is infinitely more to the endeavour than the typical professional/client relationship. The skiers live together for a week of life-altering skiing, the staff lives together for the better part of a winter, and everyone has the common experience of being guests of the surrounding wilderness. As a result, CMH is one of the few guide services in the world whose patrons are considered guests rather than clients.

Hans found himself skiing with some of the most successful business people on the planet, and he sought their advice on many things, but by traditional business wisdom his project should have failed. The risk and cost of doing business was too high and the return on investment was too low. The magnetic draw of heli-skiing brought people by the thousands, and Hans built a business model that allowed the high-risk game to be played in a way that made it safe enough for skiers, courts and the public to accept.

Throughout his career, he worked tirelessly to improve the guiding profession. From the mid-fifties he was instrumental in the standardization of Parks Canada's mountain guide-licensing program and 40 years later advised the American Mountain Guides Association while they worked towards the UIAGM training standards and membership. Hans's goal was not to build a heli-ski empire but to show people the mountains and, like a prophet of mountain adventure, help other guides to do the same work. The heli-ski industry was almost an accident – albeit a rewarding one.

Hans made what was, for him as an environmentalist, a sacrifice to create heli-skiing as we know it. He brought people and helicopters into that wide, wintry country, but he attempted to balance the impact by endeavouring to impart a respect for the wilderness and nature into everyone who signed up for a CMH adventure – a standard that exists to this day.

To the critic, Hans's mission to lead as many people as possible into the wonders of a wilderness and his desire to preserve the environment above all else presents a mystifying duality. But Hans's strong belief that a mountain experience was beneficial to the human psyche morphed these two seemingly contradictory values into a driving force in his life. So strong was his conviction, that today many who knew him find his greatest contribution was how he brought people together. Erich Unterberger says "Hans should have been nominated for the Nobel Peace Prize because of how he brought so many influential people from so many different countries together and they all got along."

However, one of the original heli-skiers, Joe Jones, explains a disappointment that dogged Hans for much of his life after the success of heli-skiing: "He loved the mountains and was very much a purist. He used to stop and point out things to people. They would get impatient and say 'Let's go! Let's go!' It would make Hans so mad – that people didn't appreciate the mountains. After a couple of years, he gave up and wouldn't share as much anymore."

Today, many guides try to follow Hans's lead and give people a sense of the world around them and a respect for each other while skiing and hiking. They talk about the mountains and point out the grizzly bear tracks leading into avalanche debris where the bear searched for uprooted plants, or for goat or caribou that may have succumbed to the slide. They point out and name distant peaks to give people a sense of just how lucky they are to be the only people enjoying an area the size of a national park. If people choose to ignore the world around them, intoxicated by the thought of the next face shot, it's their choice; but over time, most people learn that having a helicopter to take them home at the end of the day is a great opportunity to relax a bit between turns and appreciate the gift of effortless wilderness access.

Some 5,000 years ago, on the remote island of Rodoy in northern Norway, a human carved a skier with two skis and one pole into the wall of a cave. This petroglyph was accepted as the first evidence of skiing until recently, when archaeological evidence was discovered in China that may extend the first known skiing to 22,000 years ago once the dating is verified. Either way, it's not hard to imagine a prehistoric innovator, tired of plodding through deep snow, strapping a couple of pieces of wood on her feet to move more effectively in the winter. It is one of those inventions that likely occurred separately at different times in different parts of the world.

It's equally easy to imagine various people elsewhere deciding to use helicopters as ski lifts. Heli-skiing and heli-hiking undoubtedly would exist by now with or without Hans Gmoser and his team. The real gift they gave to modern recreation was, as Hans explained, the business of it. They inadvertently built a business model for heli-sport based not on the unlimited growth and profit of traditional business, but on intimacy and adventure. Hans's team built a system knowing that endless growth would eventually destroy the very experience people today are willing to pay so much to have.

As I skied along behind Hans, I pondered his answer and thought about all the hours he'd spent pushing a ski through the snow – as much or more than any man in history. In hindsight, I realize he was pushing the last few kilometres of the long ski trail he'd broken throughout his life. Three months later, he died at age 74 following a cycling accident near Banff.

Skiers, hikers and climbers the world over mourned his passing and honoured his final wish: to have no funeral ceremony, no mountain named after him, no statues built in his likeness, and for everyone who needed closure, to celebrate his life in some small way. While it is a hard request for many people to understand, those who knew him are honouring his wish. There is a poetry to it: perhaps the most fitting monuments to his team's contribution to the mountains are the countless tracks left beside each other each winter in the snows of the Columbias, as impermanent as one man's life, yet telling a story of excitement and friendship in the mountains.

BIBLIOGRAPHY

Association of Canadian Mountain Guides. *Technical Handbook for Professional Mountain Guides*. Canmore, Alta.: Association of Canadian Mountain Guides, 1998; Golden, Colo.: American Mountain Guides Association, 1999.

Cannings, Richard, and Sydney Cannings. *British Columbia, A Natural History*. Vancouver: Greystone Books, 1996.

Caulfeild, Vivian. *Ski-ing Turns*. London: Nisbet & Co., 1922.

Grillmair, Lynne. *Gourmet in Paradise*. Brisco, BC: L. Grillmair, 1987.

Kain, Conrad, and J. Monroe Thorington. *Where the Clouds Can Go*. New York: American Alpine Club, 1935; Boston: Charles T. Branford Co., 1954.

Kauffman, Andrew J., and William L. Putnam. *The Guiding Spirit*. Revelstoke, BC: Footprint Publishing, 1986.

Lawrence, Andrea Mead, and Sara Burnaby. *A Practice of Mountains*. New York: Seaview Books, 1980.

McClung, David, and Peter Schaerer. *The Avalanche Handbook*. Seattle: Mountaineers, 1993.

Piché, Marc, and Chris Atkinson. *The Bugaboos: One of the World's Great Alpine Rock Climbing Centres*. Squamish, BC: Elaho Publishing Corp., 2003.

Scott, Chic. *Powder Pioneers*. Calgary: Rocky Mountain Books, 2005.

Trenker, Luis. *Brothers of the Snow*. New York: E.P. Dutton & Co., 1934.

PHOTOGRAPHY

Rocky Mountain Books saved the following resources
by printing the pages of this book on chlorine free
paper made with 100% post-consumer waste.

Trees • 162, Fully Grown
Water • 59,213 Gallons
Energy • 113 Million BTUs
Solid Waste • 7,604 Pounds
Greenhouse Gases • 14,265 Pounds

Calculations based on research by Environmental
Defense and the Paper Task Force.
Manufactured at Friesens Corporation